CONTENTS

INTRODUCTION

Welcome to your homework book. Although this book on its own is a very useful source of homework, it has been specifically written to be used with Letts GCSE Science classbook. You will get the most benefit if you use both books together. **The numbers before the title of each of the homework units refer to the units of the classbook.**

Like the classbook, this book has been specially written for the new GCSE Double Science specifications, at both Foundation and Higher tiers. If you are doing Single Science, your teacher will be able to tell you which parts of the book you should use.

The questions in this book have been divided into three co-ordinated sections:

1 Life processes and living things
2 Materials and their properties
3 Physical processes

Each of these sections has been split into homework topics. There is also a bank of review questions for each of the three sections of the book. These are extra exam-style questions which can be used for revision and exam practice.

Each unit begins with a topic summary to remind you of the key points from the classbook, followed by a selection of questions of varying styles and difficulty. Most units have their questions divided by a line. Questions after the line are more demanding. Your teacher will tell you which questions to do and whether you should work beyond the line.

In GCSE papers from 2003, 25% of the marks on question papers will have to be answered with longer answers called Extended and Continuous writing. In these questions marks may be awarded for 'quality of written communication'. This includes writing in sentences with proper use and spelling of scientific vocabulary.

To help you answer these questions when you are at home without your classbook, there is a reference section at the back of this book. This includes a glossary so that you can find out the meaning of any important scientific terms, a list of important formulae, physical quantities and their units, and a Periodic Table.

It is becoming increasingly important to do regular homework if you want to do well. This homework book will provide a valuable way to practise and reinforce what you learn in class, and so help you to do your best and increase your enjoyment of Science.

Life processes and living things

1 Life processes

- The characteristics of living things are: growth, respiration, sensitivity, nutrition, movement, excretion and reproduction.

Q1 Complete the following sentences.

a) The removal of waste carbon dioxide when breathing out is an example of the process called ______________________.

b) Food material is eaten, digested and absorbed. Scientists refer to this process as ______________________.

c) Plants and animals ______________________ to replace those that die.

Q2 Name an animal which moves:

a) in water **b)** in the air **c)** on land

In each case describe briefly how the animal moves.

Q3 In what ways are animals different to plants in terms of **a)** nutrition, **b)** growth and **c)** movement?

2–3 Organ systems and cells

- All living things are made up of cells.
- The structure of a cell is modified and adapted for a specific function, each part having a specific function to carry out.
- A tissue is a system composed of cells of one type whose structure is modified to perform a specialised function.
- An organ is a system composed of different tissues modified to perform specialised functions.
- An organ system is a collection of organs combining to perform specialised functions within an organism.
- The work of the body is divided up amongst the organ systems. This is known as division of labour.

Q1 Match each item in column 1 with an item in column 2.

	Column 1		Column 2
A	egg	1	male sex cell or gamete
B	sperm	2	female sex organ
C	testis	3	female sex cell or gamete
D	ovary	4	male sex organ

Q2 Match each structure labelled in the diagram to one of the organ systems listed below.
1 circulatory system
2 digestive system
3 excretory system
4 gas exchange system
5 nervous system
6 reproductive system

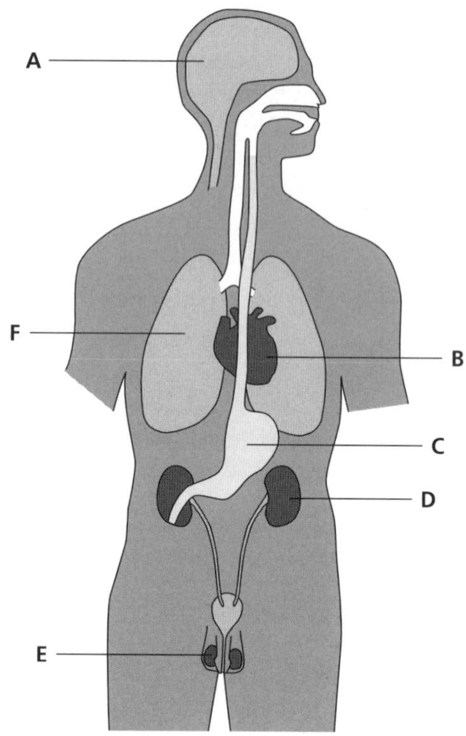

Q3 Name the organs included in each of the following human organ systems:
a) gaseous exchange system
b) nervous system
c) excretory system.

Q4 What is the biological term for a single-celled organism?

Q5 Complete the paragraph below, choosing words from the list to fill in the blank spaces.

cellulose chlorophyll chloroplast cytoplasm
fat nucleus vacuole water

A plant cell wall is made from _____________. The _____________ is found lining the cell wall. As a result a central space is created. This is called a _____________. The space is usually filled with _____________ and a variety of solutes. The solution is known as cell sap. Most cells have a large cell structure called a _____________. This contains the chromosomes.

Q6 a) Draw and label a diagram of i) a typical plant cell and ii) a typical animal cell.
b) Describe the functions of the structures you have labelled.

Q7 Explain briefly what you understand by the term **division of labour**.

4 Movement of particles

- Diffusion is the movement of particles (molecules or ions) from a region of higher concentration to a region of lower concentration down a concentration gradient.
- Osmosis is a special type of diffusion involving a selectively permeable membrane.
- Osmosis is the diffusion of water molecules from a region of higher concentration to a region of lower concentration.
- A concentration gradient exists between two areas of differing concentration.
- Active transport is an energy-consuming process by which substances are transported against a concentration gradient.

Q1 Choose the correct word(s) to complete each statement.

a) The wall of a plant cell allows water, sugars and ions to pass through it in either direction. Such a wall is said to be ______________.

non-porous   **selectively permeable**   **permeable**

b) The movement of water and solutes into and out of a cell is called ______________.

convection   **diffusion**   **radiation**   **transpiration**

Q2 Complete the sentence below, choosing words from the list to fill in the blank spaces.

concentrated   **dilute**   **insoluble**   **selectively permeable**
permeable   **soluble**   **solute**   **solvent**

Osmosis occurs when a ______________ membrane separates a more ______________ solution from a more ______________ solution or from pure ______________.

Q3 A visking tubing sac (A) was filled with distilled water. Another was filled with concentrated sucrose solution (B). They were then placed in beakers as shown in the diagram. After one hour they were removed from their beakers and checked to see if they had changed in any way.

a) What special property does visking tubing have?

b) What would you expect each sac to be like after an hour in the liquid in the beaker? Give the reasons behind any suggestions you make.

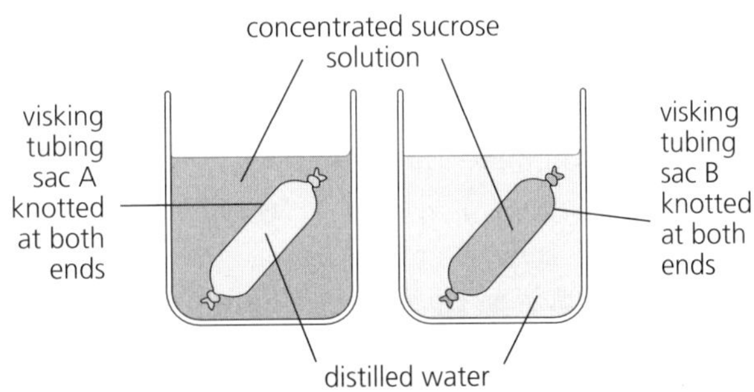

Q4 Match the definitions below with the processes listed A to C.

A active transport
B diffusion
C osmosis

a) movement of particles or ions down a concentration gradient across a permeable membrane
b) movement of water down a concentration gradient across a selectively permeable membrane
c) movement of particles across a membrane against a concentration gradient.

Q5 What do the terms **concentration gradient** and **equilibrium** mean with respect to osmosis?

Q6 Potato discs were cut from fresh potato tuber tissue. Seven sets of discs were cut and weighed. Each set was placed in a different concentration of sugar solution. The discs were removed from their solution after one hour, carefully blotted dry and re-weighed. The table (right) shows the percentage change in mass in each of the seven samples.

a) Plot a graph of these results.
b) From your graph determine at what concentration of sugar there would have been no change in mass.
c) Explain the significance of the result to **b)**.

Concentration (arbitrary units)	% change in mass of potato discs
0 (distilled water)	22
1	17
2	9
3	3
4	–3
5	–10
6	–15

Q7 Why is it not possible to explain the uptake of certain ions into root hair cells by diffusion alone?

5–7 Chromosomes, mitosis, meiosis

- Chromosomes are found in the nucleus of plant and animal cells.
- A gene can be defined as a short section of DNA. The DNA code is passed on to the next generation of cells or organisms by DNA (genetic) replication.
- Mitosis involves the replication (exact copying) of genetic material.
- Mitosis is important in growth, repair and asexual reproduction.
- Meiosis must occur somewhere in the life cycle of a sexually reproducing organism to halve the chromosome number in the formation of gametes.

■ **Variation arises in meiosis as a result of exchange of parts of chromosomes and random assortment.**

Q1 Complete the following sentences.

a) In a human cell I would expect the chromosomes to be contained in the ______________ .

b) The number of chromosomes I would expect to find in a normal, human body cell would be ______________ .

Q2 Complete the paragraph below, choosing words from the list to fill in the blank spaces.

poles replicated spindle fibres chromosomes
contraction chromatids equator relaxation

Mitosis involves a series of processes. Each of the ______________ is ______________ to form a pair of ______________. A system of ______________ is set up in the dividing cell in order to bring about their separation. The separation is achieved by ______________ of these structures. As a result two sets of chromosomes are organised at the ______________ of the cell. The cytoplasm is then divided in two to produce two daughter cells.

Q3 Complete the table to summarise the differences between mitosis and meiosis.

	Mitosis	Meiosis
Where?		
Why?		
Chromosome number of new cell?		

Q4 Why is it important that cells needed for growth and repair are produced by mitotic divisions?

Q5 Explain briefly how it is that the cells produced by a mitotic division are genetically identical to each other and to the cell from which they were formed.

Q6 Analysis of the bases found in a section of DNA showed that the percentage for adenine was 15. What would the other values have been? Explain your reasoning.

8–9 Nutrients and human diet

- Carbohydrates, fats and proteins contain the elements carbon, hydrogen and oxygen. Proteins always contain a fourth element, nitrogen.
- Carbohydrates as a group include, as examples, simple sugars such as glucose and more complex substances such as starch and glycogen.
- Fats are formed from fatty acids and glycerol. Proteins are formed from amino acids.
- Vitamins are complex organic compounds which are essential nutrients. Mineral ions can be classified as macro- or micronutrients.
- A balanced diet must include carbohydrates, fats, proteins, vitamins, minerals, water and dietary fibre. These substances must be eaten in sufficient quantities to meet the needs of the individual, for growth, repair and energy, and essential health factors.
- Obesity, anorexia nervosa and bulimia are eating-related disorders.

Q1 Complete the paragraph below, choosing words from the list to fill in the blank spaces.

carbohydrates starch glucose fats digestion
maltose sugars polymerisation proteins

A nutrient which contains carbon, hydrogen and oxygen only, is likely to belong to either the food class called ______________ or the food class ______________. Glucose and maltose are commonly known as ______________. Maltose is formed from two ______________ molecules which combine together. The two monosaccharides can be reformed by a process known as ______________ which takes place in the gut. ______________ is formed from a very large number of glucose molecules. The reaction which creates the links between them is called a ______________ reaction.

Q2 State two ways in which glucose differs from starch.

Q3 Write a word equation to show how fats are formed.

Q4 Match each item in column 1 with an item in column 2.

	Column 1		**Column 2**
A	dietary fibre	1	provide the highest energy yield
B	fats	2	provide amino acids for growth
C	proteins	3	are essential in very small quantities
D	vitamins	4	encourages improved peristalsis

Q5 Complete the following sentences.

a) Iron is an essential dietary mineral because it is an important part of the ______________ molecule.

b) Calcium plays an important part in the formation of bones and teeth. One good source of calcium is ______________.

Q6 Which important classes of food would be obtained from:

a) steak and chips

b) a green salad

c) a slice of wholemeal bread and butter

d) a glass of milk?

Draw up a results table with the following headings: food source; carbohydrates; fats; proteins; vitamins; minerals; water; dietary fibre. Complete the table for the meal described in **a)** – **d)** by ticking the appropriate boxes.

10 Digestive system

- **The five basic processes involved in human nutrition are: i) ingestion, ii) digestion, iii) absorption, iv) assimilation, v) egestion.**
- **The gut is a tube, modified along its length, each part carrying out specific functions.**
- **Several structures play an important role in connection with the gut. These include: salivary glands, teeth, tongue, epiglottis, liver, gall bladder, bile duct, pancreas, and pancreatic duct.**

Q1 List the parts of the gut, in order, through which food passes on its way from mouth to anus.

Q2 List three structures which are linked to the gut by means of ducts.

Q3 The diagram shows the mammalian gut and associated organs. In which part of the gut, labelled A to F, do the following processes occur?

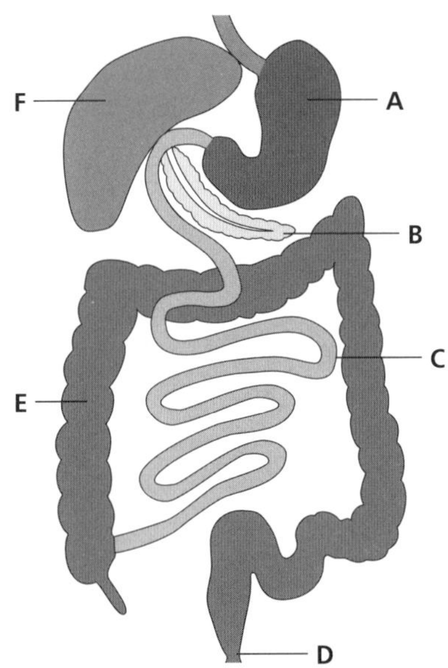

a) storage of glycogen

b) absorption of digested food

c) reabsorption of water

d) temporary storage of ingested food

e) secretion of gastric juice

f) egestion

Q4 What are the functions of the following structures?

a) an incisor
b) a canine tooth
c) a molar tooth
d) epiglottis
e) oesophagus

Q5 **a)** Explain the significance of the colon in terms of water balance.

b) Occasionally it is necessary to perform a colostomy to remove the rectum and or part of the colon as a result of cancerous growth. Gut content is diverted into an external sac from the end of the small intestine. Suggest a possible physiological problem associated with gut function which would result from such an operation.

11 Digestion in the gut

- **Digestion of food involves mechanical and chemical digestion.**
- **Mechanical digestion takes place in the mouth (chewing) and the stomach (churning).**
- **Large insoluble food molecules are digested by enzymes to form small soluble molecules.**
- **Chemical reactions in cells are speeded up by enzymes (catalysts). Enzymes are proteins. They are affected by temperature, pH and inhibitors.**
- **The end products of chemical digestion are: glucose, fatty acids and glycerol, and amino acids.**

Q1 The enzyme present in human saliva digests:

A cellulose   B protein   C starch   D sucrose

Q2 The function of bile is to:

A digest fat
B emulsify fat
C add mucus to the small intestine
D keep the small intestine contents acid

Q3 Complete the passage below, choosing words from the list to fill in the blank spaces.

insoluble absorbed mechanical stomach soluble
enzymes digestion chewing chemical muscular

Food material is made of large, ______________ molecules. Many of them are too big to pass through the wall of the gut. Food has to be broken down. The process is called ______________.

____________ digestion of food is brought about by ____________ and by the ____________ activity of the ____________. ____________ bring about ____________ digestion. The products of digestion are molecules which are ____________ and in a form which can be ____________.

Q4 Complete the following table, using words from the list.

amylase amino acids fat maltose mouth starch

Food	Enzyme	Place	Digestion products
starch			maltose
protein	protease	stomach and small intestine	
	maltase	small intestine	glucose
	lipase	small intestine	fatty acids and glycerol

Q5 Complete the paragraph below, choosing words from the list to fill in the blank spaces.

specific particular proteins shape unchanged
pH temperature catalysts rate

Enzymes only alter the ____________ of a reaction, remaining ____________ at the end of the reaction. They make reactions go faster by acting as ____________. All enzymes are ____________ and are molecules which have a very special ____________. This means that they are very ____________ and can only affect the rate of a ____________ reaction. Enzymes are sensitive to ____________ and ____________.

Q6 An experiment was carried out to investigate the effect of temperature on the action of a digestive enzyme. A fixed quantity of distilled water, enzyme and food chemical was kept at a fixed temperature in a water bath. The time taken for the enzyme to complete its action was noted. The results are recorded in the table below. (× = no change after 10 minutes.)

Temperature/°C	5	10	15	20	25	30	35	40	45	50	55	60	65	70
Time taken to complete the change/minutes	×	×	×	6.5	4.0	3.5	1.5	1.5	2.0	3.5	×	×	×	×

a) On graph paper, choose suitable scales for the temperature (x-axis) and the time taken (y-axis). Plot the results and draw a line of best fit.

b) Between which temperatures was the enzyme most active?

c) Suggest a reason why there was no change after 10 minutes in the first three and last four temperatures.

d) Suggest an explanation for the results for the first three and the last four temperatures.

Q7 Write an account of what happens to the starch and protein in a cheese sandwich when it is eaten.

12 Absorption and assimilation

- **The small intestine is long, has a folded internal surface and is lined with structures called villi providing a very large surface area for absorption.**
- **An arteriole, venule and a lacteal lie inside each villus.**
- **The venule transports sugars and amino acids away from the villus. The lacteal carries fats into circulation in the lymph system.**
- **Absorbed food is first taken to the liver, which controls how it is put to use.**

Q1 Which one of the following processes works more efficiently because of the large surface area of the small intestine?

A absorption B assimilation C egestion D ingestion

Q2 Complete the paragraph below, choosing words from the list to fill in the blank spaces.

absorbed small intestine projections area folded
surface time microvilli wider narrow large

Digested food has to be ____________ before it leaves the gut. Two things which affect how well this happens are the nature of the ____________ through which it is absorbed and the ____________ for it to take place. The section of the gut where this happens is the ____________. This is a long, ____________ tube. More of the food will be in contact with the wall as a result and for a longer time than it would be in a ____________ tube. The surface ____________ through which food is absorbed is very ____________ for a number of reasons. The inner surface of the intestine here is ____________. The surface layer forms finger-like ____________ called villi. These too have projections on their surface called ____________.

Q3 Explain why starch has to be digested to sugar before it can be absorbed by the body.

Q4 Read the following passage and suggest suitable words to replace the letters A to F.

Branches of the artery which goes to the small intestine form ___A___ which deliver blood to each villus. Blood drains away from the villus to join blood from other villi before it leaves the small intestine. A ___B___, a fine branch of the lymphatic system, lies in the centre of each villus.

____C____, amino acids, fatty acids and glycerol diffuse across the thin membranes of the villus surface cells. They enter the blood and are carried away. Their immediate removal helps to maintain a ____D____ gradient. This makes sure that more digested food can be taken into the blood by diffusion. Some absorption of digested food is by ____E____ transport. Cells at the surface of the villus absorb fatty acids and glycerol. These are used to synthesise ____F____ and the droplets formed are transferred to the lacteal.

Q5 a) Name two substances added to the blood as it flows through the blood vessels of the small intestine.

b) Where are these substances taken to first after leaving the small intestine?

c) Which blood vessel takes them there?

d) State what each of these two substances is used for in the body.

Q6 The diagram shows the liver and its blood supply. Name the parts labelled A to E.

Q7 Write an account of the way the liver controls the use of food sent to it.

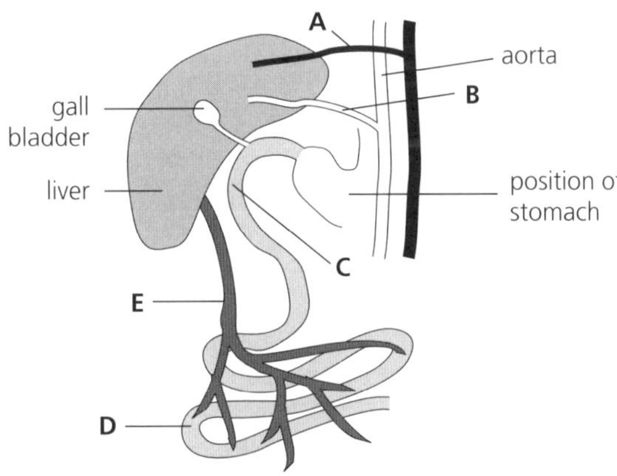

13–14 The circulatory system

- **A circulatory system allows rapid movement of materials in the right direction.**
- **The human circulatory system involves double circulation through the pulmonary and systemic circuits.**
- **The human heart has two atria above two ventricles. Each atrium communicates with a ventricle on the same side through valves.**
- **The valves prevent backflow of blood when the ventricle contracts.**
- **Diet, exercise, smoking and stress can affect the circulatory system.**

Q1 Complete the paragraph below, choosing words from the list to fill in the blank spaces.

lungs twice systemic venae cavae heart
deoxygenated vein oxygenated aorta pulmonary

Blood flows through the human heart ______________ on each complete circuit. The ______________ circuit takes blood from the ______________ to the ______________ in the pulmonary artery. The blood returns to the heart from the lungs in the pulmonary ______________. The ______________ circuit takes ______________ blood to the organs and returns ______________ blood to the heart. Oxygenated blood leaves the heart for the body in the ______________. Blood returns to the heart in the ______________.

Q2 Match each item in column 1 with an item in column 2.

	Column 1		Column 2
A	pulmonary artery	1	contains blood at highest pressure
B	hepatic vein	2	drains blood from the head
C	renal artery	3	carries blood to a lung
D	aorta	4	drains blood from the liver
E	jugular vein	5	supplies blood to a kidney

Q3 Rearrange the following words into a list to show the correct direction of the circulation of blood through the body, heart and lungs.

left ventricle lungs right ventricle left atrium right atrium

Q4 a) From what parts of the body does the blood entering the heart at i) the right and ii) the left atria come?

b) Describe the way the valves between the atria and ventricles move i) when the atria contract and ii) when the ventricles contract.

c) Although both ventricles pump the same amount of blood, the wall of the left ventricle is thicker than the wall of the right ventricle. Explain briefly why this is so.

Q5 The diagram shows a mammalian heart and associated blood vessels. Name the parts labelled A to G.

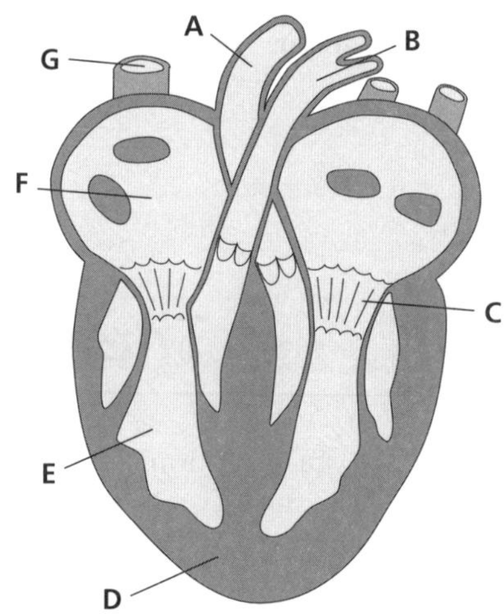

Q6 Write an account of how it is that a unicell can function without a circulatory system but we cannot.

Q7 Write an account to explain the term **double circulation**.

15–16 Blood and its transportation

- Arteries carry blood at high pressure away from the heart. Veins carry blood at lower pressure back to the heart.
- Capillaries leak tissue fluid.
- The structure of a blood vessel is related to its function.
- Blood consists of plasma, red blood cells, platelets and two types of white blood cells called phagocytes and lymphocytes.
- The structure of a red blood cell (haemoglobin, large surface area and no nucleus) is related to its function.

Q1 Complete the paragraph below, choosing words from the list to fill in the blank spaces.

valves plasma capillaries arteries low relax
contract carbon dioxide high oxygen veins

The muscles of the heart ____________, pushing blood into arteries under ____________ pressure. ____________ carry blood to organs. ____________ leaks out of ____________ to supply ____________ to the tissues. ____________ take ____________ away from the tissues. Blood in veins is under ____________ pressure. ____________ stop the blood moving backwards in veins when the heart muscles ____________.

Q2 Complete the following table comparing the structure of an artery and a vein.

Feature	Artery	Vein
wall		
elastic tissue		
lumen		
valves		

Q3 The following structures are found in blood.

a) What is A's job?

b) Cell B can escape from a capillary. Why is this important?

c) What do cells like cell C make?

d) When do structures D become important?

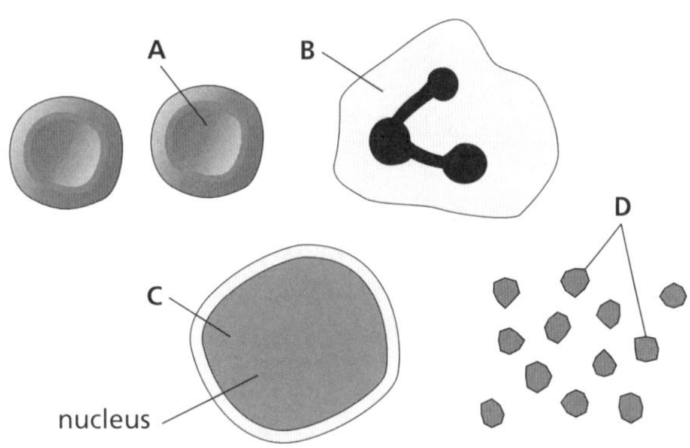

Q4 Give two features which enable you to distinguish clearly between each of the following pairs:

a) arteries and capillaries **b)** red blood cells and white blood cells.

Q5 Carbon monoxide is a gas given out by car engines. It combines with haemoglobin in the red blood cells.

Explain briefly why it is dangerous to stay in a garage with the doors and windows closed while a car engine is running.

17–18 Breathing and gas exchange

- **The structures of the parts of the breathing system are related to their functions.**
- **Movements of the rib cage and diaphragm alter the volume of the thorax, and its pressure. This causes air to move in and out of the lungs.**
- **The same amount of nitrogen, more carbon dioxide and less oxygen is breathed out than breathed in.**
- **High concentrations of carbon dioxide or lactic acid in the blood cause the rate of breathing to increase.**
- **The large, moist, thin, permeable lung surface and associated blood supply enables efficient gas exchange.**
- **There is a link between smoking and respiratory disease.**

Q1 Complete the paragraph below, choosing words from the list to fill in the blank spaces.

cartilage alveoli trachea large bronchus lungs
exchanging collapsing small bronchioles nose

Air enters the breathing system through the ______________ or mouth. The air passes along a tube called the ______________. There are rings of ______________ around the trachea to prevent it from ______________. Air then passes into the right or left ______________. These supply air to the ______________. Inside the lung, the tubes divide to form narrower tubes called ______________. At the end of each of these there are ______________ sacs known as ______________. Together the air sacs provide a ______________ surface for ______________ gases.

Q2 a) Which gas is essential for all living things?

b) Where exactly is this gas taken into i) *Amoeba* and ii) a human?

c) State **five** ways in which the surface through which the gas enters humans and *Amoeba* is similar.

Q3 The diagram shows a detailed section of one air sac.

a) Copy the diagram and label it fully to describe gas exchange at the lung surface.

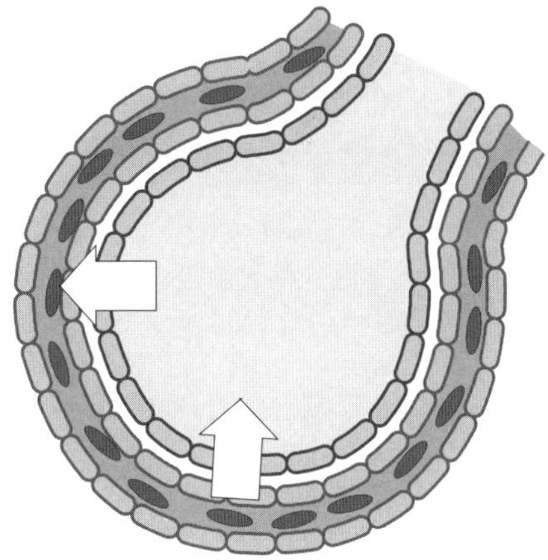

The alveoli, or air sacs, in the lung provide a large, moist surface for gas exchange during breathing. The walls of the air sacs contain many blood capillaries.

b) Why must the surface be moist?

c) What benefit is there in having many blood capillaries present?

Q4 One method of artificial respiration is called **mouth to mouth**. Air is blown into the lungs of the patient.

a) Why must the patient's nose be closed?

b) How can exhaled air be of any use to the patient?

Q5 Write an account to explain how breathing is brought about in humans.

Q6 Explain briefly the link between respiration and breathing rate.

19–20 Respiration: aerobic, anaerobic

- **Respiration provides the energy needed for life processes.**
- **Glucose and oxygen are needed for aerobic respiration. Carbon dioxide and water are produced as wastes.**
- **Anaerobic respiration releases much less energy than aerobic respiration.**
- **Cells can run up an 'oxygen debt' in the absence of oxygen, producing lactic acid which causes muscle fatigue.**
- **Baking and fermentation are employed in bread making, wine making and brewing.**

Q1 Aerobic respiration requires:

A carbon dioxide B heat energy
C oxygen D water

Q2 Respiration always involves:

A oxidation of fats B oxidation of proteins
C production of ATP D production of lactic acid

Q3 Complete the passage below, choosing words from the list to fill in the blank spaces.

long glucose yeast oxidise water more
anaerobic oxygen short aerobic

Cells need to release energy from food chemicals such as ___________. The process which does this is called respiration. Cells use oxygen to ___________ the food. Carbon dioxide and ___________ are produced as waste. This type of respiration is called ___________ respiration. Muscle cells can respire without oxygen, but only for a ___________ time. When they do they are carrying out ___________ respiration. Some cells, e.g. ___________ cells, can respire without oxygen for a ___________ time. Aerobic respiration in muscle cells releases ___________ energy than anaerobic respiration. Muscle cells respiring anaerobically create an ___________ debt.

Q4 A tuna fish is a very active hunter. Although fish are described as cold-blooded the tuna fish's body temperature is usually a few degrees higher than the water around it. How would you explain that?

Q5 a) Describe the chemical changes which take place in an actively contracting muscle which result in an oxygen debt.

b) How is the debt paid off?

21–2 Senses and the eye

- **Sense organs (receptors) detect stimuli and convert the energy from a stimulus into nerve impulses.**
- **Nerve cells, called neurones, have a structure adapted to collect and transfer impulses, some of them over long distances.**
- **A typical nerve pathway includes a stimulus, a receptor, neurones, and an effector leading to a response.**
- **The iris and pupil control the amount of light entering the eye. The lens and retina produce a focused image on the retina.**
- **There are two types of light-sensitive cells in the retina. Rods provide black and white vision. Cones provide colour vision.**

Q1 The diagram shows a motor neurone.

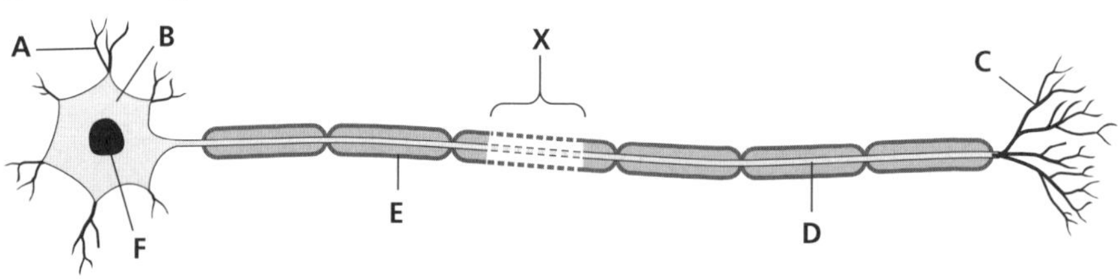

a) Match parts of the neurone, labelled A to F, with the label descriptions numbered i) to vi).
i) cytoplasm of cell body ii) point of contact with muscle or gland
iii) receptive dendrite iv) axon v) nucleus vi) myelin sheath

b) What does the feature labelled X suggest about the neurone?

c) Nerve messages transferred to A and from C cross a space. What is this space called?

Q2 Complete the paragraph below, choosing words from the list to fill in the blank spaces.

neurones central relay spinal cord glands
effectors sense muscles sensory brain
nerve motor respond stimulus

Changes in the environment are recognised by ___________ organs.
Light is one _____________ which we _____________ to.
A _____________ neurone passes impulses from a sense organ to the _____________ nervous system. The _____________ and _____________ form the central nervous system of a human.
_____________ neurones pass impulses to the brain. The brain sends impulses to _____________ by means of _____________ neurones.
Effectors can be _____________ or _____________.
A _____________ is a collection of _____________.

Q3 The diagram shows a section through a human eye.

a) Name parts A, C, F and G.

b) Which label indicates:
i) an area with the highest concentration of cone cells
ii) a part which contains muscles
iii) a part which contains pigments (colour)
iv) suspensory ligaments?

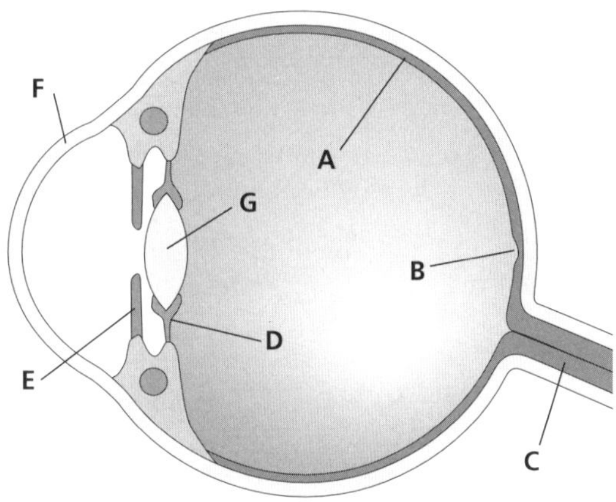

Q4 a) What is the job of the retina?

b) What adjustment do the eyes make when a person moves into a brighter light?

c) How are these adjustments brought about?

d) How does the shape of the lens differ when focused on a close object compared to its shape when focused on a distant object?

e) How is this change brought about?

Q5 You should be able to stand on one leg without falling over.
a) Name two sense organs which help you to do this.
b) Describe briefly how parts of the central nervous system are involved in controlling your balancing movements.

Q6 Explain briefly how looking slightly to one side of a dim light source, such as a star, enables you to see it better.

23–4 Reflex action and hormones

- **A reflex is an automatic means of rapid coordination by nervous control.**
- **Human reflexes include sneezing and the response of the iris to changes in light intensity.**
- **Hormones are chemical messengers carried in blood plasma.**
- **Hormones affect specific groups of cells known as target cells.**
- **Hormone and nervous coordination differ with respect to nature of transmission, speed of message, duration of message and specificity.**

Q1 Each of the following statements tells you something about a reflex action. Each statement has a letter. The statements are not in the correct order. Write down a list of letters which will be the correct order for a reflex action.

A Motor neurone is stimulated.
B Impulses are generated in a relay neurone in the central nervous system.
C The organism responds.
D Impulse passes along a sensory neurone.
E Sense organ detects a stimulus.
F A muscle contracts.

Q2 Complete the following table. Name **two** hormones produced by the human body. For each, name the gland which produces it and briefly state what effect it has.

Hormone	Gland	Effect

Q3 The diagram shows the reflex arc.

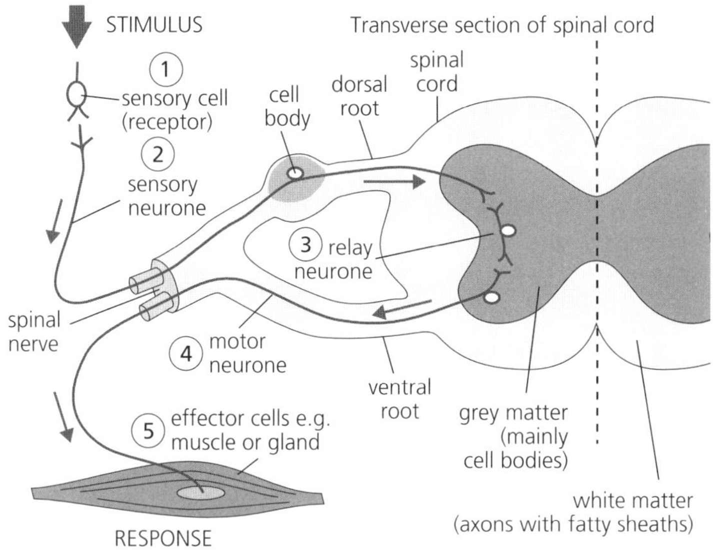

Write a short paragraph describing the sequence of events in the reflex arc. Use the words in the labels.

Q4 **a)** If you touch a very hot object the muscles of your arm very quickly move your hand away. What is this type of nervous response called?

b) Sometimes you move your hands towards a fire and keep them there to warm them. Explain briefly how the nervous activity involved differs from that named in part **a)**.

Q5 Write an account to describe the differences between hormonal and nervous coordination.

25–6 Insulin and sex hormones

- **Insulin is produced by the pancreas and controls blood glucose concentration.**
- **Liver cells respond to the level of insulin in the blood and convert glucose to glycogen.**
- **Testosterone is the male sex hormone. Oestrogen and progesterone are female sex hormones.**
- **Sex hormones control secondary sexual characteristics and the production of gametes.**
- **Female sex hormones control the menstrual cycle.**

Q1 Which organ in the body produces insulin?

A adrenal gland B duodenum C liver D pancreas

Q2 Match each item in column 1 with an item in column 2.

	Column 1		Column 2
A	endocrine	1	involved in control of blood glucose
B	exocrine	2	female sex hormone
C	insulin	3	ducted gland
D	progesterone	4	male sex hormone
E	testosterone	5	ductless gland

Q3 Complete the passage below, choosing words from the list to fill in the blank spaces.

endocrine testosterone progesterone exocrine
oestrogen glucose insulin testes

The pancreas is an ____________ gland which secretes the hormone ____________. This hormone plays a part in controlling blood ____________ concentration. ____________ is a male sex hormone produced in the ____________. Gamete formation in females involves two sex hormones. They are ____________ and ____________.

Q4 How could transplanting a pancreas avoid the need for a diabetes sufferer to inject insulin?

Q5 Draw a diagram to summarise the way in which the pancreas and the liver stop blood glucose concentration from rising too high.

Q6 Explain briefly how *in vitro* fertilisation (IVF) may be used to help someone to have a baby.

27–8 Homeostasis and the kidney

- **Human cells are surrounded by tissue fluid. It is important therefore that tissue fluid is kept constant.**
- **The ability which complex animals have to control their internal environment is described as homeostasis.**
- **Homeostatic systems often involve negative feedback.**
- **Waste materials including urea are removed from the blood by the kidneys.**
- **The kidneys filter blood at high pressure and then reabsorb water and other substances to meet the body's needs.**

Q1 Complete the passage on the next page, choosing words from the list to fill in the blank spaces.

homeostasis more composition tissue fluid
temperature negative less heat

Cells remove essential raw materials from the ______________ which surrounds them. They release carbon dioxide and other wastes into the tissue fluid. Respiration generates ______________. Therefore the ______________ and ______________ of tissue fluid around a cell will vary. The raw materials must be replaced and the wastes removed and the temperature reduced if the cell is to function efficiently.
Keeping things in a steady state is known as ______________. The kidney is one organ which is involved. The kidney keeps the concentration of water in the body in balance. If there is too much water in the blood the kidney excretes ______________. When the concentration of water is ______________ than it should be the kidney stops excreting water and actively keeps it. This type of control involves ______________ feedback.

Q2 The diagram shows the human urinary system. Name the parts labelled A to F.

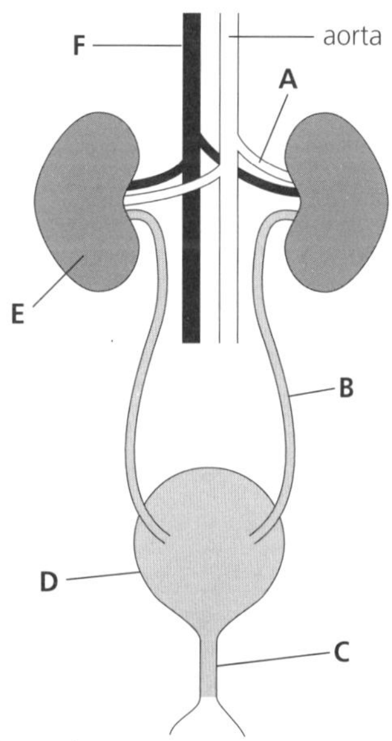

Q3 Complete the paragraph below, choosing words from the list to fill in the blank spaces.

Bowman's capsule decreases
glomerulus increases renal artery
renal vein ureter urethra

The tube which carries blood to the kidney is known as the ______________. Inside the kidney there are a very large number of capillary knots, each called a ______________. At each knot the blood pressure initially ______________. Urine passes from the kidney to the bladder in the ______________.

Q4 State **two** ways in which water is gained by the body and **two** ways in which water loss occurs.

Q5 The table shows data on three mammals.

Animal	Relative length of kidney tubule	Urea concentration (units per litre urine)	Habitat
beaver	short	500	water
human	medium	1150	land
desert rat	long	6000	land

a) Which animal produces the most dilute urine?
b) What is the relationship between length of kidney tubule and concentration of urine?

c) Humans and desert rats live on land. Suggest an explanation for the difference in urine concentration in the two animals.

Q6 What do you understand by the terms **ultrafiltration** and **selective reabsorption**?

29 Homeostasis and the skin

- **The human body gains and loses heat. This must be controlled and kept in balance.**
- **Human skin has structures in it which are involved in maintaining a constant body temperature.**
- **The skin assists in controlling body temperature through the involvement of hairs, sweat glands and blood capillaries.**

Q1 Which of the following adult animals is likely to lose heat fastest?
A horse B dog C rat D mouse

Q2 The diagram shows a section through mammalian skin.

a) Name the parts labelled A–E.

b) What parts do A and B play in temperature control?

c) When are structures C most active?

d) State two functions of D.

e) What part does structure E play in temperature control?

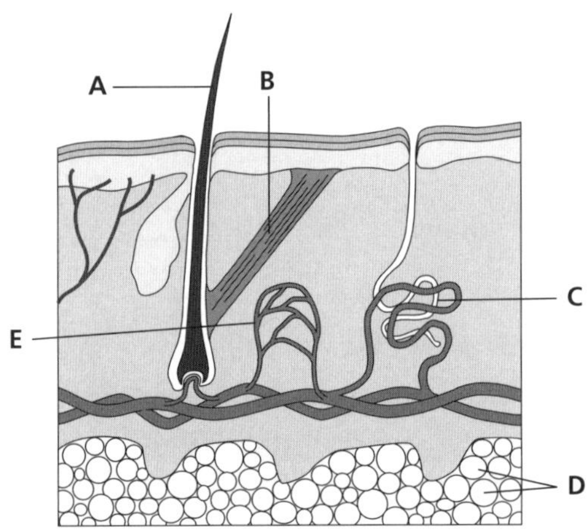

Q3 Complete the paragraph below, choosing words from the list to fill in the blank spaces.

more raised less insulates conserve constrict warm sweating

When the body needs to ______________ heat the hairs are ______________. This traps a layer of warm air which ______________ the skin. Blood capillaries in the skin ______________ and so ______________ blood flows near the surface. As a result ______________ heat is kept in. During ______________ weather the opposite happens and in addition more ______________ takes place.

Q4 A whale is a mammal which has lost its covering of hair and developed a thick layer of fat beneath its skin.
  a) What advantage has the whale gained by losing its fur?
  b) What advantage does the blubber (fat) give to the whale?

Q5 a) What is the average body temperature for a healthy human being?
  b) Mammals are sometimes described as **warm-blooded**. What does this really mean?

---

  c) Very cold conditions are never very pleasant. For newborn babies and elderly people low temperatures can be extremely dangerous. Explain briefly why this is so.

Q6 Write an account of the way the body maintains a constant temperature.

30 Defence of the body

- **The skin and the formation of clots act as barriers to prevent the entry of potential pathogens (disease-causing organisms).**
- **Some body secretions such as tears and stomach acid kill bacteria.**
- **Phagocytes engulf and kill bacteria.**
- **Pathogens produce antigens which affect body cells.**
- **Lymphocytes produce antibodies which kill bacteria or counter the effect of antigens.**

Q1 Which one of the following glands can produce white blood cells?
A endocrine B lymph C sweat D tear

Q2 Match each item in column 1 with an item in column 2.

	Column 1		**Column 2**
A	antibody	1	disease-causing organism
B	antigen	2	produced by lymphocytes
C	phagocyte	3	foreign material
D	pathogen	4	engulf bacteria

Q3 Complete the paragraph below, choosing words from the list to fill in the blank spaces.

phagocytes neutralise lymphocytes antibodies enzymes antigens

When bacteria get into the body through a cut, white blood cells attempt to prevent infection. _____________ can move about. When they find bacteria they enclose them in a food vacuole. _____________ are released into the food vacuole. The enzymes kill and digest the bacteria. _____________ make _____________ which _____________ the _____________ produced by pathogens.

Q4 a) How does the structure of a phagocyte cell differ from the structure of a lymphocyte?
b) What job do both phagocytes and lymphocytes do?
c) How do phagocytes and lymphocytes carry out this job?

Q5 a) What part do platelets play in protecting the body?
b) Where does fibrinogen occur in the body?
c) What is the difference between fibrinogen and fibrin?

Q6 Write an account of the way a clot forms when the skin is cut.

31 Drugs and solvent abuse

- **Drugs and solvents may affect human behaviour and cause damage to the brain, liver and kidneys.**
- **Body reactions are affected by alcohol and other drugs.**
- **Alcohol is a commonly used drug which adversely affects ability to drive.**
- **The legal driving limit in the UK is a blood alcohol concentration (BAC) of 80 mg per 100 ml of blood.**
- **Some drugs are harmful and habit forming. A person may become physically or psychologically dependent on a drug.**

Q1 Complete the paragraph below, choosing words from the list to fill in the blank spaces.

habit-forming physically dependent tolerance
withdrawal symptoms psychological dependence

Drugs used wrongly are harmful and often ______________. When the body gets used to having a drug in circulation the person has to keep taking it otherwise they suffer from ______________. A person in this state is ______________ on the drug. Withdrawal symptoms are what happens, i.e. the way the body reacts, when the cells are not getting any more of the drug. Sometimes people think that they need to keep on taking the drug in order to cope with life. This is described as ______________. One of the many problems linked to drug abuse is that the body's ______________ to the drug increases. This means that ever larger doses are needed to get the same effect.

Q2 a) What does **addicted** mean?
b) What is the addictive drug in cigarettes?

Q3 a) What is the highest legal blood alcohol concentration permitted for someone to drive a car?

b) In what way does alcohol affect a person's ability to drive?

Q4 Complete the following table.

Substance	Effect on the body
alcohol	
nicotine	
solvents	

Q5 Write an account of the biological and social problems associated with smoking.

32 Photosynthesis – 1

- **Plants need carbon dioxide, water and light for photosynthesis.**
- **Chlorophyll is a green pigment which absorbs light for photosynthesis.**
- **Different colours of light produce different rates of photosynthesis.**
- **Photosynthesis produces glucose and oxygen.**
- **The structure of a leaf is adapted to promote efficient photosynthesis.**

Q1 Which one of the following substances is needed for photosynthesis and is not used up or made by the process?

A oxygen B carbon dioxide C chlorophyll D light energy

Q2 Large numbers of structures containing a green pigment are found in the mesophyll cells of leaves. What are these structures likely to be?

Q3 Complete the paragraph below, choosing words from the list to fill in the blank spaces.

respiration chlorophyll starch light photosynthesis sugar carbon dioxide

Plants make their own food by a process called ______________. Plants need ______________ and water as raw materials. Only those cells which have the pigment ______________ can take part and then only if they are in the ______________. The products of this process are ______________ and oxygen. Some of the sugar is used for ______________ and some is stored as ______________.

Q4 The diagram shows a section through part of a leaf.

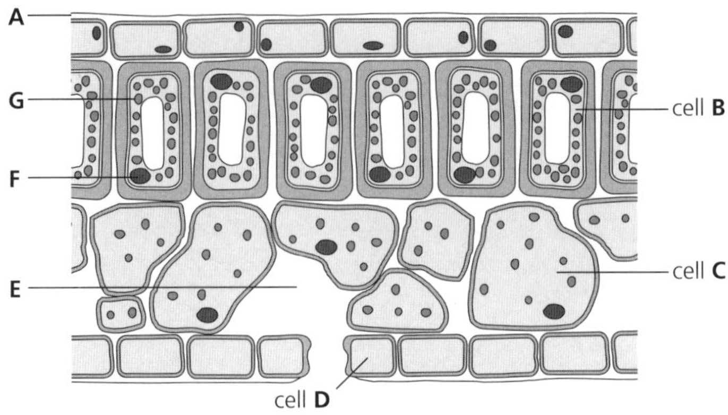

a) Name the parts labelled A to G.
b) Which cells have the most chloroplasts?
c) Which raw materials for photosynthesis would you expect to be in E?
d) Which product of photosynthesis would you expect to be in E?
e) What do a pair of Ds form?
f) Which tissues, not shown in the diagram, are vital for transporting raw materials for photosynthesis to the leaf and removing a product?
g) Where are the tissues in your answer to **f)** concentrated in the leaf?

---

h) How does photosynthesis benefit from cells like cell C having an irregular shape?

Q5 Describe the way leaves are adapted to be efficient structures for photosynthesis.

33–5 Photosynthesis – 2

- Sometimes the overall rate of a process is held back because of a shortage of one essential factor. Such a factor is described as a limiting factor.
- Plants require nitrogen, phosphorus and potassium in addition to carbon, hydrogen and oxygen. Other elements, including magnesium, are required in smaller amounts for healthy plant growth.
- Natural and artificial fertilisers provide minerals and can lead to better yields even in monocultures.
- Plants make many different organic compounds from glucose, the first being starch.
- Humans take advantage of the wide range of organic compounds made by plants.

Q1 Complete the table below, choosing words from the list to fill in the blank spaces.

membranes ATP proteins chlorophyll nucleic acids

Mineral	Used by plants
nitrogen	to make ______________ and ______________
phosphorus	to make ______________ which is produced in respiration
potassium	in the formation of cell ______________
magnesium	to make ______________

Q2 Which factors can be used to measure photosynthetic rate?

Q3 Name two limiting factors for photosynthesis.

Q4 The diagram shows the relationship between rate of photosynthesis and carbon dioxide concentration.

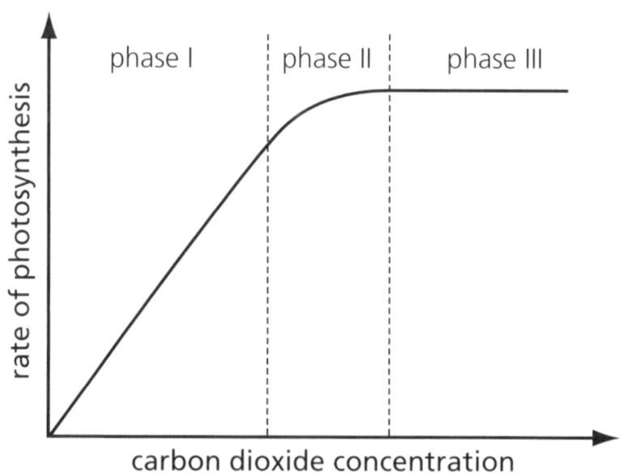

a) In which phase is photosynthesis limited by carbon dioxide concentration?

b) What could be limiting the rate of photosynthesis in phase III?

Q5 Tomatoes can be grown inside a greenhouse or outside in the garden. Relate your answers to the following questions to photosynthesis.

a) Give **two** advantages of growing tomatoes inside a greenhouse.

b) Give **one** disadvantage of growing tomatoes inside a greenhouse.

c) Explain briefly why extra carbon dioxide added to the air in a greenhouse increases the tomato crop.

Q6 What is happening in a plant at **compensation point** light intensity?

Q7 Explain briefly why heating a greenhouse in winter without giving extra artificial light could lead to a reduction in the crop produced.

36–7 Plant hormones

- Plants are sensitive to environmental stimuli such as light and gravity.
- Plants produce growth substances (plant hormones) that regulate cell growth and development.
- Rooting powders contain growth substances which promote root growth in shoot cuttings.
- Selective weedkillers contain synthetic growth substances.
- Growth substances can be applied artificially to unpollinated flowers to set fruit and produce seedless fruits. Grapes and citrus fruits provide examples.

Q1 Match each item in column 1 with an item in column 2.

	Column 1		**Column 2**
A	auxins	1	are positively geotropic
B	geotropism	2	are positively phototropic
C	phototropism	3	are growth hormones
D	roots	4	is a growth response to gravity
E	shoots	5	is a growth response to light

Q2 Complete the table by naming **two** examples of growth movements shown by a plant. In each case name the type of growth movement, the stimulus which causes it and the benefit to the plant.

Name	Stimulus	Benefit to the plant
1		
2		

Q3 Why do gardeners pinch the tips out of plants?

Q4 The diagram shows a simple demonstration of the effect of unidirectional light, i.e. light from one side.

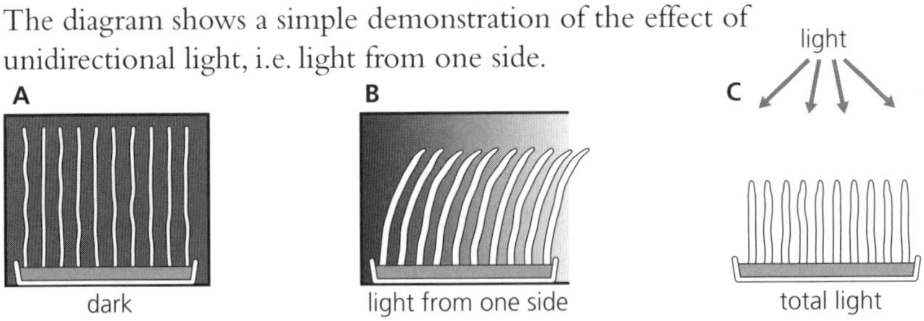

a) In which Petri dish are the seedlings tallest?

b) Using information from A and C, what effect does light appear to have on growth?

c) Which side of each seedling in B will receive the more light?

d) Which side of each seedling in B appears to have grown more?

e) Use your answers to explain the curvature of each seedling shown in B.

Q5 **a)** When would you use a selective weedkiller on a lawn?
b) How do selective weedkillers work?

38–9 Transport in plants

- Root hair cells are modified for the absorption of water by osmosis.
- Transpiration is the evaporation of water from shoot systems (leaves in particular).
- Xylem and phloem are found in the vascular bundles of plant stems and are continuous with xylem and phloem in leaves and roots.
- Water and minerals are transported up xylem vessels which are dead with no cytoplasm.
- Phloem tissue is alive and transports sugars up and down stems to regions of growth or storage.

Q1 Complete the paragraph below, choosing words from the list to fill in the blank spaces.

lignin atmosphere xylem minerals osmosis transpiration stomatal

Water enters the root hair cell by ____________. It passes across the root into the xylem. Mature ____________ cells are dead because their walls are waterproofed with ____________. Leaves lose water to the ____________ by evaporation. The loss of water through the open ____________ pores of leaves is called ____________. Transpiration pulls water and dissolved ____________ up the xylem from the roots.

Q2 State **two** adaptations shown by leaves to reduce water loss.

Q3 The diagram shows a transverse section through a stem.
a) Name the parts labelled A, B, C and D.
Which tissue:
b) transports water
c) transports sucrose
d) is covered by a layer of wax
e) provides support for the stem by turgor pressure
f) provides support for the stem because its cells are lignified (woody)?

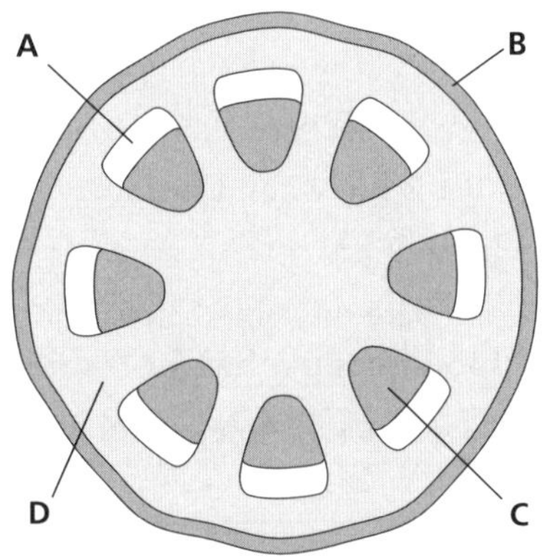

Q4 Which of the following describes one function of xylem?

	Substance transported	Source	Destination
A	sucrose	leaves	roots
B	water	leaves	roots
C	sucrose	roots	leaves
D	water	roots	leaves

Q5 **a)** Draw **two** views of the lower surface of the leaf of a plant to show the position and shape of the guard cells when:

i) the stomata are open

ii) the stomata are closed.

b) Give **one** example of environmental conditions in which the stomata are likely to close during the day in summer.

c) Why would this benefit the plant?

Q6 Draw a diagram of a root hair cell. Label the drawing with notes which together describe how the structure of the root hair cell enables it to carry out its job efficiently.

40 Variation

- **There are two types of variation: continuous and discontinuous.**
- **Continuous variation results in a graded effect in the organism, e.g. height in humans, which can be affected by the environment during the lifetime of the individual.**
- **Discontinuous variation results in large, clear-cut differences between individuals, e.g. blood group in humans, and cannot be altered by the environment during the lifetime of the individual.**

Q1 Which of the following is an example of continuous variation in humans?
A blood group B body mass C ability to taste PTC D gender

Q2 What is the main difference between continuous and discontinuous variation?

Q3 Complete the table below, choosing words from the list.
blood group height ability to taste PTC body mass gender

Continuous variation	Discontinuous variation

Q4 The table shows the heights in centimetres of 30 pupils.

Pupil	Height/cm	Pupil	Height/cm	Pupil	Height/cm	Pupil	Height/cm
1	152	9	150	17	154	25	150
2	148	10	152	18	152	26	154
3	150	11	152	19	160	27	152
4	152	12	140	20	136	28	158
5	144	13	144	21	142	29	160
6	150	14	144	22	144	30	158
7	154	15	148	23	148		
8	146	16	152	24	146		

a) What was the smallest height recorded in the group?
b) What was the biggest height recorded in the group?
c) Make a table to find out how many pupils were at each of the heights recorded (not just the smallest and biggest).
d) Use graph paper to draw a histogram of your results.

Q5 Briefly explain how continuous variation in a feature, such as body mass, can come about.

41 Reproduction and mutation

- **Sexual reproduction in animals and plants involves gamete formation and fertilisation.**
- **Non-identical twins are formed when two eggs are fertilised each by a different sperm. Identical twins are formed when an embryo divides into two parts, each part then developing independently.**
- **Random fusion of gametes gives rise to variation in the offspring.**
- **Mistakes can occur randomly when chromosomes are copied. These mistakes are called mutations.**
- **Down's syndrome is caused by the zygote having an extra chromosome.**

Q1 Match each item in column 1 with an item in column 2.

	Column 1		**Column 2**
A	ovary	1	produces sperms
B	oviduct	2	site where fetus develops
C	testis	3	carries sperms to the urethra
D	uterus	4	produces eggs
E	vas deferens	5	usual site of fertilisation

Q2 Write out the following list of parts of the male and female reproductive system under three headings: 'male', 'female' and 'both':

cervix Cowper's gland epididymis funnel ovary oviduct penis prostate gland scrotal sac seminal vesicle testis ureter urethra urinary bladder uterus vagina vas deferens

Q3 The diagram shows a vertical section through a flower.

a) Name parts A–F.

b) Which labelled structure contains male gametes?

c) Which labelled structure contains female gametes?

d) Where will seeds be formed?

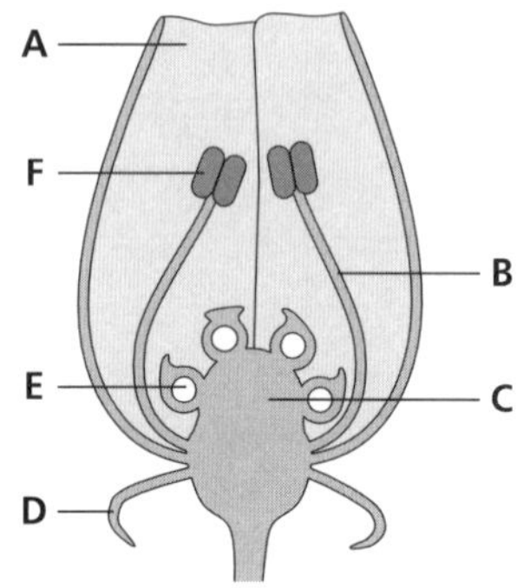

Q4 Complete the paragraph below, choosing words from the list to fill in the blank spaces.

oviduct testes embryo uterus vagina ovaries

Sperms are produced in the ____________. Eggs are produced in the ____________. Sperms are released into the ____________ during sexual intercourse. The sperms swim through the ____________ to meet the egg. Fertilisation usually takes place in the ____________. Development of the ____________ takes place in the uterus.

Q5 What is the difference between the way identical and non-identical twins are formed?

Q6 Name one mutagen and suggest how it might bring about a genetic change.

42 Monohybrid inheritance

- A monohybrid cross considers the inheritance of features which are controlled by single genes. Examples in humans include ear lobe attachment, folding of the upper eyelid and the ability to taste a chemical known as PTC.
- It is possible to demonstrate the expected outcome of a monohybrid cross using a checkerboard diagram.
- The checkerboard diagrams demonstrate probable outcomes only.
- A 3:1 phenotypic ratio is expected when both parents are heterozygous for the characteristic considered.
- A 1:1 phenotypic ratio is expected when one parent is heterozygous and the other is homozygous recessive.
- The inheritance of X and Y chromosomes results in male (XY) and female (XX) offspring (expected ratio 1:1).

Q1 Match each term in column 1 with a statement in column 2.

	Terms		**Statements**
A	Allele	1	The outcome of a particular gene. The feature shown
B	Dominant	2	Allele which works only when it is partnered by another like itself
C	Gene	3	A section of the nucleic acid, of a chromosome
D	Genotype	4	Symbols representing the alleles present for a particular gene
E	Heterozygous	5	A condition where both the alleles for a particular gene are the same
F	Homozygous	6	Feature controlled by a single gene
G	Monohybrid	7	A condition where the alleles for a particular gene are different
H	Phenotype	8	One form of a gene
I	Recessive	9	Always expresses itself

Q2 In fruit flies, the allele for grey body colour is dominant. Black body colour is recessive.
Two grey-bodied flies were mated and they produced 75 grey-bodied and 25 black-bodied flies. Which of the following possible crosses was the cross described likely to have been?

A GG × GG B GG × gg C Gg × GG D Gg × Gg

Q3 Some humans can roll their tongue longways. Some cannot. Those who can, possess at least one dominant allele.

a) What are the two possible genotypes for 'rollers'?

b) What is the genotype of a 'non-roller'?

c) Does it necessarily follow that the children of two 'rollers' will be able to roll their tongue longways?

d) Give a reasoned explanation for your answer to **c)**. Use the checkerboard to help you with your explanation.

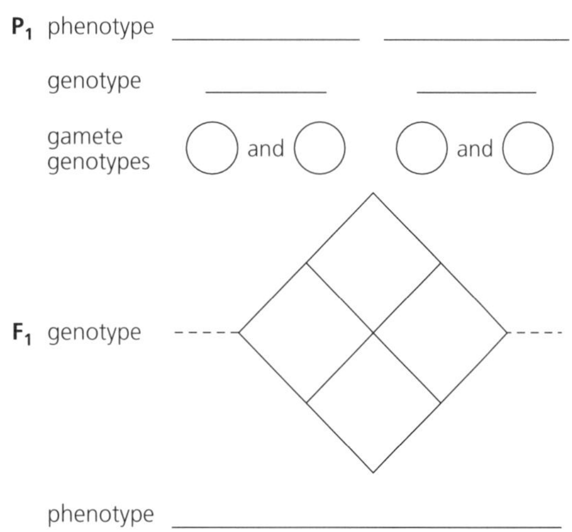

Q4 Using a copy of the checkerboard above, show how sex is determined in human beings.

43 Inheritance and disease

- Some diseases, including sickle-cell anaemia, cystic fibrosis, muscular dystrophy and haemophilia, are genetic in origin and can be inherited.
- Sickle-cell anaemia and cystic fibrosis are caused by recessive alleles which are not sex-linked.
- Some disorders are more frequent in males (XY) than females (XX). These are examples of sex-linked inheritance, e.g. red–green colour-blindness.
- For some alleles on the X chromosome there are no functioning alleles on the Y chromosome.
- Muscular dystrophy and haemophilia are caused by X-linked recessives.

Q1 Complete the table by adding the names of appropriate disorders or diseases.

Genetic disorders/diseases	Sex-linked disorders/diseases

Q2 Complete the table by adding appropriate causes and symptoms.

Disease	Cause	Symptoms
sickle-cell anaemia		
cystic fibrosis		
muscular dystrophy		
haemophilia		

Q3 **a)** Draw diagrams to represent the sex chromosomes of a human male and female.

b) Label your diagrams to show why for some alleles on the X chromosomes there are no functioning alleles on the Y chromosome.

c) Draw a labelled diagram of the sex chromosomes of a female who is a carrier for haemophilia.

d) Draw a diagram of the sex chromosomes of a haemophiliac male.

Q4 Why can males **not** be 'carriers' for haemophilia?

44–5 Breeding and biotechnology

- Some plants reproduce asexually, e.g. by bulbs, stem tubers and runners.
- A collection of asexually produced offspring have identical genotypes and are referred to as clones.
- Micropropagation is a bio-technique used commercially to produce large numbers of 'copies' from a single piece of 'stock' plant.
- Plants and animals can be bred deliberately to increase or exaggerate particular desirable characteristics. This is described as selective breeding.
- Plant and animal varieties have been bred for, for example, food yield, flavour, appearance, disease resistance.

Q1 Complete the table by adding the names of appropriate plants.

Bulb	Stem tuber	Runner

Q2 What will be true about all the individual members of a clone?

Q3 One species of buttercup reproduces by runners as well as fruits.

a) Give one advantage to the plant of spreading by runners compared with fruits under natural conditions.

b) Give one advantage to the plant of spreading by fruits compared with runners under natural conditions.

Q4 Read the following passage and then answer the questions below.

Micropropagation. A **stock plant** is carefully chosen and kept free of disease. Small pieces (**explants**) of tissue are cut from the stock plant. The explants are **surface sterilised**. New shoots are encouraged to grow on an agar jelly containing nutrients and **growth hormones**. The nutrients feed the tissues. The new shoots are removed from the explant and divided up. These are then grown on on agar jelly and the process is repeated until enough **copies** have been made. Roots are then encouraged by using a different mixture of growth substances.

a) What do you think the term **stock plant** means?

b) What are **explants**?

c) Why is it necessary to **surface sterilise** the explants?

d) What will be the effect of the **growth hormones** added to the nutrient jelly?

e) Why is the use of the word **copies** a very appropriate one?

Q5 a) List the features of a domesticated plant or animal which you think may have been built into it by artificial selection.

b) Write a short account describing how this might have been done.

46–7 Evolution, natural selection

- The theory of evolution suggests that all living things have a common ancestry.
- One line of evidence which supports the theory of evolution comes from fossil records.
- The similarities shown by the limbs of members of different vertebrate groups provide additional supportive evidence, as does DNA analysis.
- Some individual members of a species will be better equipped to survive under the environmental conditions which surround them (**survival of the fittest**). These individuals survive, breed and pass on their genes, whereas less successful individuals die out and their genes are lost (**natural selection**).

Q1 Complete the paragraph below, choosing words from the list to fill in the blank spaces.

impression sedimentary fossils casting petrification

Rocks can be broken down by the action of heat, frost and water. The particles made in this way have been laid down over very long periods of time to form ______________ rock. Evidence of dead organisms trapped in these layers appears as ______________. They are the result of a process called ______________. There are other ways in which fossils may have formed. An organism may have been turned to stone by a process called ______________. A footprint in soft mud may have been preserved as an ______________.

Q2 Name **four** different methods of fossilisation.

Q3 The fossil remains of vertebrate animals are often only bones and teeth. Describe briefly how fossils may have been formed, explaining why the softer parts are not preserved as fossils.

Q4 Each of the following statements tells you something about natural selection. Each statement has a letter. The statements are not in the correct order. Write down a list of letters which will be the correct order outlining the argument for evolution by natural selection.

A The more competitive offspring survive and breed.
B Some of the offspring will have differences which give them an advantage over the others.
C Most organisms produce large numbers of offspring.
D The more competitive genes will be passed on.
E The offspring will be in competition with each other for space, food and other factors.
F There will be variation among the offspring.

Q5 Explain briefly what scientists mean by the phrase **survival of the fittest**.

Q6 What evidence do we have from electron microscopy and biotechnology that supports the idea that today's plants and animals have a common ancestry?

48 Adaptation and competition

- **Predators are adapted to catch and eat their prey. Prey animals are adapted to avoid being caught and eaten.**
- **Plants compete for space, light, water and other essential environmental factors.**
- **Some plants show adaptations, e.g. spines, stings and poisons, to deter herbivores.**
- **Some animals are adapted to life in extreme climates.**
- **The introduction of species from one ecosystem into another can have serious consequences for the native species.**

Q1 Which of the following animals is a predator?
A buzzard B mouse C rabbit D sparrow

Q2 Complete the paragraph below, choosing words from the list to fill in the blank spaces.

zebras predator prey herbivores lion

A ______________ is a carnivorous animal which eats meat from an animal that it has caught itself. Often the animals eaten are ______________. These are the predator's ______________. A ______________ would be a good example of a predator. Its prey would include ______________ or gazelles.

Q3 a) Which features shown by the skull in the diagram would lead you to think it was the skull of a predator?

b) Which other features would you expect a mammalian predator to show?

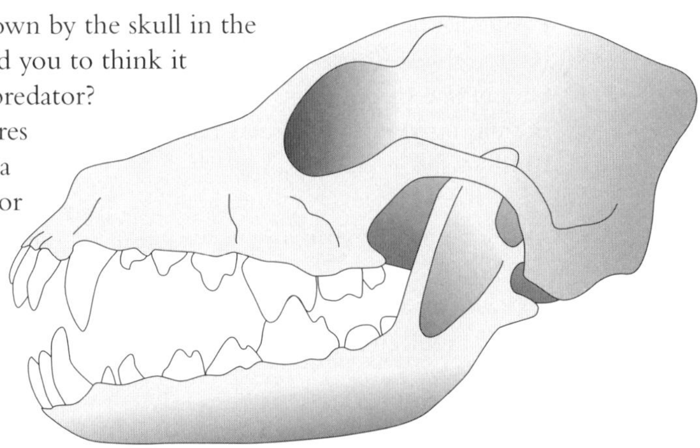

Q4 Some mammals show adaptation to extreme habitats. Complete the table to explain how the adaptations help a polar bear to survive in very cold climates.

Feature	Survival value
large body	
small ears	
thick fur	
thick layer of fat under the skin	
hibernate	

Q5 In your own words describe how plants avoid being eaten when they cannot run away.

49–50 Humans and their environment

- Human beings bring about rapid environmental changes.
- Sea levels may rise due to increased melting of ice at the Poles as a result of the greenhouse effect. The greenhouse effect is caused by an increase in the concentration of carbon dioxide in the atmosphere.
- The concentration of sulphur dioxide and nitrogen oxides in the atmosphere is rising. These gases are introduced into the air when fossil fuels are burnt, providing the chemical ingredients for acid rain. Acid rain affects the balance of metal ions in the soil and kills trees. Some freshwater organisms are also particularly affected.
- Huge areas of tropical forests have been cleared for land. This has affected not only the native species but also the carbon dioxide balance of the world.
- Pesticides have disadvantages as well as advantages.
- Renewable resources are being used faster than they can be replaced.
- Global use of energy resources is running at an unsustainable level.
- Increasing rural and urban land use is removing natural habitats.
- Biodiversity is decreasing.

Q1 Which one of the following is the major source of sulphur dioxide pollution?

A biogas converters
B coal and oil fuelled power stations
C hydroelectric power stations
D nuclear power stations

Q2 Complete the table.

Pesticide	Kills
herbicide	
fungicide	
insecticide	

Q3 Complete the table.

Example of an air pollutant	
Source of pollutant	
Damage caused	
Steps to improve situation	

Q4 Match the type of extinction A and B with the definitions 1 and 2.

A **background** B **mass**

1 Extinction caused by small changes in the environment of a species, over a period of time. These extinctions have been happening throughout time.

2 Extinction that produces a sudden loss of large numbers of different species from all over the world in a relatively short period of time. Caused by major changes in climate, or natural catastrophes such as large meteor strikes.

Q5 Read the following passage and then answer the questions below.

Herbicides are useful because weeds compete with crop plants for **essential factors**. Some fungi cause disease and reduce the **efficiency** of the crop. They may also cause **spoilage** of the final product. Insect pests cause damage during crop production and also lead to losses in storage. There are considerable advantages to be gained by using pesticides. There are also serious disadvantages. Two of these are:

1 Herbicides, fungicides and pesticides contain potentially poisonous chemicals which can **get into food chains**.

2 Pests become resistant to the pesticide as **a result of natural selection**.

a) Suggest **three essential factors** for which competition might occur in a crop field.

b) Suggest how a fungal disease might affect the **efficiency** of a crop plant.

c) Suggest a more scientific term to replace **spoilage**.

d) What might be the consequences of pesticides **getting into food chains**?

e) Explain briefly how a pest might become resistant to a pesticide as **a result of natural selection**.

51 Feeding relationships

- A community consists of populations of different species interacting with each other in an ecosystem.
- Green plants use light energy to make the organic compounds which form the basis of all feeding relationships in an ecosystem. Green plants are called producers.
- All non-photosynthetic organisms called consumers are dependent on green plants.
- Each level of feeding within an ecosystem is called a trophic level with the producer at trophic level 1.
- Organic compounds contain energy, some of which is transferred along a sequence of organisms in a food chain. A set of interconnected food chains is called a food web. Most of the energy obtained by an organism is lost to the environment as heat.
- Pyramids of number and biomass can be constructed from data about a food chain.

Q1 Complete the paragraph below, choosing words from the list to fill in the blank spaces.

herbivores omnivores producers carnivores

Plants are ______________. They make food by a process called photosynthesis. Plants are eaten by ______________. Animals that feed only on meat are called ______________. There are some animals, humans included, that eat both plants and animals. These are ______________.

Q2 Why are green plants the essential starting point for all food chains?

A They occur in larger numbers than animals.
B They can convert light energy into chemical energy.
C They release oxygen into the air.
D They remove carbon dioxide from the air.

Q3 Select items from the following list to answer the questions below.

cow dead leaves chicken grass earthworm

a) Construct two food chains, each with three trophic levels, all ending at Man.

b) Draw a pyramid of numbers for one of the food chains you have produced. You will only be able to estimate the size of each level.

c) Construct a food web ending with Man using all the items in the list.

Q4 The diagram shows a simple pond ecosystem.

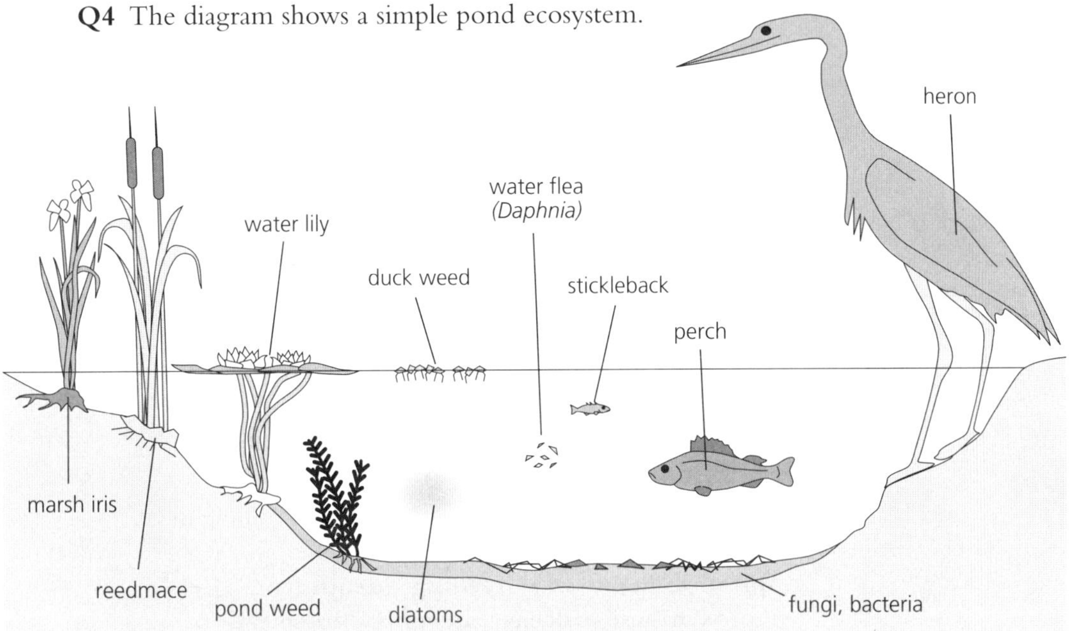

Answer the following with reference to this ecosystem.

a) Name **three** producers.

b) i) Name **three** consumers.

ii) List the three consumers in the order in which they are likely to appear in a food chain.

c) Construct **one** possible food chain.

d) Construct **one** simple food web.

Q5 Draw an inverted pyramid of numbers for a food chain based on an oak tree.

Q6 Construct a food web for a named habitat (not including a pond) such as a grassland or a woodland. Illustrate your food web with drawings or cut-out pictures.

52 The carbon cycle

- **Decomposition is important in the recycling of elements in ecosystems.**
- **Organisms which bring about the recycling of elements by decomposition are called decomposers. They include bacteria and fungi.**
- **Carbon is recycled involving photosynthesis, respiration, decomposition and burning.**

Questions for Unit 52

Q1 Complete the paragraph below, choosing words from the list to fill in the blank spaces.

inorganic oxygen photosynthesis respiration fossil fuels organic burning carbon dioxide

Plants take in ____________ food. Carbon dioxide is removed from the air by green plants. Plants make sugar from the carbon dioxide by ____________. Some of the sugar is used by the plants during ____________. Any sugar not used by the plant in this way is turned into other carbon-containing compounds. These ____________ compounds are used in the nutrition of all non-photosynthetic organisms. Respiration in plants and animals adds ____________ to the carbon in these compounds and returns it to the air as ____________. ____________ wood and ____________ also puts carbon dioxide back into the air.

Q2 Complete the following diagram of the carbon cycle by filling in the boxes with terms chosen from the following list.

respiration (use twice) **feeding death** (use twice) **photosynthesis decay burning fossilisation**

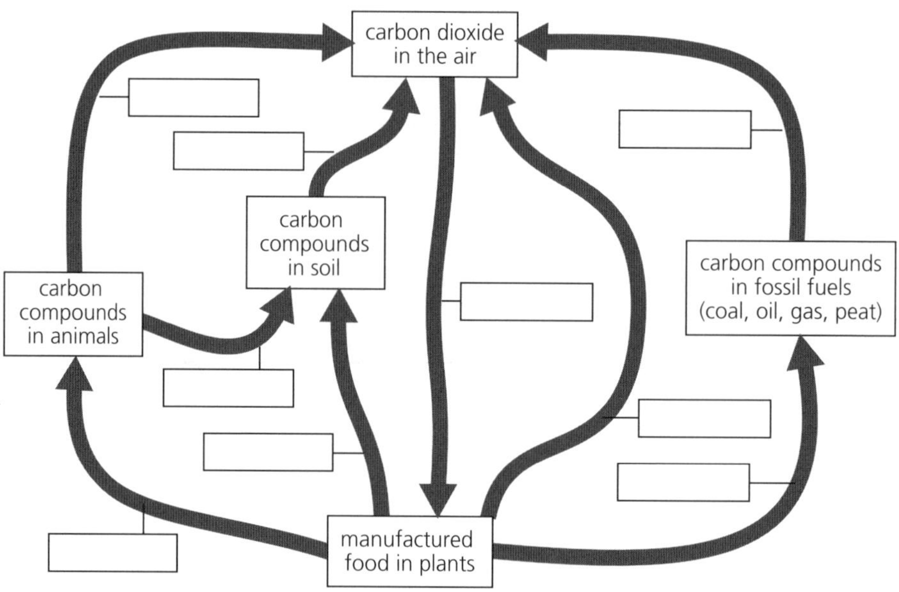

Q3 a) Which organisms are likely to be actively at work in a compost heap?

b) Why is it important for a compost heap to be well supplied with water and air?

Q4 Write an account of the way Man is affecting the balance of the carbon cycle.

53 The nitrogen cycle

- Bacteria are involved in the nitrogen cycle as decomposers, nitrifiers, nitrogen-fixers and denitrifiers.
- Leguminous plants form a symbiotic relationship with nitrogen-fixing bacteria and can be important in crop rotation as part of organic farming practice.
- Lightning adds nitrates to the soil.
- Plant roots absorb nitrates from the soil to form amino acids and proteins.
- Plant remains can be ploughed back into the soil as 'green manure' to improve nitrate levels.

Q1 Complete the paragraph below, choosing words from the list to fill in the blank spaces.

rains ammonia nitrates lightning urea
decomposers nitrifying bacteria

Bacteria in the soil convert proteins and ______________ into another nitrogen-containing substance called ______________. These bacteria are called ______________. Another group of soil bacteria, called ______________, convert ammonia to ______________. Nitrates are also put back into the soil during thunderstorms. ______________ causes chemical changes to take place in the air. The nitrates formed get into the soil when it ______________.

Q2 Complete the following diagram of the nitrogen cycle by filling in the ovals with terms chosen from the following list.

urea nitrates protein in animals nitrogen in air nitrites
ammonium compounds protein in plants ammonia

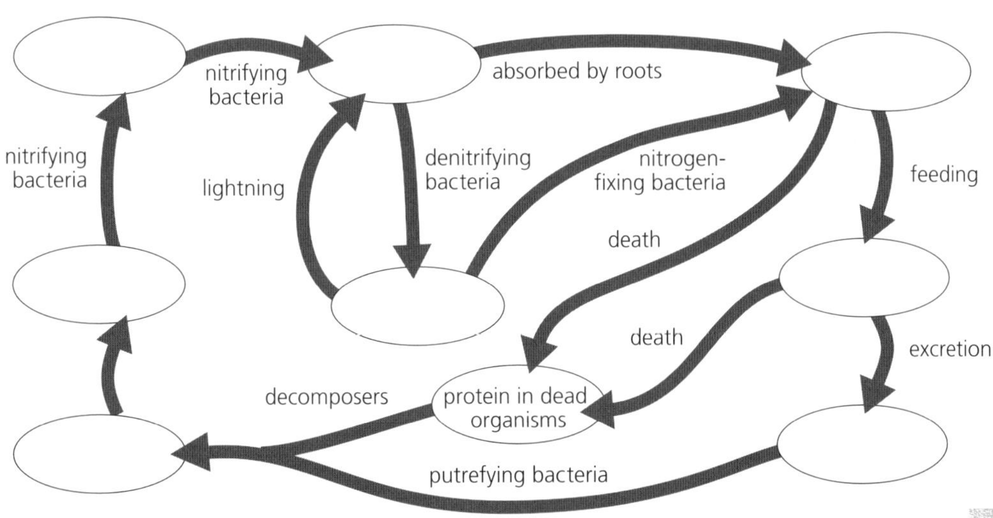

Q3 Label the diagram below. Choose your labels from the following list.

ammonia nitrates nitrogen gas
protein in dead organisms symbiosis urea

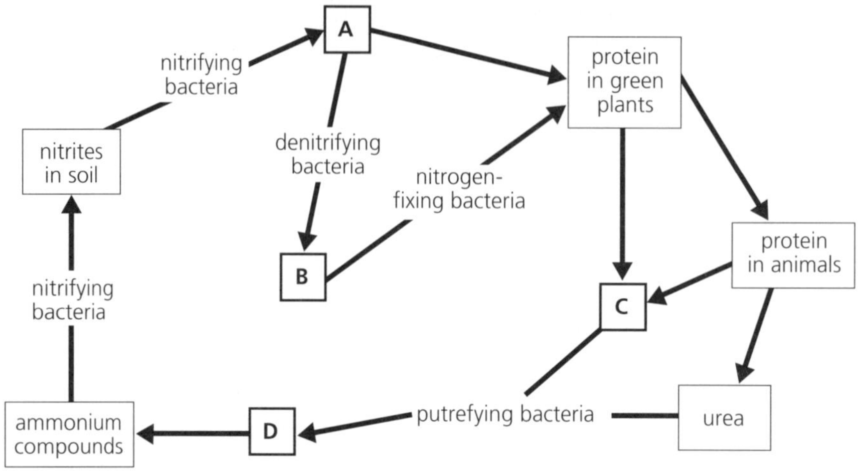

Q4 Which partners in a symbiotic relationship may be involved in the nitrogen cycle? How does each partner benefit from the relationship?

54 Artificial ecosystems

- An area of land can produce more plant food and therefore feed more people than if the area is used for producing meat.
- Crop yield increases with closer planting but it is then limited owing to competition.
- Weeds, insect pests and fungal diseases reduce crop yields but can be controlled using pesticides or by non-chemical means.
- Some areas of land, e.g. moorland and hillsides, are unsuitable for most plant crops but are useful for some production, e.g. sheep, deer and conifers.
- Animals reared intensively, e.g. chickens and pigs, are fed on cereals and therefore indirectly require 'land'.

Q1 Complete the table below, choosing terms from the following list.

farmer plus natural source total relatively low
relatively high farmer less

	Free-range pigs	Battery-unit pigs
Land used per animal		
Food supplied by		
Farmer's control over feeding		

Q2 What does the term 'leaching' mean?

Q3 Why does it take a large area of moorland to support one sheep?

Q4 Explain briefly why there are many sheep farms in the highlands of the North and West of England.

Q5 What are the problems associated with overuse of artificial fertilisers in terms of
a) soil structure
b) freshwater pollution?

Q6 What extra work do farmers have to do if they grow plant crops intensively? Why might this make the product more expensive?

Q7 Explain the possible dangers of using excessive amounts of chemicals for controlling pests.

Review questions

Cell activity (Units 1–7)

Q1 Write down the names and functions of those cell organelles visible only when viewed by an electron microscope.

Q2 Give two features which enable you to distinguish clearly between plant cells and animal cells.

Q3 **a)** List, in order, the structures through which water must pass, from the outside, before it reaches the vacuole of a plant cell.
b) Copy out the following list of structures:

cellulose cell wall **chloroplast** **cytoplasm**
mitochondrion **nucleus** **vacuole**

Underline those structures which occur in plant cells only.

Q4 Complete the following sentences. Choose your words from the list below.

diploid **doubled** **forty-six** **halved**
haploid **twenty-three**

a) Nuclei containing a number of pairs of chromosomes are called ____________________ nuclei.
b) Gametes or sex cells such as eggs and sperms have sets of single chromosomes. These cells contain ____________________ nuclei.
c) At fertilisation the number of chromosomes present in the egg is ____________________.

d) During the formation of gametes the number of chromosomes present is _____________________.

Q5 a) Describe **a different** biological example **for each** of the following processes:

i) diffusion

ii) osmosis

iii) active transport.

b) Which of the three processes in **a)** requires the use of respiratory energy?

Q6 The diagram shows a freshly peeled potato which has had a cylinder of tissue removed with a cork borer to form a 'well'.

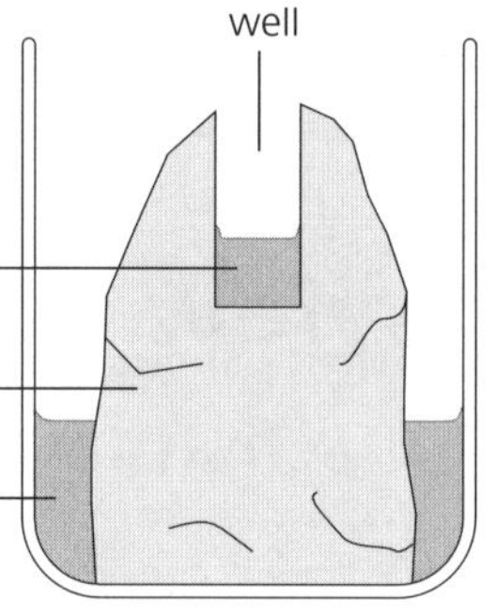

a) Suggest a change you would expect to see in the well after an hour.

b) Explain your answer to **a)**.

c) What would you expect to happen if the experiment was repeated using a previously boiled potato?

d) Explain your answer to **c)**.

Humans as organisms (Units 8–31)

Q1 Food is digested to form simple soluble compounds.

a) What are the soluble compounds absorbed when the following compounds are digested?

i) starch ii) fats iii) proteins.

b) In which organ are the soluble products of digestion absorbed?

c) What are microvilli?

Q2 The table shows the content of air breathed in and out of a human.

Gas	Air breathed in/%	Air breathed out/%
oxygen	21.00	17.00
nitrogen	78.96	78.96

a) Which sample of gas has the greater percentage of oxygen?

b) How do you account for the data given for nitrogen?

c) i) Which **two** natural components of air that humans breathe in and out is missing from the data?

ii) What values would you expect for these two components?

Q3 The diagram shows a simple piece of equipment which can be used to measure gas exchange in small animals such as blowfly larvae.

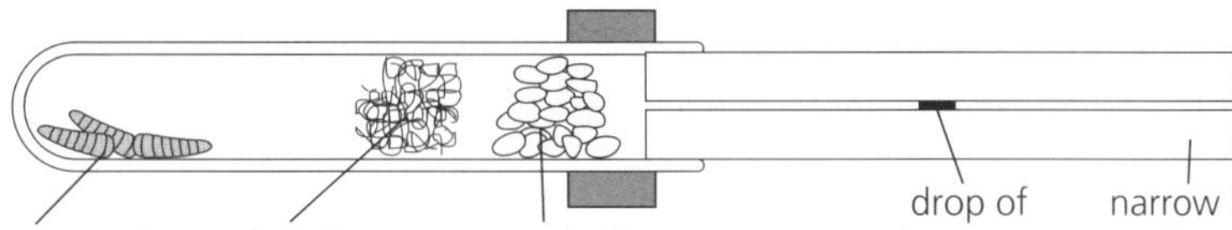

a) Which gas does soda lime remove from the air in the tube?
b) Which gas will the larvae remove from the air if they are actively respiring?
c) What will happen to the volume of gas in the tube as the experiment progresses?
d) What will happen to the marker as the experiment progresses?
e) Which two factors in the laboratory (other than the larvae) could affect the position of the marker?

Q4 The blood of a mammal contains a large number of dissolved substances. Their concentration in blood differs in different parts of the body.

The following list names some of the blood vessels of the mammalian body.

A aorta
B hepatic artery
C hepatic portal vein
D pulmonary artery
E pulmonary vein
F renal artery
G renal vein

In which of the blood vessels listed A to G, would you expect to find the highest levels of the following substances?

a) amino acids
b) carbon dioxide
c) glucose
d) oxygen
e) urea

Q5 The diagram shows some of the structures involved in a simple reflex.

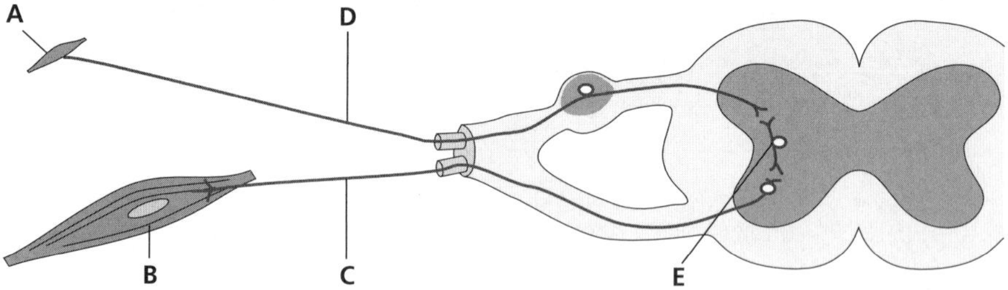

a) Name the structures labelled A to E.
b) List the labelling letters in an order which indicates the direction of the path a nerve impulse would take in a simple reflex.

Q6 a) i) Why is it dangerous to drive after consuming alcohol?
ii) Name two organs which may suffer damage as a result of long-term alcohol abuse.
b) What is meant by the following terms?
i) solvent abuse
ii) physical dependence
iii) phsychological dependence

Q7 a) i) Name a ductless gland.
ii) What is its function?
b) i) Name a gland which functions as a ducted gland and a ductless gland.
ii) Briefly describe the functions of the gland named in **b)** i).

Q8 Explain briefly why you think water might be described as the most important inorganic nutrient.

Q9 a) With the help of a large labelled diagram describe briefly how a human being breathes. In your answer make reference to the following structures:
intercostal muscles **rib cage** **sternum** **diaphragm**

b) Explain briefly how the exchange of gases takes place at the lung surface.

Q10 A girl with normal vision is reading a magazine in the shade of a beach umbrella on a sunny beach. She raises her eyes to look at a passing boy.

Changes would take place in
a) her pupils and
b) the shape of the lenses in her eyes.

In each case describe briefly the function of the change and explain how the change would be brought about.

Green plants as organisms (Units 32–39)

Q1 The diagram shows the water loss from two types of plant, A and B, over a 24-hour period.

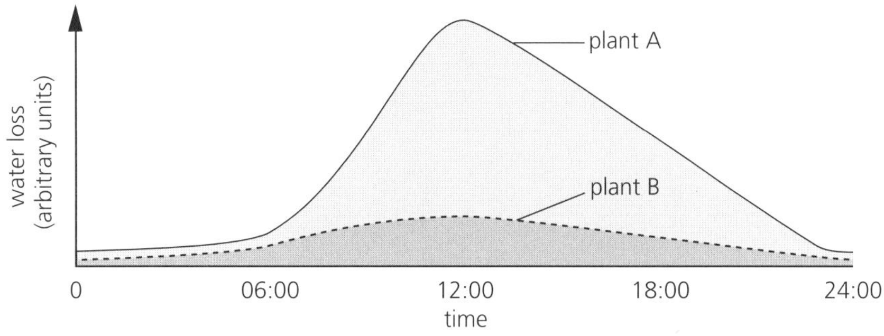

a) At what time was plant A showing its highest water loss?
b) Through which organ does a plant usually lose most water?
c) What name is given to the loss of water from a plant?
d) i) Which of the two plants would be better suited to growing in a dry habitat?
ii) Explain your choice of answer for i).

Q2 The diagram shows a section through a leaf.

a) Name the parts labelled A to H.
b) Layer A is made from wax. What is the function of the wax?
c) Tissue D provides a large surface area. How is this important for the efficiency of the leaf?
d) What part do cells like cell G play in the work of the leaf?

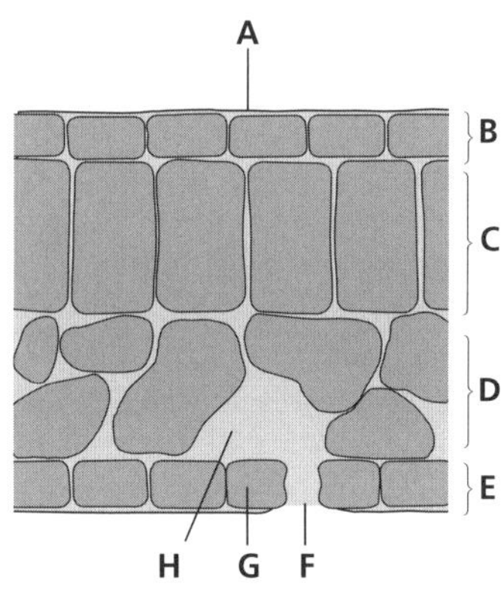

Q3 The diagram shows the apparatus used to collect the gas produced by pond weed.

a) i) How would the composition of the gas collected at A differ from the air in the laboratory as a result of the activity of the plant?
ii) What simple test could you perform to see whether you were correct?

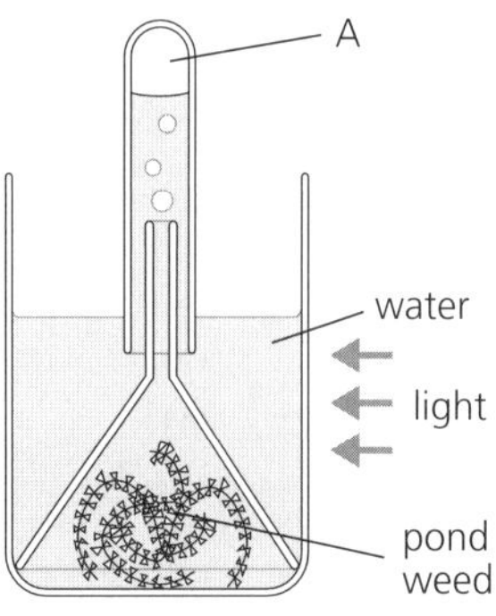

b) Which gas dissolved in the water could limit the rate of photosynthesis of the pond weed?

c) i) What would happen to the pH in the beaker as the experiment proceeds?

ii) Explain briefly your answer to i).

Q4 The diagram shows the results of growing wheat seedlings in different solutions for one month.

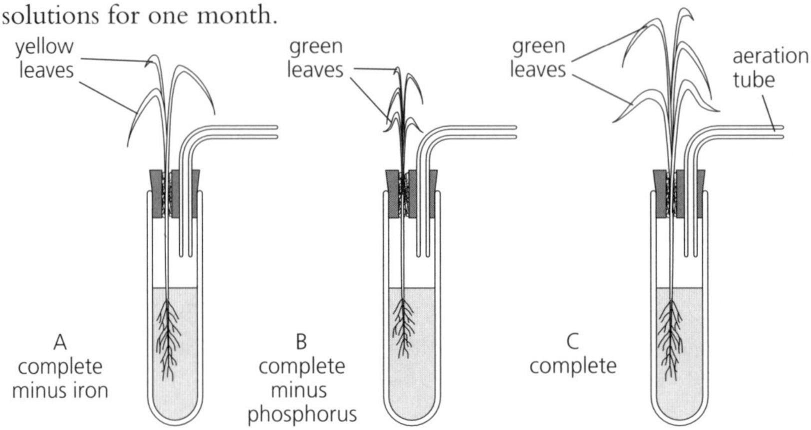

a) The complete solution contains all the mineral nutrients required by wheat for successful growth.

i) Which tube was the control?

ii) What effect does iron deficiency (lack) have on a wheat seedling?

iii) Which process is likely to be limited by iron deficiency?

iv) What effect does phosphorus deficiency have on a wheat seedling?

b) Air was bubbled into the solutions through the aeration tube every day.

i) Which respiratory gas will the seedlings need to absorb from the culture solution?

ii) 1 Why is it important that root cells respire actively?

2 Which special function of root cells depends on respiration?

Q5 Write an account of the way growth substances may be used in the commercial production of cereal crops and seedless fruits.

Variation, inheritance and evolution (Units 40–7)

Q1 **a)** Give one example of an animal and one example of a plant that Man has changed considerably by artificial selection.

b) What was the particular purpose of the selection in the examples you chose in **a)**?

Q2 **a)** Name the large molecule which forms the basis for chromosomes.

b) Name the units of heredity found on a chromosome.

c) How many chromosomes are there in a normal human sperm?

d) The parents of four children, Claire, Louise, Richard and Sarah, can taste a bitter compound known as PTC. Of their children, Louise is the only one who cannot taste PTC.
The allele for ability to taste the substance (taster) is dominant to the non-taster allele.
  i) What does the term 'allele' mean?
  ii) What does the term 'dominant' mean?
  iii) What evidence is there that both parents are heterozygous for this gene?

Q3 The diagram shows the results of a breeding experiment using black and white rabbits. Four of the rabbits have been labelled A, B, C and D.

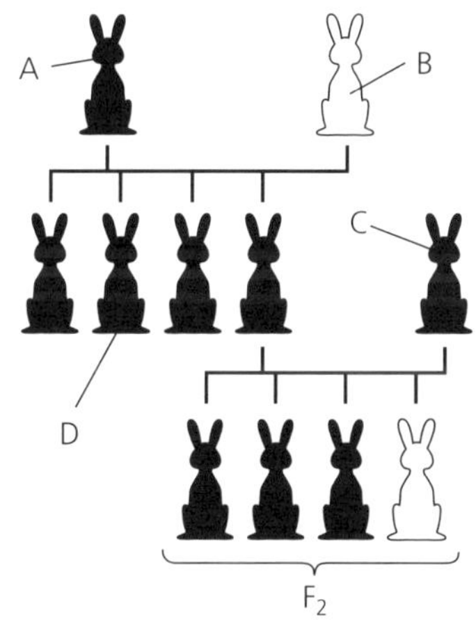

a) Which rabbit provides evidence to suggest that the black allele is dominant?
b) Using two words only, describe the genotype of rabbit B.
c) Using defined symbols state the genotypes of rabbits C and D.
d) What is the ratio of phenotypes in the F_2 generation?
e) What are the probable ratios of the genotypes in the F_2 generation?

Q4 When homozygous coloured flowers are crossed with homozygous white flowers of the same species the offspring (F_1 generation) all produce coloured flowers.
a) What does the term 'homozygous' mean?
b) Which allele is dominant in this cross?
c) What will be the genotype of the F_1 plants?

Your answers to **d)** to **f)** should include explanations. You may find it helpful to describe your crosses using checkerboard diagrams.

d) What type of flowers would you expect if the F_1 plants were self-pollinated and the resulting seeds grown?
e) What type of flowers would you expect if the F_1 plants were pollinated, by hand, with pollen from white flowers and the seeds grown?
f) What type of flowers would you expect if a clone was set up using a small piece of tissue taken from one of the F_1 plants?

Living things in their environment (Units 48–54)

Q1 a) Name two groups of organisms which play a major role in the decay of plant and animal remains.

b) State three factors which affect the rate of decay.

c) Describe briefly the process of decomposition which takes place in a compost heap.

d) In what ways does the addition of compost to a soil improve the soil?

Q2 Using named examples explain briefly what you understand by the following terms:

ecosystem producer consumer predator prey

Q3 a) Name two factors that could be responsible for background extinction.

b) Explain how these factors might bring about the extinction of a species.

Q4 a) What do you understand by the term 'competition' when applied to the organisms living in a community?

The diagram shows an arrangement of leaves shown by many plants.

b) Explain briefly how this arrangement of leaves makes the best use of available light.

c) Explain briefly how this arrangement of leaves would be an advantage in an area grazed by sheep.

d) What effect would you expect a long period of grazing in a particular area to have on the number of plants with leaves arranged like the one shown in the diagram?

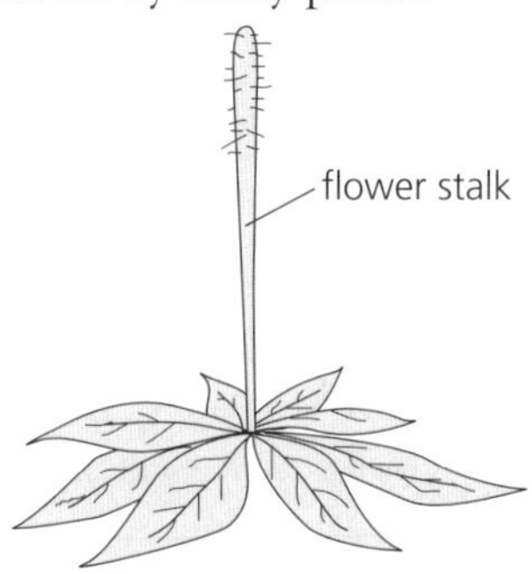

Q5 Describe briefly what can happen to the nitrogen in urine after it has been released onto the soil.

Q6 Write an account of Man's impact on the environment.

Q7 a) Describe briefly the different ways that the expansion of human settlements (towns and cities) can affect the local environment.

b) Explain briefly what scientists mean by the term 'biodiversity'.

Materials and their properties

55 Materials

- Materials used for making everyday things may be naturally occurring (raw materials) or materials made from raw materials.
- Properties can be divided into:
  Physical properties – e.g. hardness, strength, melting point, conductivity of heat and electricity, density, transparency.
  Chemical properties – e.g. does it burn, react with water, corrode?
- Composite materials (or composites) are made of two or more materials which produce a material more suitable for the job than either of the materials separately.
- There are five major groups of materials – metals, plastics, ceramics (pottery), glasses and fibres.

Q1 Each item in the left-hand column is a raw material. Each item in the right-hand column is made from raw materials. Draw lines to show which materials are made from which raw materials. One has been done for you. Remember that more than one material can be made from a raw material.

Raw materials		Materials made
		sugar
plants		
		salt
the air		metals
		coke
coal		
		road tar
crude oil	————	petrol
		plastics
the sea		
		rubber
rocks		oxygen
		roof tiles

Q2 Which of the five groups of materials should be chosen to make the items shown below? Write down the properties of the group of materials which make it suitable.

a) a vase
b) a milk bottle which will be thrown away after use
c) a milk bottle which will be washed and re-used a number of times
d) a rope which is to be used to tie up a ship.

Q3 The table gives some properties of building materials. Put a tick in the box if the material has that property and a cross if it does not. One has been done for you.

Property	Is it transparent?	Is it non-porous (waterproof)?	Is it a good insulator of heat?
brick	✘	✘	✔
glass			
roofing tiles			
wood			
plastic			

56 Solids, liquids and gases

- There are three states of matter – solid, liquid and gas.
- In a solid the particles are closely packed together. The arrangement of particles is usually regular. The particles are vibrating.
- In a liquid the particles are not as closely packed as in a solid and the arrangement is not regular.
- In a gas the particles are not regularly arranged. They are widely spaced and are moving very quickly in all directions. This movement is called random movement.
- Diffusion is the movement of the particles of a gas or liquid to fill all of the available space. It occurs quickly in gases.

Q1 Complete the diagram summarising the relationships between the three states of matter. You should use words from the following list to label the diagram.

condensation **evaporation** **freezing** **melting** **sublimation** (twice)

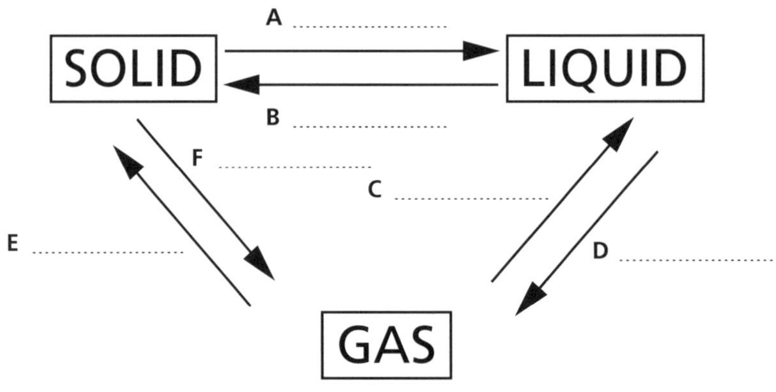

Q2 The table shows the melting and boiling points of some substances. Complete the chart below on graph paper. For each substance there is a column divided into three sections. The bottom section is labelled **solid**, the middle section **liquid**, and the top section **gas**.
The dotted horizontal line represents room temperature. The state of a substance can be found by looking at which part of the column the dotted line passes through.
For example, potassium (chemical symbol K) is a solid because the dotted line passes through the **solid** section.

Substance	Melting point/°C	Boiling point/°C
potassium	64	760
phosphorus	44	280
mercury	–39	357
bromine	–7	58
oxygen	–219	–183
chlorine	–101	–35
lead	327	1744
rubidium	39	700
helium	–270	–269
calcium	850	1440
sulphur	119	444
nitrogen	–210	–196

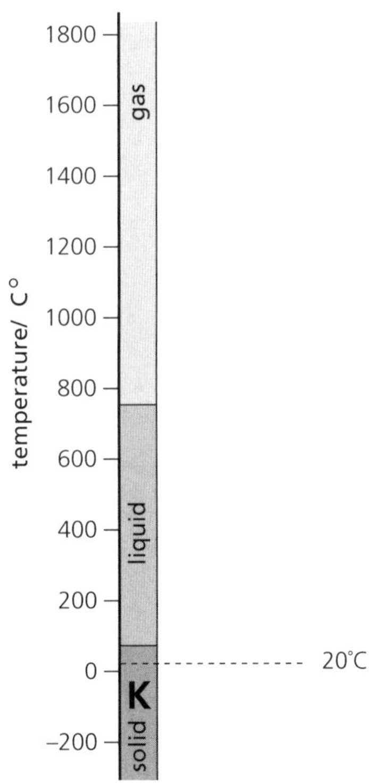

a) Complete the following table using the substances in the table above.

Solid	Liquid	Gas
potassium		

b) Draw a horizontal dotted line on your chart at –100°C. Now work out whether each substance in the table is solid, liquid or gas at –100°C.

c) Similarly, draw another horizontal line at 300°C. Work out whether each substance in the table is solid, liquid or gas at 300°C.

57 Structure of the atom

- All atoms, apart from hydrogen, are made up from three basic particles – protons, neutrons and electrons.
- All atoms are neutral and so contain equal numbers of protons and electrons.
- When an atom gains or loses electrons it forms a charged ion.
- The atomic number is the number of protons in an atom. It is also the number of electrons in an atom.
- The mass number is the total number of protons and neutrons in an atom.
- Isotopes are atoms of the same element but which contain different numbers of neutrons.

Q1 Complete the table.

Particle	Approximate mass	Charge
proton (p)		
electron (e)		
neutron (n)		

Q2 The diagram shows a simple representation of an atom. Write down:

a) the number of protons present
b) the number of electrons present
c) the number of neutrons present
d) the atomic number of the element
e) the arrangement of electrons in the atom.

Identify the element. (Use the Periodic Table on page 188 to help you.)

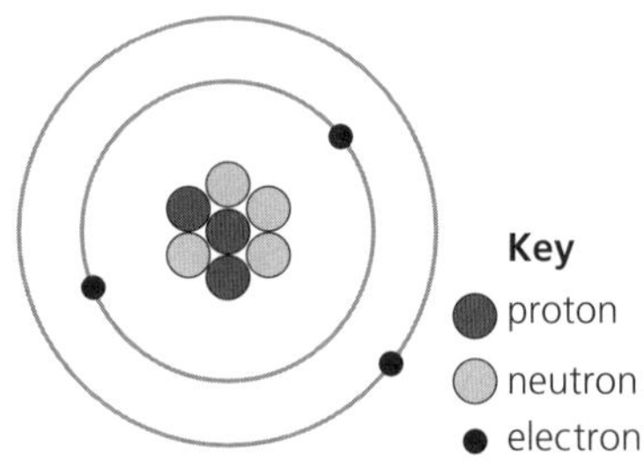

Q3 The table contains the numbers of particles in five atoms A–E. (These are not chemical symbols.) Complete the table.

Atom	Mass number	Atomic number	Number of protons	Number of neutrons	Number of electrons
A	16		8		
B		7		7	
C	19	9			
D				9	8
E			6	8	

Which of the atoms A–E are isotopes of the same element?

Q4 There are two isotopes of chlorine: chlorine-37 and chlorine-35. Draw diagrams showing the arrangement of protons, neutrons and electrons in each isotope. The atomic number of chlorine is 17.

58–9 Ionic and covalent bonding

- **Ionic bonding involves loss of one or more electrons from a metal atom to form a positive ion. The non-metal atom gains one or more electrons to form a negative ion. The ions are held together by strong electrostatic forces.**
- **Covalent bonding involves the sharing of electrons between two atoms. When one electron is given by each atom to form one electron pair, a single covalent bond is formed.**
- **Covalent bonding is particularly used to join non-metal atoms together, e.g. H_2, Cl_2.**

Q1 Complete the diagram to show how atoms of magnesium and oxygen combine together to form magnesium oxide (MgO).

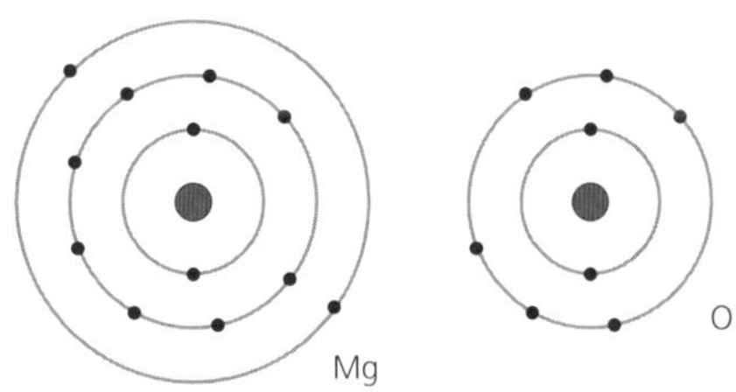

Q2 Barium fluoride, BaF_2, contains ionic bonding.

a) Describe the changes which take place when barium and fluorine combine to form barium fluoride.

b) Why would you expect barium fluoride to have a different crystal structure to sodium chloride or magnesium oxide?

c) Which of the following statements are true for barium fluoride?

A It dissolves in hexane.

B It dissolves in water to form a conducting solution.

C It conducts electricity when solid.

D It melts at a high temperature to form a liquid which conducts electricity.

Q3 Which of the substances A–D in the table is/are likely to contain covalent bonding?

	Melting point	Boiling point	Electrical conductivity when molten	Solubility in water
A	high	high	good	insoluble
B	low	low	nil	insoluble
C	high	high	nil	insoluble
D	high	high	good	very soluble

Q4 Complete the diagrams to show the arrangement of outer electrons.

a) hydrogen H H **b)** chlorine Cl Cl

c) nitrogen N N **d)** oxygen O O **e)** methane

H
H C H
H

Q5 Here are the melting points of some ionic compounds.

barium chloride $BaCl_2$	963°C	barium oxide BaO	1923°C
calcium oxide CaO	2600°C	magnesium oxide MgO	2800°C
potassium bromide KBr	730°C	potassium chloride KCl	776°C
sodium bromide NaBr	755°C	sodium chloride NaCl	808°C

Suggest why there is a wide range of melting points in these compounds.

60 Structure

- **A substance with a giant structure has a high melting point.**
- **If the melt conducts electricity, the substance has a giant structure of ions.**
- **If it does not conduct electricity it has a giant structure of atoms.**
- **A substance with a molecular structure has a low melting and boiling point.**
- **Possible structures are :**

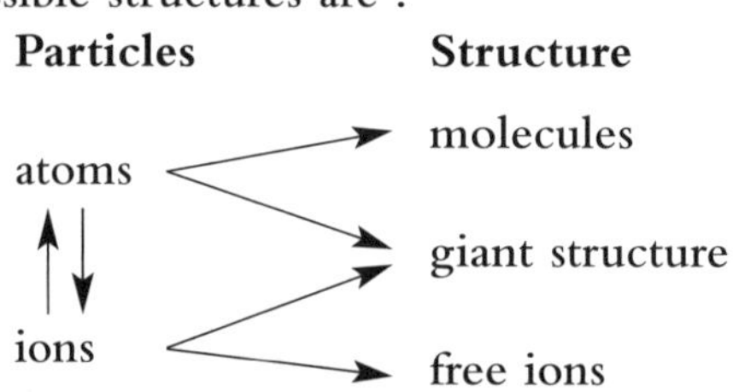

Q1 The table gives some information about four substances A–D.

Substance	Melting point/°C	Boiling point/°C	Electrical conductivity when solid	Electrical conductivity when melted
A	low	low	none	none
B	high	high	good	good
C	high	high	none	good
D	high	high	none	none

a) Which one of the substances has a metallic giant structure? Explain your answer.

b) Which one of the substances has a giant structure of ions? Explain your answer.

c) Which one of the substances has a giant structure of atoms? Explain your answer.

d) Which one of the substances has a molecular structure? Explain your answer.

Q2 Sulphur exists in two allotropic forms: α- or rhombic sulphur and β- or monoclinic sulphur. The table gives information about these two forms of sulphur.

Property	α - or rhombic sulphur	β - or monoclinic sulphur
appearance	bright yellow crystals	orange-brown, needle-shaped crystals
density/g per cm^3	2.02	1.96
solubility	Insoluble in water. Soluble in organic solvents like methylbenzene.	
effect of heat	rapidly heated it melts at 113°C	melts at 119°C
range of stability	more stable below 96°C	more stable above 96°C
burning in oxygen	Burns to produce sulphur dioxide. No residue. Equal masses of sulphur dioxide.	

a) What is meant by the term 'allotropic forms'?

b) What evidence is there in the table that both α- and β-sulphur are both molecular structures?

c) Both α- and β-sulphur are made up of rings of eight sulphur atoms. What does the information in the table suggest about the arrangement of the rings in the two forms of sulphur?

Three students, Peter, Paul and Mary carried out experiments to produce samples of sulphur.

In Peter's experiment, a saturated solution of sulphur dissolved in methylbenzene is allowed to crystallise above 96°C. Brown, needle-shaped crystals are formed.

d) Which form of sulphur did Peter produce? Give two reasons to support your answer.

In Paul's experiment, a saturated solution of sulphur in methylbenzene is allowed to cool below 96°C. Bright yellow crystals are formed.

e) Which form of sulphur did Paul produce? Give two reasons to support your answer.

In Mary's experiment, molten sulphur is poured into cold water. A brown, rubbery solid is formed. This solid turns hard and yellow when left at room temperature.

f) i) Suggest a structure for the brown, rubbery solid formed in Mary's experiment.

ii) What is formed when this brown, rubbery solid is kept at room temperature?

61 Elements and compounds

- Substances which cannot be split up into simpler substances are called elements.
- A mixture consists of several substances that are not combined together.
- A compound is a pure substance consisting of two or more elements which are chemically combined.
- The properties of a mixture are always the same as the properties of the substances which make up the mixture.
- A pure substance has a definite melting point. An impure substance (i.e. a mixture of substances) melts at a lower temperature and over a range of temperatures.

Q1 Complete the paragraph below, choosing words from the list to fill in the blank spaces.

atoms chlorine compound ions molecules silicon silicon chloride

$SiCl_4$ is the formula for the ____________ called ____________.
It is made up of ____________ each containing one ____________ atom and four ____________ atoms joined together.

Q2 Complete the table, using words from the following list.

pure water sea water crude oil air gin and tonic liquid ammonia mercury

Element	Mixture	Compound

Q3 The photograph shows a sample of granite. Why is this a mixture rather than a pure substance?

Q4 The melting points of three substances are:

A 90°C
B 82–85°C
C 114°C.

a) Which substance is **not** a pure substance? Explain your answer.

b) Which substances would melt in the apparatus shown on the right?

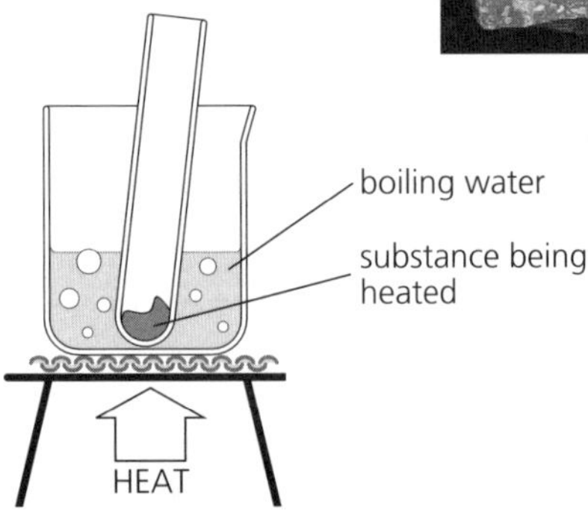

Q5 When aluminium and iodine react together, aluminium iodide, AlI_3, is formed. Complete the diagram (right) showing the changes which occur when aluminium iodide is formed.

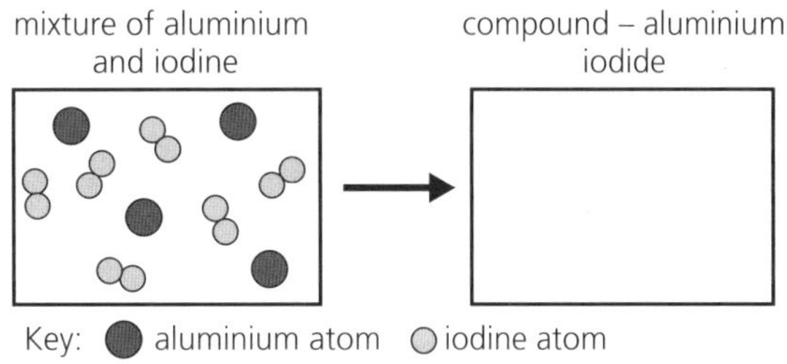

62–3 Separating mixtures – 1 and 2

- Sodium chloride (salt) can be obtained from rock salt by dissolving the salt in water, removing the insoluble residue by filtration and evaporating off the water to leave solid salt.
- Distillation is used to separate a solvent from a solution, e.g. water from salt solution.
- When two liquids form separate layers they are said to be immiscible, e.g. oil and water.
- Immiscible liquids are best separated with a separating funnel.
- When two liquids mix completely and form a single layer they are said to be miscible, e.g. ethanol and water.
- Miscible liquids can be separated by fractional distillation.

Q1 The diagram shows the processes used to obtain salt from rock salt.

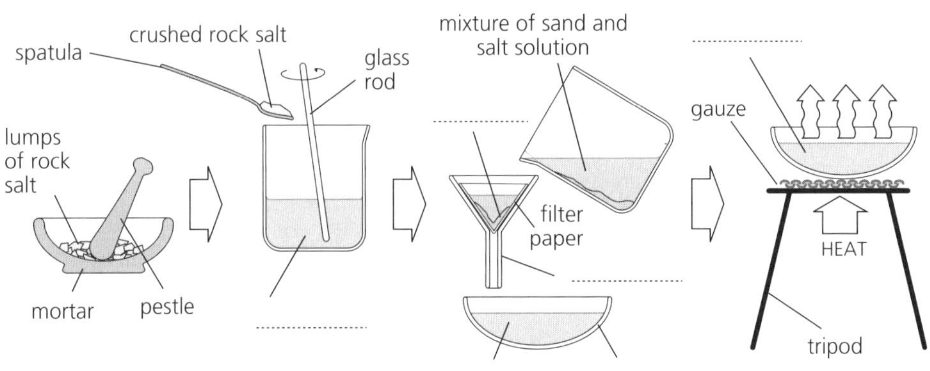

a) Draw the diagram and complete the labelling on the diagram.

b) Write a brief account of the experiment to produce pure salt from rock salt. Your account should be no more than 100 words. You should use the following words in your account:

dissolve **evaporate** **evaporating basin** **filter funnel** **solution** **residue**

Questions for Units 62–3

Q2 In Africa it is common to try to purify water by pouring it through a finely woven cloth.
a) What does this remove from the water?
b) What does this not remove from the water?

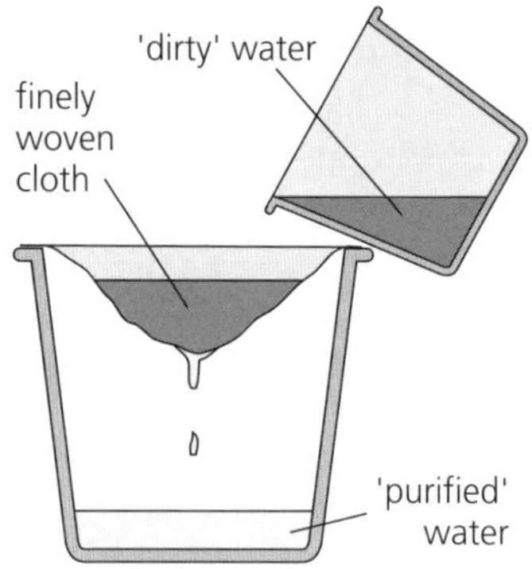

Q3 Draw a diagram using the apparatus below to show how pure water can be obtained from a solution of ink by a process of distillation.

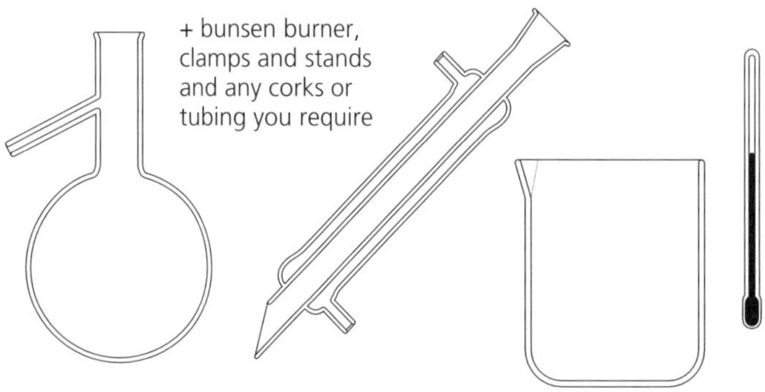

Q4 Complete the passage below, choosing words from the list to fill in the blank spaces.

boils condenses dissolves distillation distilled filter immiscible separating

Pure water can be produced from sea water by a process of ______________. The sea water is heated until it ______________.
The steam produced is cooled and it ______________ to form ______________ water.
Two liquids which do not mix are said to be ______________. They can be separated using a ______________ funnel.

Q5 Look at the ingredients on a bottle of salad cream or mayonnaise. They are emulsions. Identify substances which make up:
a) the oily layer, **b)** the watery layer and **c)** the emulsifying agent.

Q6 Phil wants to separate an organic compound from inorganic impurities. The table gives the properties of the organic compound and the impurities.

	Organic compound	Inorganic impurities
melting point	160°C	over 400°C
solubility in water	insoluble	insoluble
solubility in meths	soluble	insoluble

a) Write an account of how a pure sample of the organic compound can be made. Give any safety precautions you would take.
b) How would you attempt to show that the organic compound is pure?

64–5 Separating mixtures – 3 and 4

- Fractional distillation can be used to separate two or more liquids which have different boiling points, e.g. hexane (boiling point 69°C) and methylbenzene (boiling point 111°C).
- Whisky is a spirit produced by the fractional distillation of a mixture of ethanol (boiling point 78°C) and water (boiling point 100°C).
- Chromatography can be used to separate mixtures of substances dissolved in a solvent.

Q1 There are three forms of the compound xylene. They are liquids with boiling points of 138°C, 139°C and 144°C. Why can they not be separated by fractional distillation?

Q2 Draw a diagram using the apparatus below to show the apparatus which would be used to separate a mixture of liquids by fractional distillation.

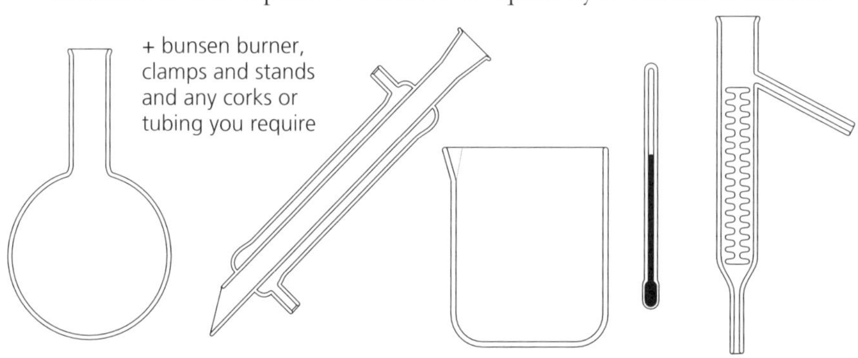

Q3 The graph below was obtained during an investigation into the separation of a mixture of three miscible liquids by fractional distillation. Every minute the temperature shown on the thermometer was recorded. The graph shows the temperature on the thermometer (on the vertical or *y*-axis) and time (on the horizontal or *x*-axis).

Study the graph carefully and answer the following questions.

a) What is room temperature?

b) After how many minutes does the first liquid start to boil off?

c) What is the boiling point of the first liquid?

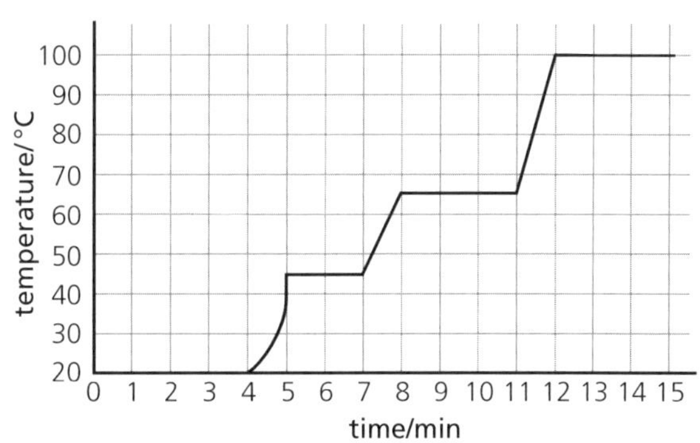

d) After how many minutes does the second liquid start to boil off?
e) What is the boiling point of the second liquid?
f) After how many minutes does the third liquid start to boil off?
g) What is the boiling point of the third liquid?
h) Suggest what this third liquid might be.
i) What is the temperature on the thermometer after seven minutes?
j) Why is the temperature shown on the thermometer unchanged after two minutes?

Q4 An experiment was carried out to find which pen had been used to write a 'poison-pen' letter.
The results of the experiment are shown in the diagram. A sample of ink from the letter was used (labelled P). Three samples were taken from pens which might have been used (labelled A, B and C).

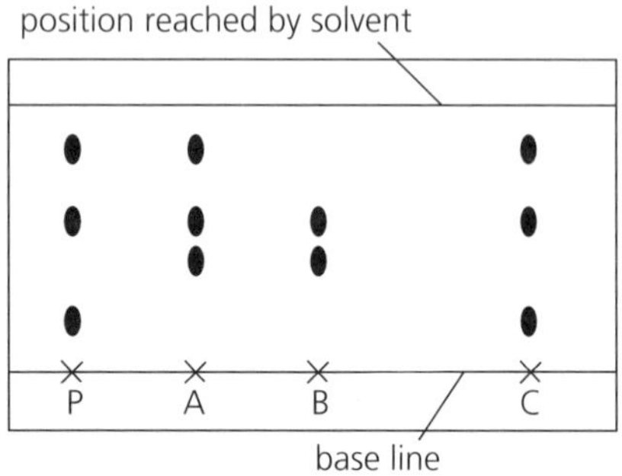

a) How many dyes are mixed in the ink in pen C?
b) How many dyes occur in **both** pen A and pen B?
c) Which pen was used to write the letter? Explain your answer.
d) Why should the base line be drawn with a pencil and not a pen?

Q5 Compounds can be identified by calculating R_f values which can then be compared with R_f values from a data book. The R_f value can be calculated using the formula:

$$R_f \text{ value} = \frac{\text{distance moved by the spot}}{\text{distance moved by the solvent}}$$

An experiment was carried out to find the amino acids present in a mixture. The table gives the R_f values of five possible amino acids.

Amino acid	R_f value
histidine	0.2
glycine	0.26
glutamic acid	0.3
tryptophan	0.5
valine	0.6

a) Using the chromatogram below, calculate the R_f values of the two amino acids present.
b) Use the table to identify the two amino acids present.
c) The chromatogram is sprayed with ninhydrin and heated before being examined. Suggest why this is so.

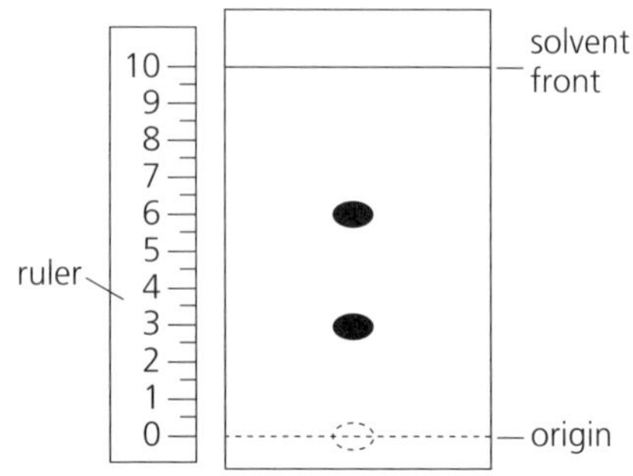

66 Solubility

- The solubility of a solute is the mass of the solute that dissolves in 100 g of solvent at a particular temperature.
- A solubility curve is a graph of solubility of a solute (on the vertical or y-axis) against temperature (on the horizontal or x-axis).
- Most solutes increase in solubility with rise in temperature.

Sample results for the calculation of the solubility of sodium chloride at room temperature

1 Mass of evaporating basin = 50.25 g
2 Mass of evaporating basin + sodium chloride solution = 118.25 g
3 Mass of evaporating basin + solid sodium chloride = 68.25 g

Mass of sodium chloride solution
= **2** – **1** = 118.25 g – 50.25 g = 68.00 g

Mass of solid sodium chloride
= **3** – **1** = 68.25 g – 50.25 g = 18.00 g

Mass of water in solution
= **2** – **3** = 118.25 g – 68.25g = 50.00 g

18.00 g of sodium chloride dissolved in 50.00 g of water at room temperature.

Therefore, $^{18}/_{50} \times 100$ g of sodium chloride dissolved in 100 g of water at room temperature.

The solubility of sodium chloride at room temperature is 36.0 g of sodium chloride per 100 g of water.

Q1 Use the following results to calculate the solubility of potassium nitrate at room temperature.

1 Mass of evaporating basin = 67.55 g
2 Mass of evaporating basin + potassium nitrate solution = 144.55 g
3 Mass of evaporating basin + solid potassium nitrate = 88.55 g

Q2 The results in the table give the solubility of ammonium chloride in water at different temperatures.

Temperature/°C	0	10	20	40	60	80
Solubility/g per 100 g water	30	33	37	46	55	66

a) Use a piece of graph paper. Choose suitable scales for the temperature (x-axis) and the solubility (y-axis). Plot the results and draw a solubility curve.

b) Complete the following sentence.
As the temperature rises the solubility of ammonium chloride in water ______________.

Q3 The graph shows the solubility curves of three solutes: potassium nitrate, copper(II) sulphate and sodium chloride.

a) Which one of the substances:

i) has almost the same solubility at all temperatures

ii) is least soluble at 0°C

iii) is most soluble at 60°C?

b) What is the solubility of potassium nitrate at 0°C?

c) At what temperature is the solubility of copper(II) sulphate 24 g per 100 g of water?

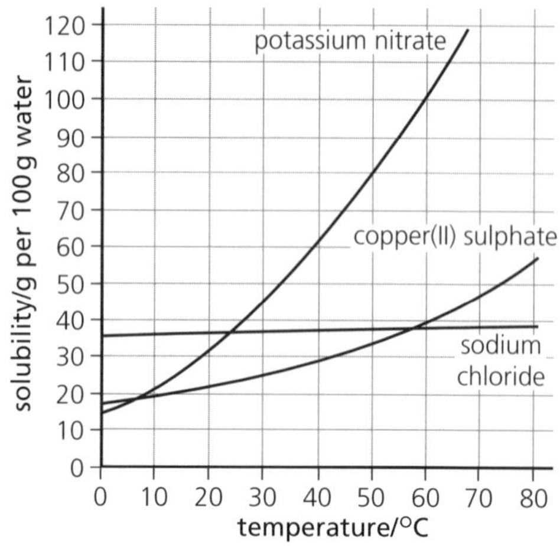

d) What is the maximum mass of copper(II) sulphate which will dissolve in 25 g of water at 70°C?

e) At what temperature is the solubility of copper(II) sulphate and the solubility of sodium chloride the same?

f) How could you obtain a pure sample of potassium nitrate from a saturated solution of potassium nitrate and sodium chloride at 80°C?

67 Change

- There are two types of change:
  Temporary (or physical) change. No chemical reaction has taken place. It is easy to reverse. Example: melting water.
  Permanent or chemical change. It is usually accompanied by an energy change with energy being lost to the surroundings. It is usually impossible to reverse the change. Example: burning wood.
- The sum of the masses of the reacting substances = the sum of the masses of the substances produced. This is called the Law of Conservation of Mass.
- Decomposition is the breaking down of a substance into simpler substances. There are three types of decomposition: thermal (heat) decomposition, catalytic decomposition and electrolytic decomposition.
- Reduction is the opposite of oxidation. A substance which gains oxygen or loses hydrogen is oxidised.

Q1 The table shows the action of heat on five substances.

Substance	Original appearance	Change on heating	Change on cooling	Residue
potassium manganate(VII)	purple crystals	darkens on heating; fine black powder and oxygen gas produced	very dark green	potassium manganate(VI) and manganese(IV) oxide
zinc oxide	white powder	turns to yellow powder	white powder	zinc oxide
silicon(IV) oxide	yellowish powder	yellowish powder	yellowish powder	silicon(IV) oxide
zinc carbonate	white powder	on gentle heating a colourless gas is given off which turns limewater milky (carbon dioxide); yellow residue	white powder	zinc oxide and carbon dioxide
copper metal	reddish-brown solid	glows red on heating	black coating on metal	copper(II) oxide

a) Which substance is unchanged on heating?
b) Which substance undergoes a temporary change on heating and turns back to the original substance on cooling?
c) Which substance reacts with oxygen from the air on heating?
d) Which substances are thermally decomposed on heating?

Q2 a) A reaction takes place when burning magnesium ribbon is lowered into carbon dioxide gas. The word equation for the reaction is:

magnesium + carbon dioxide ⟶ carbon + magnesium oxide

Which one of the substances is:
i) oxidised
ii) reduced
iii) the oxidising agent
iv) the reducing agent?

b) A mixture of copper(II) oxide and carbon is heated together. The word equation for the reaction is:

copper(II) oxide + carbon ⟶ carbon dioxide + copper

Which one of the substances is:
i) oxidised
ii) reduced
iii) the oxidising agent
iv) the reducing agent?

Q3 Oxidation and reduction can be defined in terms of loss and gain of electrons. Oxidation is a process where electrons are lost and reduction is a process where electrons are gained.
(Remember: OIL RIG **o**xidation **i**s **l**oss of electrons
reduction **i**s **g**ain of electrons)
Explain in each of the following whether oxidation or reduction have taken place. In one case no oxidation or reduction has occurred.

a) $Na \longrightarrow Na^+ + e^-$

b) $O_2 + 4e^- \longrightarrow 2O^{2-}$

c) $H^+ + OH^- \longrightarrow H_2O$

d) $2Fe^{2+} + Cl_2 \longrightarrow 2Fe^{3+} + 2Cl^-$

e) $Zn + Cu^{2+} \longrightarrow Zn^{2+} + Cu$

68–9 Chemicals from oil

- **Crude oil (petroleum) is a complex mixture of hydrocarbons (compounds of carbon and hydrogen only).**
- **Crude oil is separated into useful saleable fractions by the process of fractional distillation.**
- **Each fraction has a range of boiling points. The fractions produced contain hydrocarbons called alkanes.**
- **Hydrocarbons burn well to produce energy. Burning or combustion of hydrocarbons, including alkanes, requires oxygen from the air. Providing there is a plentiful supply of oxygen, then water vapour and carbon dioxide are produced.**

Q1 a) Complete the table, which contains information about the first six members of the alkane family.

Alkane	Formula	Structure	Melting point/°C	Boiling point/°C	Mass of 1 mole/g	State at room temperature and pressure
methane		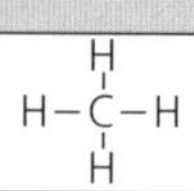	–182	–161	16	gas
ethane	C_2H_6		–183	–89	30	gas
propane	C_3H_8	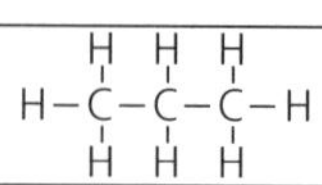	–188	–42	44	
butane		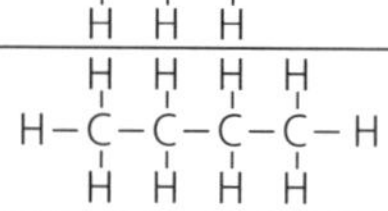	–138	0	58	gas
pentane	C_5H_{12}		–130	36	72	liquid
hexane	C_6H_{14}	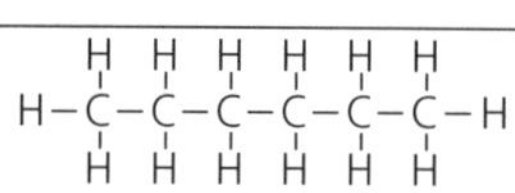	–95	68	86	

b) How do the melting and boiling points of the alkanes change with increasing molar mass (mass of 1 mole)?
c) Write down the formula of the alkane that contains *n* carbon atoms. This is called the general formula of the alkane family.
d) Which of the following are alkanes?
C_6H_6 $C_{15}H_{30}$ $C_{20}H_{42}$ $C_{17}H_{36}$ $C_{40}H_{78}$

Q2 Draw a graph of boiling point of alkanes (on the *y*-axis) and the number of carbon atoms in the molecule (on the *x*-axis) up to eight carbon atoms. Predict the boiling points of heptane (containing seven carbon atoms) and octane (containing eight carbon atoms).

Q3 Complete word equations for the burning of methane.
Plentiful supply of air:
methane + ____________ ⟶ ____________ + ____________
Limited supply of air:
methane + ____________ ⟶ ____________ + ____________

Q4 Explain why:
a) there are NO SMOKING signs on garage forecourts
b) it is dangerous to run a car engine in an enclosed garage
c) diesel fuel may freeze in a lorry in winter but petrol does not
d) gas fires should be regularly serviced.

Q5 Copy out the structural formula of butane. It is possible to draw out an alternative butane structure which has the same molecular formula but does not have four carbon atoms in a chain. These two forms are called **isomers**.
Draw out the other isomer of butane.
Now draw out the three isomers of pentane.

70 Cracking hydrocarbons

- **Industrial processes such as cracking and reforming in the oil industry produce more petrol, gas and other important chemicals using naphtha, paraffin and heavy gas oil.**
- **Cracking is a process which breaks down long-chain alkanes into smaller molecules. Alkane vapour is passed over a catalyst at high temperature and high pressure.**
- **Some of the products are unsaturated. That is, they contain one or more carbon–carbon double bonds (alkenes).**
- **Alkenes can be distinguished from alkanes by their addition reaction with bromine.**

Q1 The diagram shows the apparatus required to produce ethene from liquid paraffin.

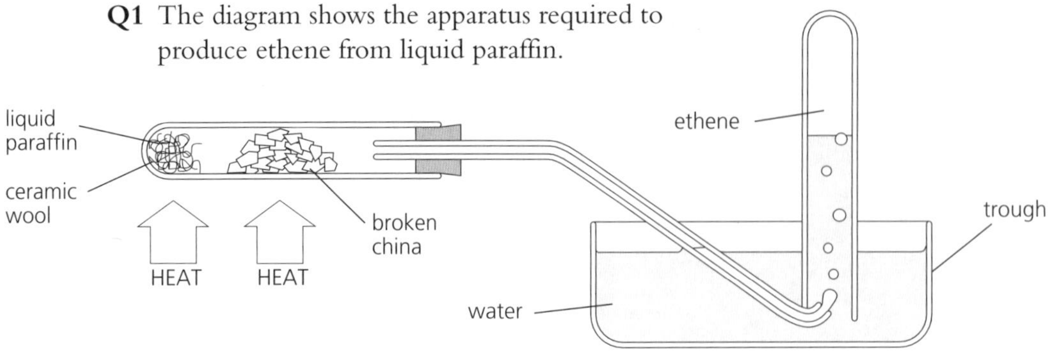

a) For what purpose is ceramic wool included in the apparatus?
b) What process is taking place when liquid paraffin turns to ethene?
c) At the end of the experiment a liquid was found floating on the water in the trough. What is this liquid and how is it formed?

Q2 Complete the table comparing the properties of ethene and ethane.

Hydrocarbon	Formula	Structural formula	Test with bromine	Products of complete combustion
ethene		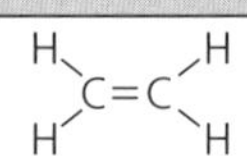		
ethane	C_2H_6			carbon dioxide and water

Q3 The structural formula of dodecane is 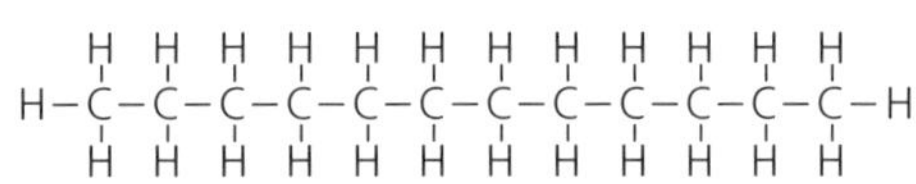

a) Write down the molecular formula of dodecane.
Dodecane can be broken into two molecules each containing six carbon atoms. One molecule is an alkane and one is an alkene.
b) Draw the structures of the two molecules produced when dodecane breaks into two molecules each containing six carbon atoms.
c) One compound decolourises bromine and the other does not. What is the significance of this observation?
d) Hydrocarbons containing six carbon atoms have names containing the prefix hex-. Write down the names of the two molecules formed when dodecane breaks.
e) Write down the structural formulae of the molecules produced when dodecane breaks into six smaller molecules each containing two carbon atoms.

71 Addition polymerisation

- Polymerisation involves the joining together of small molecules called monomers to form long chains by a series of reactions.
- A polymer formed by a series of addition reactions is called an addition polymer.
- The monomer molecules contain a carbon–carbon double bond but the polymer does not contain double bonds.
- The properties of the polymer will depend upon the reaction conditions.

Q1 Complete the following table.

Monomer	Polymer	Structure of monomer	Structure of polymer
ethene			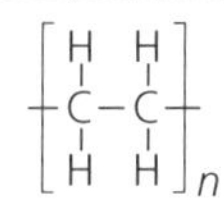
propene		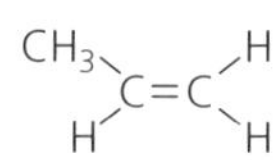	
	poly(chloroethene)	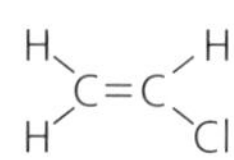	

Q2 A modern car contains over 2700 different components, of which over 750 are probably made of some type of polymer.
Write an account of the advantages of using polymers rather than metals in car manufacture. You should consider the following in your answer: cost of making; ease of production; fuel economy of the car; corrosion.

Q3 Polymers can be divided into two types – thermoplastics and thermosetting. A thermoplastic polymer melts on heating. A thermosetting polymer does not melt but on further heating may decompose.
Complete the following table by writing **thermoplastic** or **thermosetting** against each type of polymer. The first one has been done for you.

Polymer	Thermoplastic or thermosetting
poly(ethene) in plastic bags	thermoplastic
Bakelite in light fittings	
poly(propene) in washing-up bowls	
Formica on kitchen working surfaces	

Q4 Draw a diagram to show the structure of the copolymer formed when 2-methyl-1,3-butadiene and 2-methylpropene form a copolymer with alternating monomers.

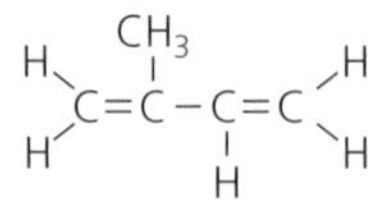

2-methyl-1,3-butadiene

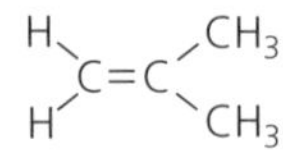

2-methylpropene

72 Ethanol

- **Ethanol can be prepared by the process of fermentation. This involves the action of enzymes in yeast on sugar or carbohydrate solution.**

  sugar (glucose) ⟶ ethanol + carbon dioxide + energy

  $C_6H_{12}O_6$ (aq) ⟶ $2C_2H_5OH$ (aq) + $2CO_2$ (g) + 84 kJ
- **Ethanol can be produced from ethene by reaction with steam at 300°C and very high pressure:**

  C_2H_4 (g) + H_2O (g) ⟶ C_2H_5OH (g)

Q1 Choose compounds from the list below to answer the questions which follow. All compounds in the list contain molecules with two carbon atoms. You may use each compound once, more than once or not at all.

ethane ethanol ethene 1,2-dibromoethane

Which compound:

a) is an alkene

b) contains carbon, hydrogen and oxygen

c) is produced when ethene reacts with steam

d) contains a carbon–carbon double bond

e) is produced when hydrogen reacts with ethene?

Q2 The conversion of starch to poly(ethene) can be brought about in four stages. These four stages involve:

dehydration fermentation hydrolysis polymerisation

The three intermediate compounds are:

ethene ethanol glucose

Complete the following flow diagram.

starch ⟶ (.................) ________ ⟶ (.................) ________ ⟶ (.................) ________ ⟶ (polymerisation) poly(ethene)

Q3 Jay carried out an experiment with a spirit lamp containing ethanol.

He weighed the spirit lamp before and after use and measured the temperature of the water at the start and end of the heating. The results were:

Mass of spirit lamp before = 45.45 g
Mass of spirit lamp after = 45.05 g
Temperature of water at start = 20°C
Temperature of water at end = 32°C

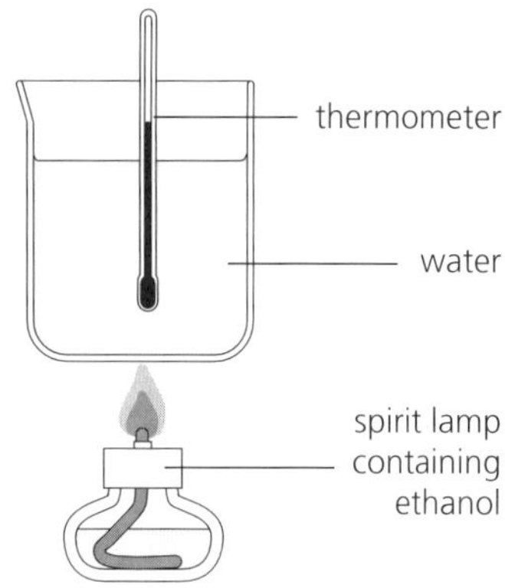

a) Why is the spirit lamp covered during the weighing?

b) What mass of ethanol was used up?

c) What temperature rise of the water was recorded?

d) What temperature rise would you expect if the same mass of ethanol was used to heat twice the mass of water?

---

e) Copy and complete the energy level diagram for the combustion of ethanol.

ethanol + oxygen

73–4 Reactivity series

- A list of metals in order of reactivity is called the reactivity series.
- A displacement reaction is a reaction where one metal replaces another during a chemical reaction. For example, if an iron nail is put into blue copper(II) sulphate solution, a displacement reaction takes place and iron sulphate and copper are formed.
- Metals high in the reactivity series are most reactive. When reactive metals react to form compounds, they produce the largest energy losses.
- Compounds of metals high in the reactivity series are difficult to split up.
- The method used to extract a metal from its ores depends upon the position of the metal in the reactivity series.

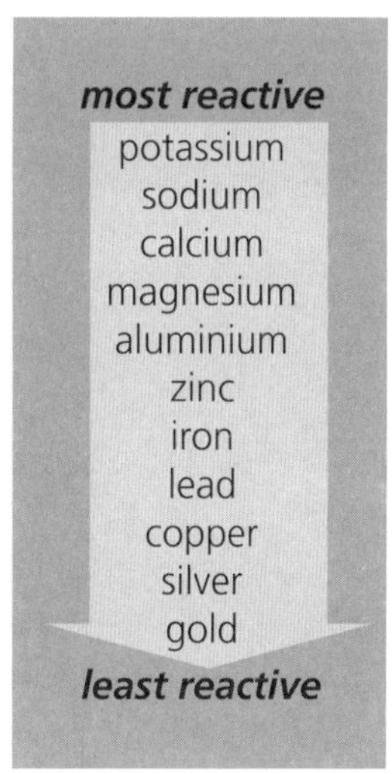

Q1 The table compares the reactivity of some metals.

<table>
<tr><th>Metal</th><th>Reaction with air</th><th>Reaction with water</th><th>Reaction with dilute hydrochloric acid</th></tr>
<tr><td>potassium</td><td rowspan="6">Burn in air or oxygen to form an oxide</td><td>Reacts violently with cold water to produce hydrogen. Hydrogen burns with a lilac flame</td><td rowspan="2">Violent reaction to produce hydrogen (dangerous)</td></tr>
<tr><td>sodium</td><td>Reacts quickly with cold water to produce hydrogen. Hydrogen does not ignite</td></tr>
<tr><td>calcium</td><td>Reacts slowly with cold water to produce hydrogen</td><td rowspan="4">React with acid to produce a metal chloride and hydrogen. React more slowly down list</td></tr>
<tr><td>magnesium</td><td>Reacts very slowly with cold water. Violent with steam</td></tr>
<tr><td>zinc</td><td>Fairly fast with steam</td></tr>
<tr><td>iron</td><td>Reacts only reversibly with steam</td></tr>
<tr><td>lead</td><td rowspan="2">Converted to the oxide by heating in air or oxygen but do not burn</td><td rowspan="3">No reaction with water</td><td>Exceedingly slow reaction to produce hydrogen</td></tr>
<tr><td>copper</td><td rowspan="2">Hydrogen not produced. No reaction with dilute hydrochloric acid</td></tr>
<tr><td>silver</td><td>Not affected by oxygen or air</td></tr>
</table>

Tin is between iron and lead in the reactivity series. Use the table to predict how tin will react with:

a) air **b)** water **c)** dilute hydrochloric acid.

Q2 The table shows the reactions of four metals W, X, Y and Z with metal salt solutions.

Metal salt solution	W	X	Y	Z
Solution of nitrate of W	–	✗	✗	✓
Solution of nitrate of X	✓	–	✗	✓
Solution of nitrate of Y	✓	✓	–	✓
Solution of nitrate of Z	✗	✗	✗	–

Use this information to arrange the four metals in order of reactivity, with the most reactive metal first.

Q3 Four metals A, B, C and D have the following properties:
A does not react with cold water or dilute hydrochloric acid.
B reacts steadily with cold water and rapidly with dilute hydrochloric acid.

C does not react with cold water or steam but reacts slowly with dilute hydrochloric acid.
D reacts rapidly with cold water and dilute hydrochloric acid.
Arrange the four metals in order of reactivity.

Q4 Describe how you would find out where manganese fits in the reactivity series without using voltage measurements of simple cells.

75 – 6 Extraction of metals

- Most metals are usually present in the Earth as rocks containing compounds of a metal. These are called ores.
- Sodium is extracted from molten sodium chloride by electrolysis in the Downs cell:

  cathode $Na^+ + e^- \longrightarrow Na$

  anode $2Cl^- \longrightarrow Cl_2 + 2e^-$
- The extraction of aluminium is carried out by electrolysis of molten aluminium oxide dissolved in molten cryolite (sodium aluminium fluoride):

  cathode $Al^{3+} + 3e^- \longrightarrow Al$

  anode $2O^{2-} \longrightarrow O_2 + 4e^-$
- Iron is extracted in a blast furnace. Iron ore, coke (carbon) and limestone are added to the blast furnace. Hot air is blown into the base of the furnace.
- Copper is purified by electrolysis, with the anode made of impure copper and the cathode made of pure copper. The electrolyte is copper(II) sulphate solution:

  anode $Cu \longrightarrow Cu^{2+} + 2e^-$

  cathode $Cu^{2+} + 2e^- \longrightarrow Cu$

Q1 The table shows the percentage of metal in samples of different rocks.

Rock	Metal in rock	Percentage
haematite	iron	45
rutile	titanium	20
cassiterite	tin	1.5
bauxite	aluminium	28
zinc blende	zinc	20

a) Complete the sentence by choosing the **best** words from this list.

an element **a pure substance**
an ore **a mineral**

Cassiterite is an example of ____________ of tin.

b) Suggest **two** reasons why tin is an expensive metal.

c) i) Cassiterite contains tin dioxide. Tin is extracted from tin dioxide by heating with carbon. What **type** of chemical reaction takes place when tin is obtained from tin dioxide?

ii) Here are five sentences about the making of tin. They are in the wrong order.
A The mixture is heated until the tin is molten.
B The rock is mixed with coke (carbon) and heated.
C The rock is crushed.
D Molten tin is poured off.
E Rock is dug out of the ground.
Fill in the boxes to show the right order. The first one has been done for you.

E → ☐ → ☐ → ☐ → ☐

Q2 The Earth's crust contains 7.5% of aluminium and 4.7% of iron.

a) Suggest a reason why aluminium is much more expensive than iron.
Aluminium is obtained from bauxite, $Al_2O_3.2H_2O$. The bauxite is added to sodium hydroxide solution and the impurities remain undissolved. The impurities are removed and aluminium oxide precipitated.
The melting point of aluminium oxide is 2045°C. Aluminium is extracted by the electrolysis of a melt containing aluminium oxide dissolved in molten cryolite (sodium aluminium fluoride). The temperature of the molten electrolyte is below 1000°C. The products of the electrolysis are aluminium (at the cathode) and oxygen (at the anode).

b) Aluminium oxide dissolves in both alkalis and acids. What name is given to oxides which dissolve in acids and alkalis?

c) Name a procedure for removing insoluble impurities from the solution.

d) Why is there a sloping floor to the electrolysis cell?

e) Why is it economic to extract aluminium from aluminium oxide dissolved in cryolite but not from molten aluminium oxide?

f) Write ionic equations to show the changes taking place at each electrode.

Q3 These questions refer to the extraction of iron in the blast furnace.

a) Why do you think the furnace is called a blast furnace?

b) Write down the three raw materials which are added to the top of the furnace.

c) Write down the name of the gas which is blown into the furnace.

d) What are the two liquids which are tapped off from the furnace?

e) What is the reducing agent in the process?

f) Suggest what the waste gases from the furnace can be used for.

g) The main reactions in the blast furnace are:

$$C\ (s) + O_2\ (g) \longrightarrow CO_2\ (g)$$
$$CaCO_3\ (s) \longrightarrow CaO\ (s) + CO_2\ (g)$$
$$CO_2\ (g) + C\ (s) \longrightarrow 2CO\ (g)$$
$$Fe_2O_3\ (s) + 3CO\ (g) \longrightarrow 2Fe\ (l) + 3CO_2\ (g)$$
$$CaO\ (s) + SiO_2\ (s) \longrightarrow CaSiO_3\ (l)$$

Which equation represents:

i) the reduction of iron oxide to iron

ii) the reduction of carbon dioxide to carbon monoxide

iii) the decomposition of calcium carbonate

iv) the reaction of an acidic oxide with a basic oxide?

h) What is the advantage of a continuous process?

77–9 Rocks and the rock cycle

- Most rocks are usually made up of a mixture of chemicals called minerals.
- A sedimentary rock is formed when a layer of mud, sand or other natural debris is compressed, e.g. limestone, sandstone and conglomerate.
- New sedimentary rocks are deposited on existing rocks. Therefore the older rocks are, the lower they are in the Earth's crust.
- An igneous rock is a hard rock formed when the molten magma inside the Earth's crust crystallises, e.g. granite and basalt.
- The size of the crystals in an igneous rock is determined by the rate of cooling of the magma.
- A metamorphic rock is a hard rock formed when high temperatures and high pressures act on other rocks, e.g. marble.

Q1 The key below can be used to identify minerals.

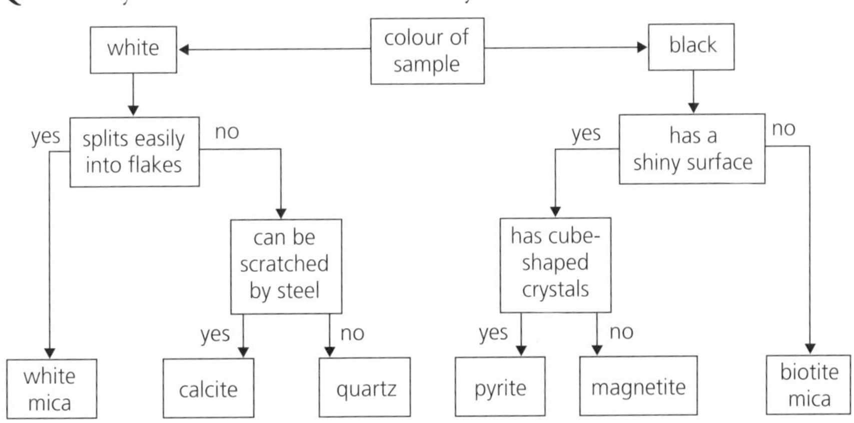

Use the key to identify the minerals A and B:
A is black with shiny cube-shaped crystals.
B is white, does not split into flakes and is not as hard as steel.

Q2 Rocks are made up from minerals. The table compares the properties of five minerals: calcite, fluorite, barite, galena and sphalerite.

Property	Mineral				
	calcite	**fluorite**	**barite**	**galena**	**sphalerite**
colour	white, pink, colourless	blue, yellow, green, colourless	white, pink	dark grey	black to brown
streak	white	white	white	thick grey	pale brown or off-white
lustre	glassy	glassy	glassy to dull	metallic	metallic to glassy
hardness	3	4	3.5	2.5	3.5
density	moderate	moderate	surprisingly dense for a white material	very dense	moderate
acid test	fizzes violently	nil	nil	**do not test**	nil
habit (shape)	'dog tooth' shape, or more often rhombus-shaped cleaved fragments	cubic sometimes with corners missing	often 'cocks-comb' structure, otherwise layered	often broken into cubic cleavage fragments	good shapes rare

a) Which of the five minerals is the hardest?
b) The table (right) gives some results for tests on a mineral.
Which mineral was being tested?

Colour	white
Streak test	white
Lustre	glassy
Acid test	no gas produced
Shape	layered

Q3 The diagram shows part of a rock face in Derbyshire.
a) Explain how you can tell that these rocks are sedimentary.
b) Suggest a reason why in rock C the sandstones are coarse-grained at the bottom, medium-grained in the middle and fine-grained at the top. What other evidence supports your suggestion?
c) Write down the order in which the rocks were formed, starting with the oldest rock.

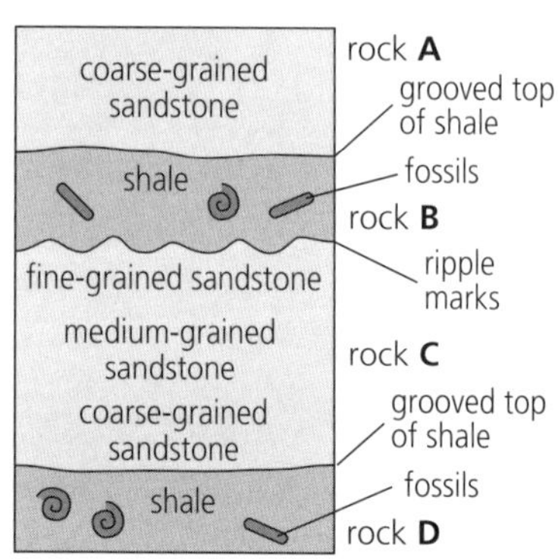

Q4 Metamorphic and igneous rocks are usually hard, while sedimentary rocks are soft.

a) Why do some metamorphic rocks contain fossils but igneous rocks do not?

b) The diagram shows an intrusion. Use the diagram to help you describe how metamorphic rocks are formed.

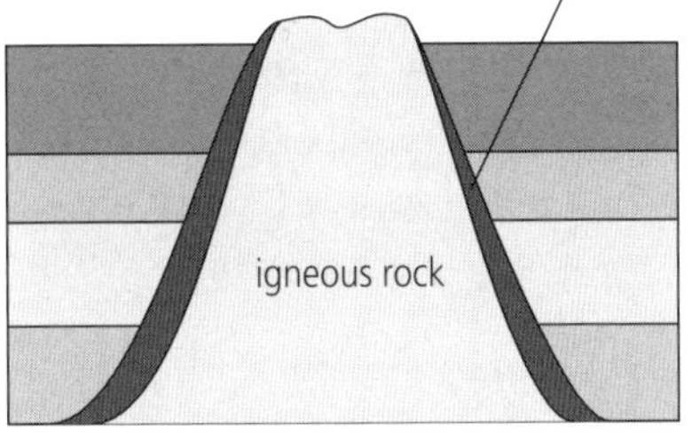

c) The table compares the properties of limestone and marble.

	Limestone	Marble
Grain size	fine to medium	fine to coarse
Density in g/cm^3	2.3	2.7
Hardness	medium	hard
Colour	light in colour, often grey or yellow	light in colour but varied
Reaction with dilute hydrochloric acid	fizzes producing carbon dioxide	fizzes producing carbon dioxide

i) Use the information in the table to identify similarities and differences between limestone and marble.

ii) Are limestone and marble igneous, sedimentary or metamorphic rocks?

Q5 Cement is produced in large factories close to limestone deposits in areas of natural beauty. Suggest advantages and disadvantages to a rural community of building a new cement factory.

Q6 The table gives information about four rocks frequently used.

Rock	Type of rock	Minerals present	Properties
granite	igneous	feldspar, quartz	very hard, attractive when polished
marble	metamorphic	calcite	hard, attacked by acid rain, attractive appearance, slippery when wet
limestone	sedimentary	calcite	widely available, quite hard, attacked by acid rain, relatively cheap
sandstone	sedimentary	quartz	moderately hard but crumbles to form sand, relatively cheap

a) What problem could be caused when using marble for paving around a swimming pool?

b) A plaque is going to be placed on a statue in the centre of a city. The plaque is exposed to all weathers. Which of the four rocks would you choose? Explain your answer.

c) A long path is going to be made across a park, using rock chippings. Which rock would you recommend for these chippings?

80 The rock record

- When tectonic plates move, layers of rock can break (called faulting) or bend (called folding).
- Fossils are the remains of plants and animal bodies that have not decayed but have been preserved.
- Fossils can be used to date rocks.

Q1 Geologists looking for deposits of crude oil try to find suitable rock structures where oil can be trapped. The diagram below shows such a structure.

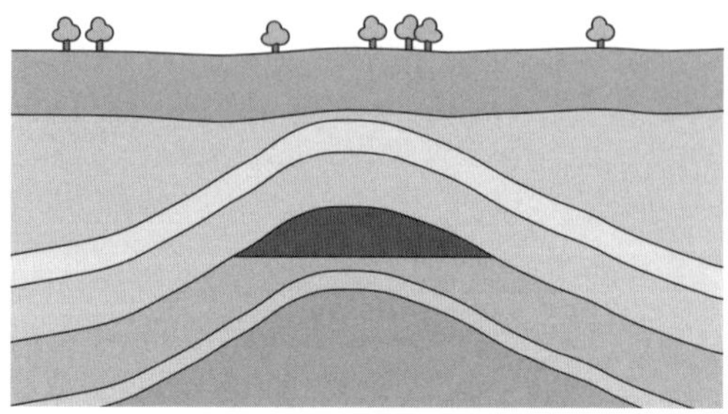

Explain how crude oil becomes trapped in the rock structure shown above.

Q2 Earthquakes occur when plates of rock slide past each other at a fault. Despite the risk of earthquakes, cities such as San Francisco are still built in areas where earthquakes are likely.

a) Suggest some of the things that can be done during the construction of buildings to minimise the damage caused by earthquakes.

b) Suggest some of the things that can be done after the city has been built to minimise the effects of an earthquake.

Q3 The diagram below shows some rock structures where coal is found. Which of the places A, B or C would be the best place to site a shaft for a coal mine? Explain your choice.

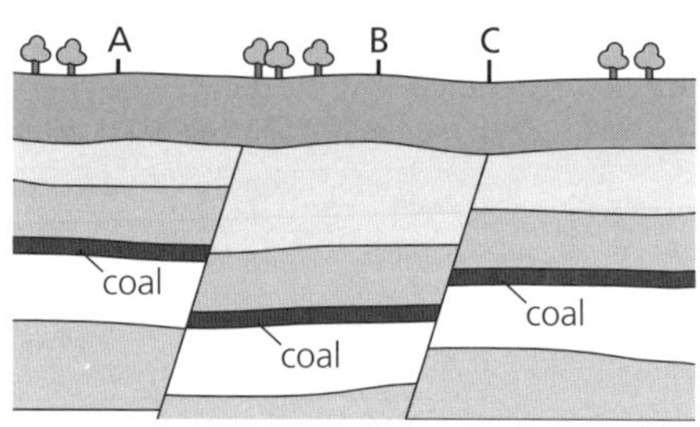

81 Composition of the atmosphere

- Over millions of years the composition of the atmosphere has changed. At first the atmosphere consisted of hydrogen and helium.
- Oxygen started to form in the atmosphere when green plants converted carbon dioxide into oxygen.
- Dry air contains approximately 78% nitrogen and 21% oxygen. It contains smaller amounts of carbon dioxide and the noble gases.
- The percentage of oxygen gas in the air can be found by passing air over heated copper.

Q1 An experiment was carried out to compare the time taken for a candle flame to go out when it was covered with beakers of different sizes. The results are shown in the table below.

Volume of beaker in cm^3	100	250	400	600	800
Time in s	20	40	70	105	140

a) Use this data to draw a graph. Put time along the x-axis(horizontal).
b) How long would it take for a candle to go out if it was covered with a 500 cm^3 beaker?
c) What can be concluded from the results shown in the graph?
d) If a very large beaker (e.g. 2000 cm^3) is used the time is much less than expected. Suggest how this could be explained.

Q2 An experiment was carried out to find the percentage of oxygen in a sample of air. The apparatus used is shown in the diagram.

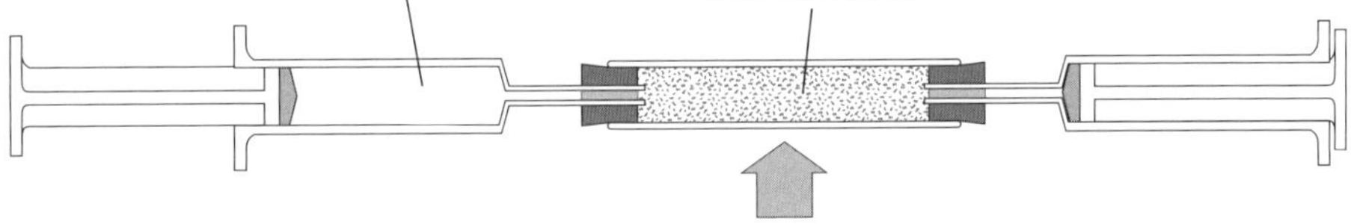

One of the gas syringes was filled with 100 cm^3 of air. The air was passed backwards and forwards over heated iron wool in a hard glass tube. **The iron wool started to glow, and the glow spread throughout the iron wool even when the flame was removed.**
On cooling, the volume of air remaining was 80 cm^3 and a black solid residue remained in the hard glass tube.

a) i) Write down the name of the metal more commonly used in this experiment.
ii) Write down the name of the gas removed from the air by the heated iron wool.
iii) Name two gases present in the air left at the end of the experiment. One should be an element and one should be a compound.
b) What can be concluded from the information in bold type?
c) Why was the apparatus allowed to cool to room temperature before the final volume of gas was measured?
d) Why is the reaction faster with iron wool than with an iron nail of the same mass?
e) How would the result have been different if exhaled air had been used? Give an explanation.

82 The oceans

- The dissolved ions in sea water come from rocks that dissolve or are broken down and dissolved in rivers.
- The composition of ions in the oceans is fairly constant.
- Despite the large amount of calcium and sulphate ions in rocks, the composition of these ions in the oceans is much less.
- Phytoplankton in the oceans help to maintain the oxygen content of the atmosphere.

Q1 The table below gives the composition of common ions in sea water.

Ion	Concentration of ion in g/1000g of sea water
Chloride Cl^-	19.2
Sodium Na^+	10.7
Sulphate SO_4^{2-}	2.7
Magnesium Mg^{2+}	1.4
Calcium Ca^{2+}	0.4
Potassium K^+	0.38
Hydrogencarbonate HCO_3^-	0.14
Bromide Br^-	0.07

a) Calculate the mass of sodium chloride that could be obtained from 1 dm^3 of sea water.

b) Magnesium is extracted from sea water by electrolysis of magnesium chloride. What is the minimum volume of sea water needed to produce 1 tonne of magnesium? (1 tonne = 1000 kg).

c) Bromine is extracted by sea water. The sea water is concentrated by evaporation. The solution is then acidified . Chlorine is bubbled through the solution. Heating the solution then evolves bromine as a gas. This gas is then condensed to produce liquid bromine.

i) Why is it necessary to concentrate the solution before extracting bromine?

ii) Write a word and ionic equation for the reaction that takes place when chlorine is bubbled through sea water.

iii) Write down the name of the process used to extract liquid bromine from the solution.

d) The Earth's crust contains 5.1% calcium, but less than 1% of the material dissolved in sea water is calcium. Explain why there is such a large difference.

Q2 It is believed that phytoplankton have an important part to play in maintaining the balance of oxygen and carbon dioxide in the atmosphere.
Phytoplankton grows better as temperature increases, but can be destroyed by pollution.
Explain how burning fossil fuels could cause environmental problems and how these problems could be solved by phytoplankton.

83 Chemical equations

- **In a chemical reaction new substances are formed. The substances that react are called reactants and the new substances made are called products.**
- **A chemical reaction can be represented by a chemical equation which summarises, in words or symbols, the change taking place.**
- **Substances which remain unchanged during the reaction are not shown in the equation.**
- **State symbols may be shown in equations: (s) solid; (l) liquid; (g) gas; (aq) aqueous solution.**

Q1 Some of the following formulae are correct and some are incorrect:
$MgSO_4$ $MgOH_2$ $MgNO_3$ $MgCl$ $MgCO_3$ Mg_3N_2
Correct any formulae that are wrong.

Q2 Complete the table by adding the formula of each compound.

	Chloride Cl^-	Carbonate CO_3^{2-}	Phosphate PO_4^{3-}
ammonium NH_4^+			
copper Cu^{2+}			
chromium Cr^{3+}			

Q3 What is wrong with the following equation? Write out the correct equation.
$HCl(aq) + NaOH(aq) + H_2O(l) \longrightarrow NaCl(aq) + 2H_2O(l)$

Q4 Complete the following equations:
a) aluminium + oxygen ⟶ aluminium oxide
$Al \longrightarrow Al_2O_3$
b) sodium + hydrogen ⟶ sodium hydride
$\longrightarrow NaH$
c) sodium + chlorine ⟶ sodium chloride
$\longrightarrow$
d) potassium chlorate ⟶ potassium chloride + oxygen
$KClO_3 \longrightarrow$

e) potassium + water ⟶ potassium hydroxide + hydrogen
⟶ KOH

f) calcium + water ⟶ calcium hydroxide + hydrogen
⟶

g) zinc + hydrochloric acid ⟶ zinc chloride + hydrogen
⟶ $ZnCl_2$

h) zinc oxide + hydrochloric acid ⟶ zinc chloride + water
⟶

i) zinc hydroxide + hydrochloric acid ⟶ zinc chloride + water
$Zn(OH)_2$ ⟶

j) zinc carbonate + hydrochloric acid ⟶ zinc chloride + water + carbon dioxide
⟶

Q5 Balance the following equations. Add the appropriate state symbols.

a) $Mg + N_2 \longrightarrow Mg_3N_2(s)$
b) $NH_3 + O_2 \longrightarrow NO + H_2O$
c) $C_4H_{10}(g) + O_2 \longrightarrow CO_2 + H_2O$
d) $Mg_3N_2 + H_2O \longrightarrow MgO + NH_3$
e) $Pb(NO_3)_2(s) \longrightarrow PbO + NO_2 + O_2$

84 The mole

- Avogadro's number (L) is approximately 6×10^{23} or 600 000 000 000 000 000 000 000.
- The amount of a substance which contains Avogadro's number of particles is called 1 mole. For example:
  1 mole of hydrogen atoms weighs 1 g.
  1 mole of magnesium atoms weighs 24 g.
  1 mole of sulphur atoms weighs 32 g.
- The mass of 1 mole of compounds can be calculated using the correct formula. For example, calcium carbonate $CaCO_3$:
  The masses of 1 mole of calcium, carbon and oxygen are 40, 12 and 16, respectively.
  The mass of 1 mole of calcium carbonate = 40 + 12 + (3 × 16) = 100 g.

Use the Periodic Table (page 188) to help you answer these questions.

Q1 What mass of carbon atoms contains the same number of atoms as:

a) 32 g of sulphur atoms
b) 4 g of calcium atoms
c) 10 g of bromine atoms
d) 2 g of hydrogen atoms?

Q2 Work out the mass of:

a) 1 mole of lithium atoms, Li
b) 1 mole of bromide ions, Br^-
c) 1 mole of iron(III) ions, Fe^{3+}
d) 1 mole of nitrogen molecules, N_2
e) 1 mole of aluminium oxide, Al_2O_3
f) 0.5 moles of copper(II) oxide, CuO
g) 0.1 moles of copper(II) sulphate, $CuSO_4$
h) 0.2 moles of carbon dioxide, CO_2
i) 2 moles of ammonia, NH_3
j) 0.1 moles of sodium hydroxide, NaOH.

Q3 Calculate the mass of a nickel atom.

Q4 Copper consists of a structure of tightly packed copper atoms. The density of copper is 9 g per cm^3. Calculate the approximate volume of a copper atom.

Q5 Calculate the percentage of water in copper(II) sulphate crystals, $CuSO_4.5H_2O$.

85 Chemical formulae

- **Theoretically every chemical formula can be found as a result of a chemical experiment.**
- **These experiments usually involve a series of weighings.**
- **Sample calculation for the formula of magnesium oxide:**

1	**Mass of crucible + lid**	=	**25.15 g**
2	**Mass of crucible, lid and magnesium**	=	**25.27 g**
	Mass of magnesium 2 – 1	=	**0.12 g**
3	**Mass of magnesium, lid and magnesium oxide**	=	**25.35 g**
	Mass of magnesium oxide 3 – 1	=	**0.20 g**

From these results:

0.12 g of magnesium combines with (0.20 – 0.12 g) of oxygen to form 0.20 g of magnesium oxide.

0.12 g of magnesium combines with 0.08 g of oxygen.

0.12/24 moles of magnesium combines with 0.08/16 moles of oxygen atoms.

0.005 moles of magnesium combines with 0.005 moles of oxygen atoms.

The simplest formula of magnesium oxide is, therefore, MgO.

Refer to the Periodic Table (page 188) to find the relative atomic masses of the elements.

Questions for Unit 85

Q1 The diagrams summarise the method used to find the formula of magnesium oxide.

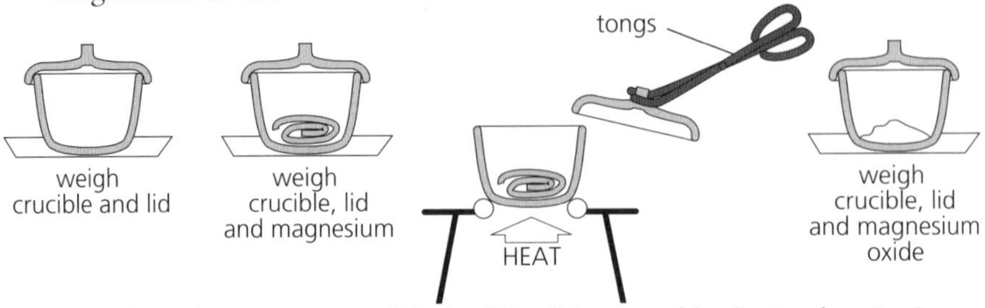

a) Why is it important to lift the lid of the crucible during heating?

b) Five groups of students (A–E) carried out the experiment. Each group burned different masses of magnesium ribbon in air to form magnesium oxide. Their results are shown in the table.

	A	B	C	D	E
Mass of magnesium/g	0.9	1.2	1.5	1.8	2.1
Mass of magnesium oxide formed/g	1.5	2.0	2.5	2.7	3.5
Mass of oxygen/g	0.6				

i) Complete the table by working out the mass of oxygen combined in each experiment. One has been done for you.

ii) Plot these results on graph paper. Draw the best straight line through the points.

iii) From the graph, why do you think that the results of group D are not correct?

iv) Use the graph to work out the mass of oxygen which combines with 2.4 g of magnesium.

c) Show that these results prove that the formula of magnesium oxide is MgO.

d) During the experiment the students were told to lift the crucible lid from time to time.
What do you think remained at the end of the experiment in the crucible of group D apart from magnesium oxide?

e) On the same grid, draw a straight line showing the results which you would expect if the oxide has a formula of Mg_2O.

Q2 Calculate the simplest formulae from the following data:

a) 6 g of carbon combines with 1 g of hydrogen.

b) 0.7 g of nitrogen combines to form 1.5 g of nitrogen oxide.

c) 4.14 g of lead combines with 0.64 g of oxygen to form a lead oxide.

d) 0.02 g of hydrogen combines with 0.32 g of oxygen to form a hydrogen oxide.

e) 1.12 g of iron combines with oxygen to form 1.60 g of iron oxide.
f) 2.00 g of mercury combines with chlorine to form 2.71 g of mercury chloride.

86 Calculations from equations

- The masses of substances that react and the masses of the products formed can be calculated using a balanced symbol equation.
- At room temperature and atmospheric pressure, one mole of any gas has a volume of 24 dm^3.
- Sample calculations:
  The equation for the reaction between calcium carbonate and dilute hydrochloric acid is

$$\text{calcium carbonate} + \text{hydrochloric acid} \longrightarrow \text{calcium chloride} + \text{water} + \text{carbon dioxide}$$

$$CaCO_3\,(s) + 2HCl\,(aq) \longrightarrow CaCl_2\,(aq) + H_2O\,(l) + CO_2\,(g)$$

Mass of 1 mole of calcium carbonate	= 40 + 12 + (3 × 16)	=	100 g
Mass of 2 moles of hydrochloric acid	= 2(1 + 35.5)	=	73 g
Mass of 1 mole of calcium chloride	= 40 + (35.5 × 2)	=	111 g
Mass of 1 mole of water	= (2 × 1) + 16	=	18 g
Mass of 1 mole of carbon dioxide	= 12 + (2 × 16)	=	44 g

Calculate the mass of calcium chloride produced when 50 g of calcium carbonate reacts with excess hydrochloric acid

From the equation:

100 g of calcium carbonate reacts to produce 111 g of calcium chloride.

1 g of calcium carbonate reacts to produce 111/100 g of calcium chloride.

50 g of calcium carbonate reacts to produce 111 × 50/100 g of calcium chloride = 55.5 g.

Refer to the Periodic Table (page 188) to find the relative atomic masses of the elements.

Q1 The equation for the reaction of copper(II) oxide and dilute hydrochloric acid is

$$CuO\,(s) + 2HCl\,(aq) \longrightarrow CuCl_2\,(aq) + H_2O\,(l)$$

Work out the mass of copper(II) chloride produced when 20 g of copper(II) oxide reacts with excess hydrochloric acid.

Q2 The equation for the thermal decomposition of potassium hydrogencarbonate is

$$2KHCO_3\,(s) \longrightarrow K_2CO_3\,(s) + H_2O\,(l) + CO_2\,(g)$$

a) Work out the mass of 1 mole of potassium hydrogencarbonate and 1 mole of potassium carbonate.
b) What mass of potassium carbonate would be produced from 20 g of potassium hydrogencarbonate?
c) What mass of carbon dioxide would be produced when 20 g of potassium hydrogencarbonate is decomposed?
d) What volume, at room temperature and atmospheric pressure, of carbon dioxide would be produced when 20 g of potassium hydrogencarbonate is decomposed?

Q3 $$2NO\,(g) + O_2\,(g) \longrightarrow 2NO_2\,(g)$$

If 40 cm^3 of oxygen and 40 cm^3 of nitrogen monoxide are allowed to react, what will be:
a) the volume of oxygen reacting with 40 cm^3 of nitrogen monoxide
b) the volume of oxygen unused
c) the volume of nitrogen dioxide produced
d) the final volume of the gas mixture?
(All volumes are measured at room temperature and atmospheric pressure.)

87 Mole calculations

- **Concentrations of solutions can be expressed in different ways.**
- **One way is mass of solute per unit volume of liquid, e.g. g per dm^3 or g/dm^3.**
- **Concentrations in moles per dm^3 allow a direct comparison of the number of particles present in different solutions to be made.**
- **The concentration in moles per dm^3 can be calculated by dividing the mass in 1 dm^3 by the mass of 1 mole of the solute.**

Refer to the Periodic Table (page 188) to find the relative atomic masses of the elements.

Q1 $$HCl + NaOH \longrightarrow NaCl + H_2O$$

25 cm^3 of sodium hydroxide solution (0.1 mole per dm^3) were titrated with hydrochloric acid (0.5 mole per dm^3).
a) What mass of sodium hydroxide is needed to make 1 dm^3 of the sodium hydroxide solution used in the titration?
b) How many moles of sodium hydroxide are present in 25 cm^3 of sodium hydroxide solution (0.1 mole per dm^3)?
c) How many moles of hydrochloric acid will react with this amount of sodium hydroxide?
d) What volume of hydrochloric acid would be needed?

Q2 Vinegar contains ethanoic acid. An experiment was carried out to find the concentration of ethanoic acid in a sample of white vinegar. 50 cm^3 of the vinegar was added to a flask and sodium hydroxide (1 mole per dm^3) was added until the indicator changed colour. The volume of sodium hydroxide added was 20 cm^3.

The equation for the reaction is

$$CH_3COOH + NaOH \longrightarrow CH_3COONa + H_2O$$

a) How many moles of sodium hydroxide are present in 20 cm^3 of 1 M sodium hydroxide solution?
b) How many moles of ethanoic acid are present in 50 cm^3 of vinegar?
c) How many moles of ethanoic acid are present in 1000 cm^3 of vinegar?
d) What is the mass of 1 mole of ethanoic acid?
e) What is the concentration of ethanoic acid, in g per dm^3, in vinegar?

88–9 The Periodic Table

- **In the Periodic Table the elements were originally arranged in order of increasing atomic weights with elements having similar properties in the same vertical columns.**
- **In the modern Periodic Table the elements are arranged in order of increasing atomic number. This avoids some anomalies caused by varying numbers of neutrons in atoms.**
- **The vertical columns of elements are called groups. The horizontal rows are called periods.**
- **There is a relationship between the electron arrangement in an atom and its position in the Periodic Table. The number of electron shells is the same as the period number and the number of outer electrons is the same as the group number.**
- **When physical properties of the elements are plotted against atomic mass, periodic graphs are produced which consist of repeating patterns of peaks and troughs. Elements in the same group occupy similar positions on the graph.**

Q1 Dobereiner found he could find three elements with similar properties. He called these triads. Two such triads are:

calcium, strontium, barium
chlorine, bromine, iodine

a) Look up the relative atomic masses of the three elements in each triad. What is the relationship between the atomic masses of the three elements?

b) Which of the following sets of elements are triads?
A lithium, sodium, potassium
B copper, silver, gold
C iron, cobalt, nickel

Q2 Use the Periodic Table to identify the elements whose atoms have electron arrangements of:
a) 2, 8, 6
b) 2, 8, 18, 1
c) 2, 8, 18, 18, 4

Q3 In 1864 Lothar Meyer calculated the volume that one mole of atoms of each element would occupy if it were a solid. He called this atomic volume. He plotted atomic volume against atomic weight. The graph is shown opposite.
Find the position on the graph of the first five elements in group 1 of the Periodic Table (lithium, sodium, potassium, rubidium and caesium). What is similar about the position of these elements on the graph?

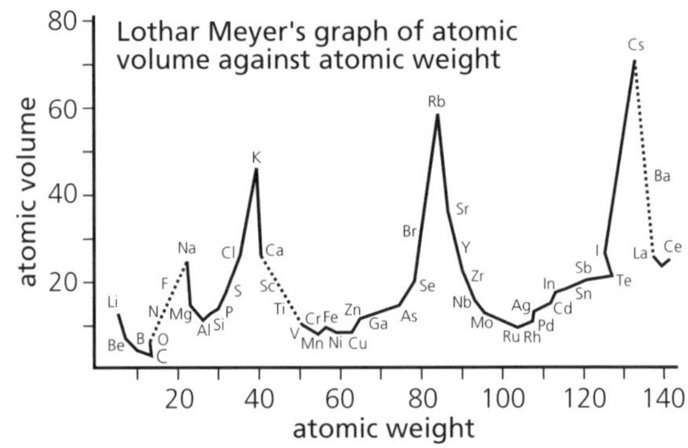

Q4 The table gives some physical properties of the first twenty elements.

Element	Order of increasing atomic weight (atomic mass)	Melting point/°C	Boiling point/°C	Density at room temperature and pressure/g per cm³
hydrogen	1	–259	–253	0
helium	2	–270	–269	0
lithium	3	180	1360	0.53
beryllium	4	1285	2470	1.85
boron	5	2030	3700	2.47
carbon	6	3500	4827	3.53
nitrogen	7	–210	–196	0
oxygen	8	–219	–183	0
fluorine	9	–220	–188	0
neon	10	–249	–246	0
sodium	11	98	900	0.97

Element	Order of increasing atomic weight (atomic mass)	Melting point/°C	Boiling point/°C	Density at room temperature and pressure/g per cm^3
magnesium	12	650	1100	1.74
aluminium	13	660	2350	2.7
silicon	14	1410	2620	2.33
phosphorus	15	44	2280	1.82
sulphur	16	115	444	1.96
chlorine	17	−101	−34	0
argon	19	−189	−186	0
potassium	18	63	777	0.89
calcium	20	840	1490	1.53

Note that when the elements are arranged in order of increasing atomic mass, argon and potassium are the wrong way round.

Use the information in the table to plot graphs like the one Lothar Meyer plotted. You should see how **a)** melting points, **b)** boiling points and **c)** densities of the first twenty elements vary with increasing atomic mass. (The densities of all of the gases can be taken as zero for this exercise.)

Q5 Place the elements in the list below in the correct columns of the table.

arsenic bromine calcium copper iodine manganese phosphorus silicon silver tin

Metal	Non-metal

Q6 Look at the modern Periodic Table. Which elements are gases in the Periodic Table at room temperature and atmospheric pressure? Where are they all placed in the Periodic Table?

Q7 Here is a table which shows patterns of hydrides of some of the main block elements.

Group	1	2	3	4	5	6	7	0
period 2		BeH_2	BH_3	CH_4	NH_3	OH_2	FH	no hydrides
period 3	NaH	MgH_2	AlH_3	SiH_4		SH_2	ClH	no hydrides
period 4	KH		GaH_3	GeH_4	AsH_3	SeH_2	BrH	no hydrides

a) Complete the table.

b) Use the modern Periodic Table to write the formulae of:

i) caesium hydride

ii) hydrogen telluride

iii) hydrogen iodide

iv) strontium hydride.

Q8 The elements potassium and argon appear to be the wrong way round. Look in the Periodic Table (page 188) and find other examples where the atomic masses are out of order.

Can you suggest why some elements are out of order? (*Hint:* Look at Unit 57.)

90–1 Alkali metals and noble gases

- **Lithium, sodium, potassium, rubidium and caesium all belong to the family of elements called alkali metals. They are all in group 1 of the Periodic Table.**
- **Down group 1 there is increasing reactivity and this is most clearly seen by the reactions of the metals with water.**
- **The noble gases are a family of unreactive gases placed in group 0 of the Periodic Table.**
- **Noble gases can form compounds, e.g. xenon tetrafluoride, XeF_4.**

Q1 Here is some information about five alkali metal elements.

Element	Symbol	Atomic number	Melting point/°C	Boiling point/°C	Density /g per cm^3	Date of discovery
lithium	Li	3	181	1331	0.54	1817
sodium	Na	11	98	890	0.97	1807
potassium	K	19	63	766	0.86	1807
rubidium	Rb	37	39	701	1.53	1861
caesium	Cs	55	29	685	1.87	1861

a) Which of these alkali metals:
  i) has the greatest density
  ii) has the highest melting point
  iii) has the largest atoms?

b) Suggest a reason why sodium and potassium were discovered before the other three metals.

Q2 The table gives some information about the atomic and ionic radii of the alkali metals. It also gives the energy, in kJ, required to remove an electron from a mole of atoms for each metal.

	Lithium	Sodium	Potassium	Rubidium	Caesium
Atomic radius/pm	152	186	231	244	262
Ionic radius/pm	60	95	133	148	169
Ionisation energy/ kJ per mole	519	494	418	402	376

a) How does i) the atomic radius, ii) ionic radius and iii) ionisation energy change down group 1?

b) Use this data to explain why the reactivity of the alkali metals increases down the group.

Q3 Unlike other alkali metals, lithium burns in nitrogen to form a white solid. When water is added to this white solid, a strong-smelling gas is produced which turns damp red litmus paper blue.

a) Identify the white solid produced when lithium burns in nitrogen and the strong-smelling gas produced when water is added to the white solid.

b) Write word and balanced equations for the reactions taking place.

Q4 a) Draw a labelled diagram of apparatus which could be used to make xenon tetrafluoride from xenon and fluorine.

b) Write equations for the formation of xenon tetrafluoride, XeF_4, and xenon hexafluoride, XeF_6, from xenon and fluorine.

c) Suggest a reason why xenon and fluorine react but helium and iodine do not.

92–3 The halogens

- The halogens are a family of reactive, non-metallic elements placed in group 7 of the Periodic Table.
- The order of reactivity of the halogens is:

  most reactive
  fluorine
  chlorine
  bromine
  iodine
  least reactive

- A displacement reaction takes place when a halogen is added to a salt containing a halogen if the halogen in the salt is less reactive than the halogen added.
  For example:

$$\text{potassium iodide} + \text{chlorine} \longrightarrow \text{potassium chloride} + \text{iodine}$$
$$2KI\,(aq) + Cl_2\,(g) \longrightarrow 2KCl\,(aq) + I_2\,(s)$$

- The high reactivity of halogens compared with many other elements can be related to electronic structure. All halogens, in group 7 of the Periodic Table, have seven electrons in their outer shell. Halogens gain one electron to form an ion with a single negative charge (e.g. F^-, Cl^-, Br^-).
- Chlorides, bromides and iodides can be tested for in aqueous solution by using silver nitrate solution. A white precipitate of silver chloride confirms chloride, a cream precipitate of silver bromide confirms bromide and a yellow precipitate of silver iodide confirms iodide.

Questions for Units 92–3

Q1 The table confirms information about the halogens.

Element	Atomic number	Melting point/°C	Boiling point/°C	Density at room temperature and atmospheric pressure/g per dm^3	Appearance at room temperature and atmospheric pressure
fluorine F	9	−220	−188	1.58	colourless gas
chlorine Cl	17	−101	−34	2.99	greenish-yellow gas
bromine Br	35	−7	58	3.12	dark red liquid
iodine I	53	114	183	4.94	black shiny solid
astatine At	85	302	337	not available	

a) Which halogen:
   i) could be solidified in a mixture of ice and salt
   ii) has the lowest melting point
   iii) has the highest boiling point
   iv) has the lowest density at room temperature and atmospheric pressure
   v) is more reactive than chlorine?

b) Chlorine gas can be prepared by adding concentrated hydrochloric acid with a tap funnel to solid potassium manganate(VII). Draw a diagram to show how a sample of chlorine could be prepared and collected.

Q2 The diagram shows a simple diagram of a fluorine atom.

a) How many protons are there in a fluorine atom?

b) Draw a similar diagram to show the arrangement of electrons in a chlorine atom.

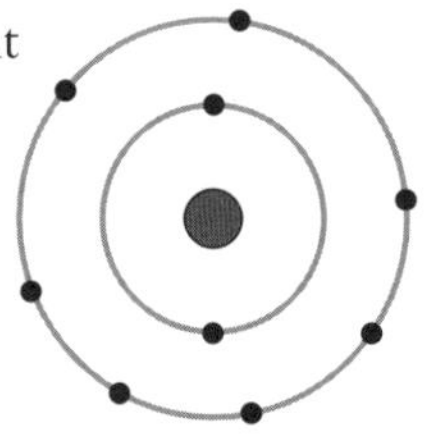

c) A fluorine atom gains an electron to form a fluoride, F^-, ion.
   i) Draw a diagram to show the arrangement of electrons in a fluoride ion.
   ii) Which element has the same electron arrangement as a fluoride ion?

Q3 A, B and C are aqueous solutions of potassium chloride, potassium bromide and potassium iodide. It is not known which solution is which. Samples of each solution were placed in separate test tubes. A couple of drops of chlorine solution were added to each test tube.
Three fresh samples of A, B and C were put into clean test tubes and a couple of drops of pale yellow bromine solution added to each test tube. The observations are shown in the table.

Solution	Add chlorine water	Add bromine water
A	orange-red solution	pale yellow solution
B	colourless solution	pale yellow solution
C	red-brown solution	red-brown solution

Use the information in the table to identify A, B and C.
Explain your answer.

Q4 The table shows the colour of the precipitate formed when silver nitrate solution is added to solutions of sodium salts.

Sodium salt	Colour of precipitate when silver nitrate solution added
sodium carbonate	white
sodium chloride	white
sodium bromide	cream
sodium iodide	yellow

a) Name the yellow precipitate formed when silver nitrate solution is added to sodium iodide solution.

b) When carrying out tests with silver nitrate solution, why is it possible to confuse a solution which contains both chloride and iodide with a solution containing bromide only?

c) When testing for halides, the solution is acidified before adding silver nitrate solution.

i) Why is the solution acidified?

ii) Why should nitric acid be used rather than hydrochloric acid?

Q5 Tin(IV) chloride, $SnCl_4$, is a liquid prepared by the action of dry chlorine on heated tin.

a) Write word and balanced symbol equations for the reaction producing tin(IV) chloride.

b) Why would you expect the reaction of tin with iodine to be slower?

c) Draw a diagram of apparatus which could be used to produce a sample of tin(IV) chloride from tin.

Tin(II) chloride, $SnCl_2$, is a solid prepared by passing hydrogen chloride, HCl, over heated tin.

d) Write word and balanced symbol equations for the reaction producing tin(II) chloride.

e) Write an ionic equation for the oxidation of tin(II) to tin(IV).

94–5 Rates of reaction

- Chemical reactions can take place at different speeds.
- A reaction which is over in a fraction of a second is a very fast reaction, i.e. it has a high rate of reaction. As the time taken for the reaction to be completed increases, the rate of reaction decreases. That is:

$$\text{rate of reaction} \propto 1/\text{time}$$

- Increasing the concentration of reactants increases the rate of reaction.
- Increasing the pressure of gases increases the rate of reaction.
- In both cases, there are more collisions between particles which could lead to more successful outcomes, and hence a faster reaction.

Q1 Explain why iron filings sprinkled into a Bunsen burner flame burn brightly but a lump of iron can be heated in a Bunsen burner without burning.

Q2 The diagram shows two sets of alternative apparatus which could be used for experiments with marble chips and hydrochloric acid. What is the advantage of using B rather than A?

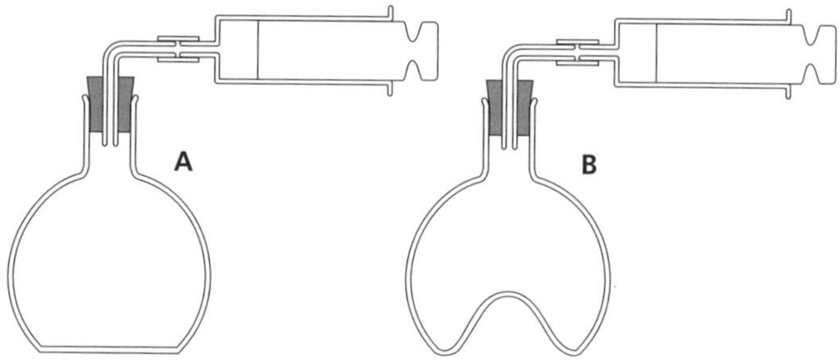

Q3 An experiment was carried out using marble chips and hydrochloric acid to investigate the effects of particle size on the rate of reaction.

$$CaCO_3\,(s) + 2HCl\,(aq) \longrightarrow CaCl_2\,(aq) + H_2O\,(l) + CO_2\,(g)$$

A large marble chip (mass 0.4 g) was placed in a conical flask and the flask placed on a top-pan balance. 25 cm^3 of dilute hydrochloric acid was added to the flask and a plug of cotton wool was placed in the neck of the flask. The reading on the balance was noted at intervals.

The following results were obtained:

Total loss of mass/g	0	2.2	2.9	3.3	3.6	3.7	3.7	3.7
Time/min	0	2	4	6	8	10	11	12

a) Why was there a loss of mass during the experiment?

b) Why was a plug of cotton wool placed in the neck of the flask?

c) Plot a graph of the total loss of mass (on the *y*-axis) against time (on the *x*-axis).

d) When was the reaction fastest?
e) After how many minutes was the reaction completed?
f) After 12 minutes a small piece of marble remained in the flask. What can be concluded about the amounts of marble and hydrochloric acid used?

The experiment was repeated using 0.4 g of powdered marble and a fresh 25 cm^3 sample of dilute hydrochloric acid.

g) What practical difficulty would be encountered in doing this?
h) On the same graph, sketch the graph that would be obtained with powdered marble.
i) What can you conclude from these two experiments?
j) How can you explain these results using a simple model?

Q4 Hydrogen peroxide solution is sold in solutions of different concentrations. On standing, hydrogen peroxide decomposes slowly into water and oxygen.

Buying a concentrated solution of hydrogen peroxide is much better value than buying dilute solutions. Why is it advisable to dilute the concentrated solution before storage?

Q5 The table gives results of an experiment between a mixture of two gases A and B. The rate in each case is the rate of disappearance of A at the start of the reaction.

Initial concentration of A/mol m^{-3}	Initial concentration of B/mol m^{-3}	Relative rate initially
0.2	0.2	1
0.4	0.2	4
0.2	0.4	2

a) What is the effect on the relative rate of reaction of doubling the concentration of A while keeping the concentration of B unchanged?
b) What is the effect on the relative rate of reaction of doubling the concentration of B while keeping the concentration of A unchanged?
c) What would be the relative rate of reaction if both A and B were doubled?

The rate of reaction can be expressed by a rate equation

$$\text{rate} = k\,[A]^x\,[B]^y$$

where [A] and [B] represent the concentrations of A and B.

d) What are the values of x and y for this reaction?

x and y are called the order of reaction with respect to A and B. The total order of the reaction is $x + y$.

e) Suggest factors which might affect the rate of this reaction apart from concentration.

96–8 Catalysts and enzymes

- Increasing the temperature increases the rate of reaction.
- Increasing the temperature increases the average speed of particles and their kinetic energy. Faster moving particles result in more collisions. More collisions are successful because the particles possess the activation energy necessary for reaction.
- A catalyst is a substance which alters the rate of a chemical reaction without being used up.
- Catalysts are often finely divided powders, pellets and fine gauzes. This suggests the importance of surfaces for catalysis to take place.
- Catalysts are often transition metals or transition metal compounds.
- Enzymes are proteins that control vital biological processes. They often act as biological catalysts.

Q1 In an experiment to investigate the effect of temperature on the rate of reaction, the volumes and concentrations of sodium thiosulphate solution and dilute hydrochloric acid are kept the same. The time is taken until a cross just disappears from view through the beaker. The table of results is shown below.

Temperature/°C	Time for the cross to disappear/s	Rate of reaction 1/time per s
20	280	
30	132	
40	60	
50	33	
60	18	

Complete the table by calculating 1/time to obtain the rate of reaction. For example, at 20°C: 1/280 = 0.0036.

a) Plot graphs of:

i) the time for the cross to disappear on the *y*-axis against temperature on the *x*-axis

ii) the rate of reaction on the *y*-axis against temperature on the *x*-axis.

b) Complete the following:

Increasing the temperature of a chemical reaction ______________ the time taken for a reaction to be completed.

Increasing the temperature of a chemical reaction ______________ the rate of reaction.

Q2 In an experiment to compare different ions as a catalyst for a certain reaction, the following results were obtained.

	Temperature/°C	Substance tested as a catalyst	Time for reaction to be completed/s
A	20	cobalt chloride	18
B	20	sodium nitrate	30
C	20	cobalt nitrate	12
D	30	cobalt nitrate	8
E	20	sodium chloride	40

a) Why should D not be used in any comparison?
b) Which substance gives the greatest increase in the rate of reaction?
c) Which substance is least effective as a catalyst?
d) Which ion is the most effective as a catalyst?

Q3 An experiment was set up to investigate the effect of temperature on the activity of a protein-digesting enzyme.

The apparatus shown in the diagram (next page) was set up at a particular temperature. After 5 minutes the enzyme was added to the egg white, the tube shaken and returned to the water bath. At first the solutions were cloudy because of the egg white protein present. The time was taken for the solution to become clear. The experiment was repeated at different temperatures.

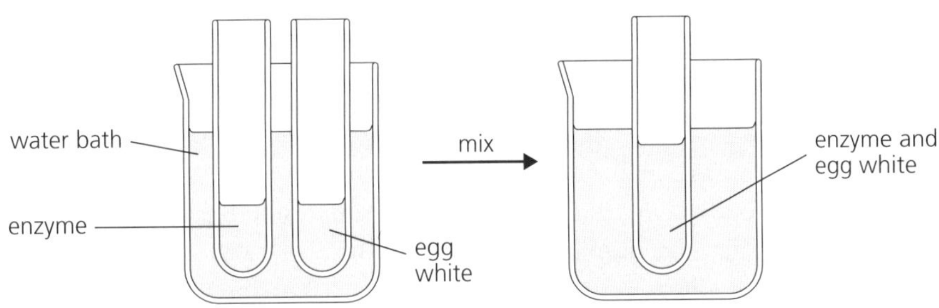

The results are shown in the table.

Temperature/°C	5	15	25	40	50	60
Time for cloudiness to disappear/min	16	10	5	1	7	still cloudy

a) Plot these results on a grid with time on the *y*-axis and temperature on the *x*-axis. Draw the best curve using these points.
b) At what temperature did the enzyme work most rapidly?
c) Why were the test tubes kept in the water bath for five minutes before mixing?

d) The mixture at 60°C did not go clear but remained cloudy. Explain why this was the case. Could the enzyme be re-used?
e) Explain how an enzyme speeds up the reaction.

99 Equilibrium

- **A reversible reaction is a reaction which can go from left to right or right to left, depending upon the conditions.**
- **A system is said to be in equilibrium when the forward and reverse reactions in a reversible reaction are still continuing at the same rate.**
- **If the equilibrium moves to produce more products (i.e. the forward reaction for a time becomes faster than the reverse reaction) the equilibrium is said to move to the right.**
- **Increasing the temperature helps to establish the equilibrium more quickly.**

Q1 The reaction between iron(III) chloride and potassium thiocyanate solutions can be represented by the following ionic equation:

$$Fe^{3+}(aq) + 3CNS^-(aq) \rightleftharpoons Fe(CNS)_3(aq)$$

pale yellow colourless blood red

What colour change would you expect if:
a) iron(III) chloride is added to an equilibrium mixture
b) potassium thiocyanate is added to an equilibrium mixture?

Q2 The reaction between silver nitrate and iron(II) sulphate can be represented by the following ionic equation:

$$Ag^+(aq) + Fe^{2+}(aq) \rightleftharpoons Ag(s) + Fe^{3+}(aq)$$

An equilibrium is established.
a) Suggest one way of making more silver solid precipitate.
b) Suggest one way of making solid silver dissolve.

Q3 $$3Fe(s) + 4H_2O(g) \rightleftharpoons Fe_3O_4(s) + 4H_2(g)$$

a) Complete the diagram to show how iron and steam can be made to react completely to produce iron oxide and hydrogen.

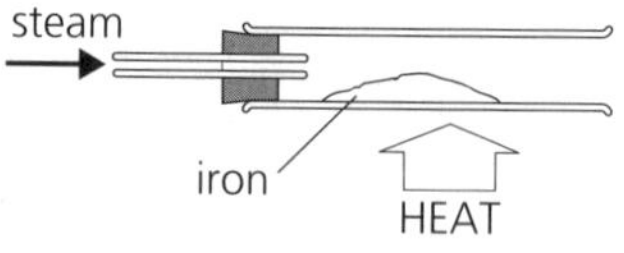

b) Complete the diagram to show how iron oxide and hydrogen can be made to react completely to produce iron and steam.

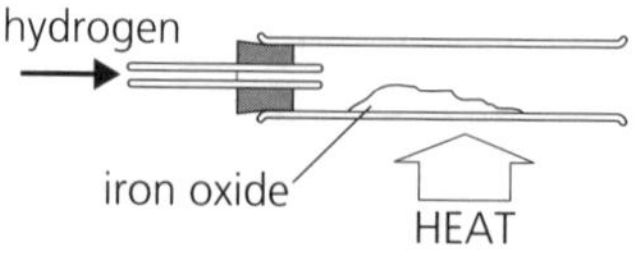

c) Explain why equilibrium is not established in **a)** or **b)**.

100 The Haber process

- The Haber process is used to manufacture ammonia from nitrogen and hydrogen.
- The equation for the reaction is:

$$\text{nitrogen} + \text{hydrogen} \rightleftharpoons \text{ammonia}$$
$$N_2\,(g) + 3H_2\,(g) \rightleftharpoons 2NH_3\,(g)$$

- Most of the ammonia produced is used to make fertilisers, e.g. ammonium sulphate and ammonium nitrate.

Q1 Complete the passage below, choosing words from the list to fill in the blank spaces.

air	**ammonia**	**catalyst**
dissolving	**hydrogen**	**iron**
liquefying	**nitrogen**	**platinum**
recycled	**vanadium(V) oxide**	

In the Haber process ______________ gas and ______________ gas react together to form ______________ gas.
______________ is obtained by fractional distillation of liquid air and ______________ from cracking natural gas.
The gases are mixed together and compressed to a high pressure. The mixture of gases is passed over a heated ______________ of finely divided ______________.

______________ is removed from the mixture of gases by ______________. The unreacted gases are then ______________.

Q2 The diagram shows the percentage yield of ammonia produced at different temperatures and pressures.

a) What percentage yield of ammonia is produced at 450°C and 200 atmospheres pressure?

b) What effect does i) increasing temperature and ii) increasing pressure have on the yield of ammonia?

c) What disadvantage is there in carrying out the process at a lower temperature?

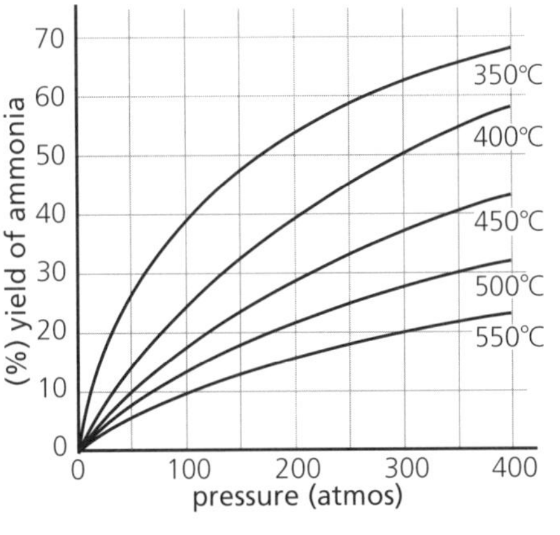

Q3 The synthesis of ammonia can be represented by:

The bond energy is the average energy required to break a covalent bond. It is also the amount of energy given out when a covalent bond is formed.

By using the average bond energies given in the table below, show that the forward reaction in the Haber process is exothermic.

	N≡N	H–H	N–H
Average bond energy/kJ per mole	+944	+436	+388

101 The Contact process

- The Contact process is a three-stage process. The second stage involves a reversible reaction.
- In Stage 1, sulphur dioxide is formed from burning sulphur or minerals rich in sulphur.
- In Stage 2, sulphur dioxide and air are passed over a heated catalyst in the catalyst chamber:

sulphur dioxide + oxygen (from the air) ⇌ sulphur trioxide + heat

$$2SO_2\,(g) + O_2\,(g) \rightleftharpoons 2SO_3\,(g) + \text{heat}$$

- In Stage 3, the sulphur trioxide is removed from the mixture of gases and converted to sulphuric acid.
- The overall reaction is:

sulphur trioxide + water → conc. sulphuric acid

$$SO_3\,(g) + H_2O\,(l) \rightarrow H_2SO_4\,(l)$$

- Because all of the impurities were removed from the gases before reaction, the acid produced is 99.5% pure.

Q1 Complete the paragraph below, choosing words from the list to fill in the blank spaces.

arsenic **concentrated sulphuric acid** **oleum**
poison **sulphur dioxide** **sulphur trioxide** **vanadium(V) oxide**

Sulphuric acid is manufactured by the Contact process. Sulphur is burned in air to produce ______________ gas. The gases contain impurities which might ______________ the catalyst. The dust containing ______________ is removed in the electrostatic dust precipitators. The gases are then washed and dried and then passed through the catalyst chamber. The catalyst is ______________. Some sulphur trioxide is formed. This is then dissolved in concentrated sulphuric acid to form ______________. This is then diluted with water to form ______________ .

Q2 The equation for the important stage in the Contact process is:

$$2SO_2(g) + O_2(g) \rightleftharpoons 2SO_3(g) + \text{heat}$$

What effect does each of the following have on the yield of sulphur trioxide? Your answer each time will be **increase the yield** or **decrease the yield** or **no change**. In each case explain your choice of answer.

a) Increase the concentration of sulphur trioxide.
b) Use a catalyst.
c) Increase the temperature.
d) Increase the pressure.
e) Remove sulphur trioxide from the mixture as it is formed.

102 Acids and alkalis

- **Acids are compounds containing hydrogen which can be replaced by a metal to form a salt.**
- **There are three common mineral acids:**

Acid	Formula	Salt produced
sulphuric acid	H_2SO_4	Na_2SO_4
hydrochloric acid	HCl	$NaCl$
nitric acid	HNO_3	$NaNO_3$

- **A base is an oxide or hydroxide of a metal. It reacts with an acid to form a salt and water only.**
- **An alkali is a base which is soluble in water. A solution of an alkali contains an excess of hydroxide, OH^-, ions. The common laboratory alkalis are potassium hydroxide KOH, sodium hydroxide NaOH, calcium hydroxide $Ca(OH)_2$ and ammonia solution (ammonium hydroxide) $NH_3(aq)$ or NH_4OH.**
- **The pH scale gives the comparative strengths of acids and alkalis.**

Q1 The table shows the results of tests with litmus paper on three solutions A, B and C.

Solution	Add red litmus paper	Add blue litmus paper
A	stays red	stays blue
B	stays red	turns red
C	turns blue	stays blue

What can you conclude about each solution from these tests?

Q2 Five test tubes labelled D, E, F, G and H contain five different liquids. These are: water, dilute hydrochloric acid, salt solution, sodium hydroxide solution and ethanoic acid. It is not known which solution is in which test tube.

The liquids were tested with:

i) litmus   ii) Universal Indicator.

The results are shown in the table.

Test tube	Colour with litmus	Colour with Universal Indicator	pH
D	red	red	1
E	blue	purple	13
F	purple	green	
G	red	orange	
H	purple	green	

a) Complete the table.

b) Which test tube contains

i) sodium hydroxide

ii) hydrochloric acid

iii) ethanoic acid?

c) Which test tubes contain either water or salt solution?

d) How, apart from tasting, could you find out which test tube contained water and which contained salt solution?

Q3 The table gives the colour of four different indicators in solutions of different pH. The gap in each case between colours corresponds to the pH at which the indicator changes colour.

<table>
<tr><th></th><th colspan="14">pH</th></tr>
<tr><td>Indicator</td><td>1</td><td>2</td><td>3</td><td>4</td><td>5</td><td>6</td><td>7</td><td>8</td><td>9</td><td>10</td><td>11</td><td>12</td><td>13</td><td>14</td></tr>
<tr><td>methyl orange</td><td colspan="3">← red →</td><td></td><td colspan="10">← yellow →</td></tr>
<tr><td>bromocresol green</td><td colspan="4">← yellow →</td><td></td><td colspan="9">← blue →</td></tr>
<tr><td>phenol red</td><td colspan="6">← yellow →</td><td></td><td colspan="7">← red →</td></tr>
<tr><td>phenolphthalein</td><td colspan="8">← colourless →</td><td></td><td colspan="5">← red →</td></tr>
</table>

a) What colour is a solution of pH 8 with a couple of drops of bromocresol green indicator added?

b) A solution turns yellow when either methyl orange or phenol red is added. What is the approximate pH of this solution?

c) A mixture of methyl orange, bromocresol green and phenolphthalein is added to pure water (pH 7). What colour is the resulting solution?

Q4 The table opposite shows the reactions of dry hydrogen chloride dissolved in methylbenzene and dry hydrogen chloride dissolved in water.

Test	Dry hydrogen chloride dissolved in methylbenzene	Dry hydrogen chloride dissolved in water
dry Universal Indicator paper	green, pH7, neutral	red, pH 1, strongly acidic
electrical conductivity	does not conduct electricity	good conductor of electricity
add magnesium ribbon	no bubbles of hydrogen gas	bubbles of hydrogen gas produced
add sodium carbonate crystals	no bubbles of carbon dioxide gas	bubbles of carbon dioxide produced

a) What can you conclude from these results?

b) In dry methylbenzene, hydrogen chloride exists as molecules:

$$H—Cl$$

Suggest what changes occur when water is added.

103 Neutralisation

- **Neutralisation occurs when an acid is mixed with an alkali, in the correct proportions, and a neutral solution is formed.**
- **One product of neutralisation is water. Any neutralisation can be represented by the ionic equation:**

$$H^+ (aq) + OH^- (aq) \longrightarrow H_2O (l)$$

- **These reactions are exothermic. There is a temperature rise when the two solutions are mixed.**

Q1 In a neutralisation experiment 500 cm^3 of hydrochloric acid (2 moles per dm^3) and 500 cm^3 of sodium hydroxide solution (2 moles per dm^3) were mixed in a poly(phenylethene) container with a lid. The temperature of both solutions before mixing was 20°C and after mixing the temperature rose to 33°C.

a) Write a balanced symbol equation and an ionic equation for the reaction taking place.

b) What is the advantage of using a poly(phenylethene) (also known as polystyrene) container rather than a metal container?

c) What was the temperature rise?

d) What was the total volume of the solution after mixing?

e) Assuming 1 cm^3 of this solution weighs 1 g, what is the mass of the final solution?

f) Work out the heat evolved on mixing these solutions. (*Remember:* heat evolved = mass × specific heat capacity × temperature rise. The heat required to raise the temperature of 1 kg of solution by 1°C is 4.2 kJ. This is the specific heat capacity of water.)

g) Suggest a reason why the experimental result is lower than the value in the data book.

Q2 The table gives the energy produced when 1 mole of acid and 1 mole of alkali are neutralised.

Acid	Alkali	Energy given out/kJ per mole
hydrochloric acid HCl	sodium hydroxide NaOH	57.2
hydrochloric acid HCl	potassium hydroxide KOH	57.2
nitric acid HNO_3	sodium hydroxide NaOH	57.2
hydrofluoric acid HF	sodium hydroxide NaOH	68.6

a) Explain why the energy given out on mixing 1 mole of acid and 1 mole of alkali is the same in the first three examples in the table. Writing balanced ionic equations may help you.

b) Why is the fourth result different?

104–5 Salt formation

- **A salt is produced when hydrogen ions in an acid are replaced by metal or ammonium (NH_4^+) ions. For example:**

  hydrochloric acid ⟶ sodium chloride

  HCl NaCl

- **The following word equations summarise the possible reactions:**

  metal + acid ⟶ salt + hydrogen

  metal oxide + acid ⟶ salt + water

  metal hydroxide + acid ⟶ salt + water

  metal carbonate + acid ⟶ carbon dioxide + salt + water

- **Insoluble salts are prepared by precipitation.**

Q1 The table shows information about the solubility of salts at room temperature.

a) Name:

i) a soluble lead salt

ii) two slightly soluble sulphates

iii) an insoluble calcium salt

iv) two insoluble silver salts.

b) Name the salt produced from each of the following pairs of chemicals:

i) magnesium and dilute hydrochloric acid

Metal	Chloride	Nitrate	Sulphate	Carbonate
sodium	s	s	s	s
calcium	s	s	ss	i
zinc	s	s	s	i
barium	s	s	i	i
magnesium	s	s	s	i
lead(II)	i	s	i	i
potassium	s	s	s	s
iron(II)	s	s	s	i
ammonium	s	s	s	s
copper(II)	s	s	s	i
silver	i	s	ss	i

Key: s soluble in water
ss slightly soluble in water
i insoluble in water

ii) zinc carbonate and dilute sulphuric acid
iii) sodium hydroxide and dilute nitric acid
iv) lead(II) oxide and dilute nitric acid.

Q2 Complete the following word equations for reactions producing soluble salts.

a) calcium carbonate + _______ ⟶ calcium chloride + _______ + _______

b) zinc + _______ ⟶ zinc sulphate + _______

c) potassium hydroxide + _______ ⟶ potassium chloride + _______

d) ammonium hydroxide + hydrochloric acid ⟶ _______ + _______

Q3 The diagram shows the method used to produce magnesium sulphate crystals, $MgSO_4.7H_2O$, from magnesium oxide.

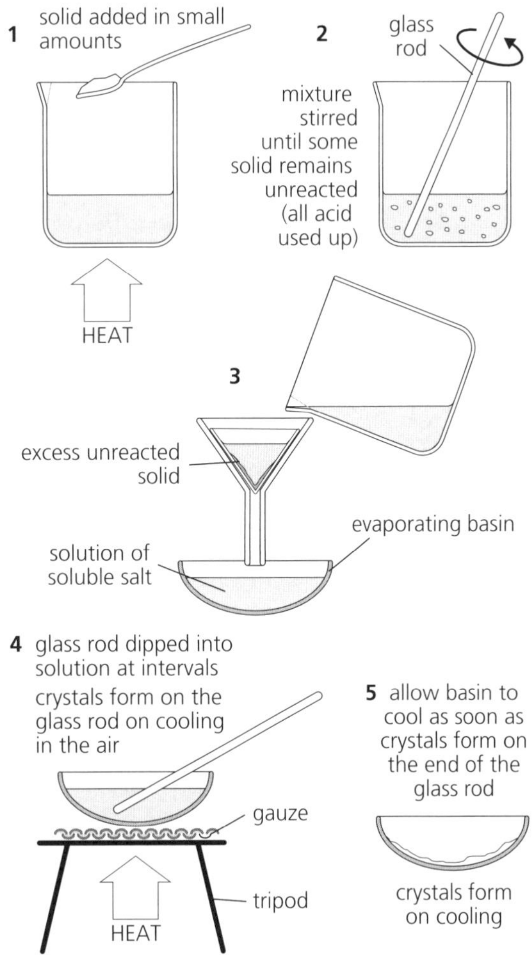

a) Why is the dilute sulphuric acid heated before the magnesium oxide is added?

b) Chris said that when magnesium oxide remained unchanged at the bottom of the beaker in diagram 2, the solution was a saturated solution of magnesium sulphate. Is this true? Explain your answer.

c) What is done to ensure that no acid remains in the solution after filtering?

d) How is excess magnesium oxide removed from the solution?

e) Why is the magnesium sulphate solution not evaporated to dryness in diagram 4?

f) Write a written account of the method you would use to produce magnesium chloride crystals from magnesium powder. Include an equation (word or balanced symbol), the steps you would use and any safety precautions you would recommend.

Q4 a) Ethanoic acid has the structure shown:

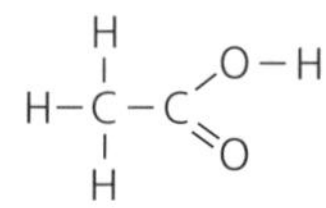

i) Why is this a monobasic acid and not a tetrabasic acid?

ii) Write down the formula of the salt of ethanoic acid, sodium ethanoate.

b) Phosphoric acid, H_3PO_4, is a tribasic acid. Write down the names and formulae of the sodium salts of phosphoric acid.

106 Fertilisers

- **Nitrogen, phosphorus and potassium are required by plants in large amounts.**
  Nitrogen is needed for the growth of stems and leaves of plants.
  Phosphorus is essential for root growth.
  Potassium is required for the production of flowers.
- **Ammonia is manufactured by the Haber process in a three-stage process.**
- **Ammonium nitrate can be prepared by reacting ammonia solution and nitric acid.**

Q1 Work out the percentage of nitrogen in ammonium sulphate, $(NH_4)_2SO_4$.

Q2 Work out the percentage of potassium in potassium nitrate, KNO_3.

Q3 The table compares three fertilisers.

Compound	Formula	Mass of 1 mole/g	Price per kg	Solubility in water
ammonium nitrate	NH_4NO_3	80	80p	readily soluble in water
calcium cyanamide	$CaCN_2$	80	60p	insoluble but reacts slowly to produce soluble products
urea	$CO(NH_2)_2$	60	40p	soluble but reacts very slowly with water

a) Calculate the percentage of nitrogen in each compound.

b) Which fertiliser would you recommend to farmers who want their grass to grow quickly in Spring? Explain your choice.

c) Which fertiliser would you recommend to farmers who want to use it in the Spring but want it to carry on acting throughout the Summer and Autumn?

Q4 Why is it unwise to spread an ammonium fertiliser and lime onto a field at the same time?

Q5 Calculate the mass of ammonium sulphate fertiliser which could be obtained by neutralising 300 cm^3 of ammonium hydroxide solution NH_4OH (1.5 moles per dm^3) with sulphuric acid.

Review questions

Classifying materials (Units 55–65)

Q1 Here is a list of methods used for purifying substances:

A chromatography B distillation C evaporation
D filtration E fractional distillation

Which method is most suitable for each of the following?

a) Removing small pieces of glass from a solution.
b) Obtaining a sample of salt from a salt solution.
c) Producing a nearly pure sample of ethanol from a sample of beer.
d) Separating the mixture of amino acids produced when a protein is split up.
e) Producing water for domestic use from water in a reservoir.
f) Producing a sample of pure water from sea water.

Q2 An experiment was carried out to identify the products obtained when starch is split up with

i) enzymes in saliva and
ii) dilute hydrochloric acid.

a) Why is the filter paper dipped into locating agent and heated?
b) What can you conclude about the products of the reactions of starch with i) enzymes in saliva and ii) dilute hydrochloric acid?

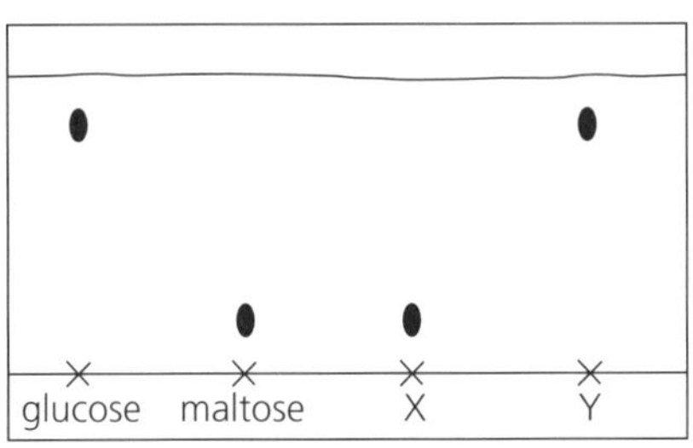

X – sample produced by hydrolysing starch with enzymes
Y – sample produced by hydrolysing starch with dilute hydrochloric acid

Q3 A chemical fertiliser contains a mixture of three substances: ammonium chloride, urea and potassium chloride. The properties of these three substances are summarised in the table.

Substance	State at room temperature	Solubility in cold water	Change on heating
ammonium chloride	solid	dissolves well	sublimes
urea	solid	does not dissolve	melts
potassium chloride	solid	dissolves well	melts

Write an account of the method you would use to produce pure samples of the three substances from the mixture in the fertiliser.

Q4 Explain each of the following:

a) A person wearing spectacles finds they 'steam up' when entering a hot, steamy kitchen.

b) Ice forms on the inside of a freezer.

c) The windows of your bedroom may be steamed up on a cold morning.

d) Puddles in the road disappear faster on a warm day than on a cold day.

e) A patch of ice on the road disappears without the temperature rising above 0°C.

f) Water from the windscreen washer bottle, when sprayed onto the windscreen on a very cold day, makes it impossible to see out.

g) Droplets of water may be seen dripping from a car exhaust pipe when a car is started but not when the engine has been running for some time.

Q5 When ammonia and hydrogen chloride gases mix, dense white fumes are formed.

$$NH_3\,(g) + HCl\,(g) \longrightarrow NH_4Cl\,(s)$$

A long, dry glass tube was clamped horizontally. A piece of cotton wool, soaked in concentrated ammonia solution, and a piece of cotton wool, soaked in concentrated hydrochloric acid, were placed at opposite ends of the glass tube at the same time. After five minutes a white solid ring was formed as shown in the diagram.

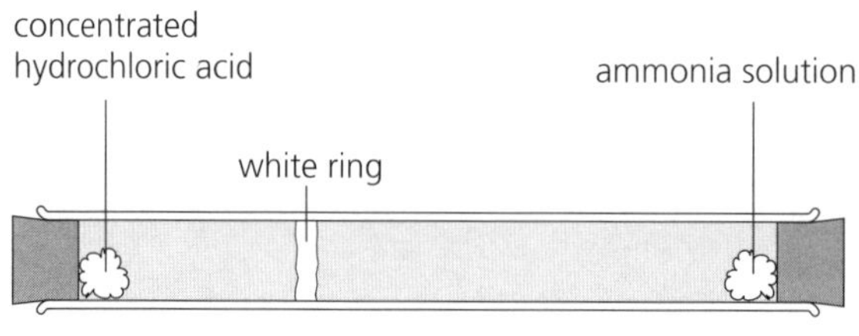

a) Name the white solid formed in the tube.

b) Explain why the white ring was formed closer to the end containing the pad of hydrochloric acid.

c) The particles of ammonia and hydrogen chloride are moving rapidly at room temperature. Give two reasons why the formation of the ring takes five minutes.

d) What name is given to this movement of particles?

A similar experiment can be carried out using saturated solutions of hydrogen sulphide (H_2S) and sulphur dioxide (SO_2) in place of ammonia solution and hydrochloric acid.

e) What is the solid formed in this case?

f) Where is the solid formed in the tube?

Changing materials (Units 66–87)

Q1 For each of the following pairs of chemicals, write down if a reaction will take place when the chemicals are mixed. In some cases the mixture may need to be heated. If a reaction does take place, write word equations or symbol equations for the reactions.

a) zinc and copper(II) sulphate solution

b) copper and iron(III) oxide

c) magnesium and copper(II) oxide

d) zinc and silver nitrate solution.

Q2 A white powder was heated in the apparatus shown in the diagram. A colourless gas was produced and collected in the gas syringe. The test tube and white powder were weighed before and after heating.

Mass of test tube + white powder = 23.19 g

Mass of test tube + white powder after heating = 23.12 g

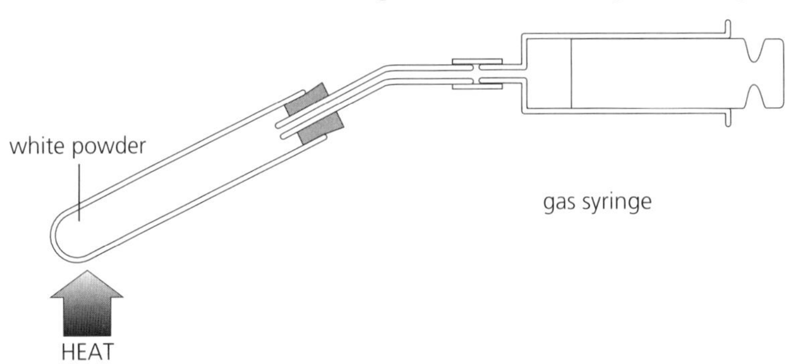

At the end of the experiment 40 cm^3 of the colourless gas (at room temperature and atmospheric pressure) were collected.

a) What mass change occurred on heating?

b) What is the mass of 40 cm^3 of the colourless gas?

c) Calculate the mass of

i) 1 cm^3 of the gas at room temperature and atmospheric pressure.

ii) 24 000 cm^3 of the gas at room temperature and atmospheric pressure.

Here are some values from a data book for the mass of 24 000 cm^3 of different gases at room temperature and atmospheric pressure.

hydrogen	2 g
oxygen	32 g
nitrogen	28 g
carbon dioxide	44 g
sulphur dioxide	64 g

d) Which one of these gases is most likely to be lost when the white powder is heated?

Q3 Titanium is an important metal in industry. It can be extracted from titanium ore in a two-stage process.

Stage 1. Titanium dioxide is heated with carbon in a stream of dry chlorine. Titanium chloride is formed, together with carbon dioxide. Titanium chloride is a low boiling point liquid. It can be separated from impurities by fractional distillation.

Stage 2. Titanium chloride is heated with sodium. A displacement reaction takes place and titanium is produced.

a) Write a word equation for the reaction taking place in Stage 1.

b) Write a word equation for the reaction taking place in Stage 2.

c) How could titanium be removed from the products of Stage 2?

d) Suggest a reason why sodium is used as the reducing agent, rather than carbon.

Q4 An experiment was carried out to arrange five metals P, Q, R, S and T in order of reactivity by measuring the voltages of simple cells using the apparatus shown in the diagram.

In each case a copper rod was used, and the other metals were used, in turn. The results are shown in the table.

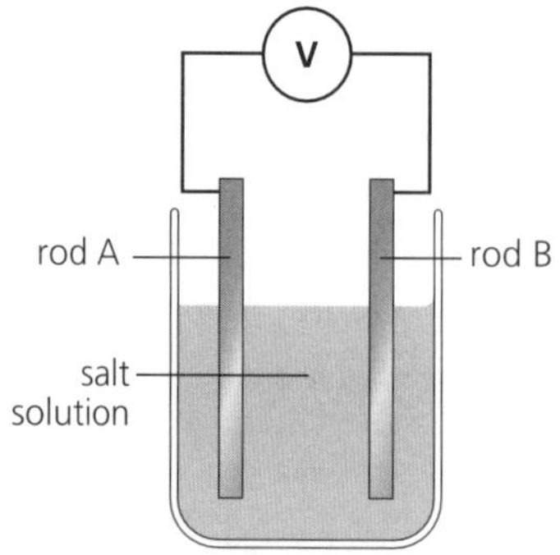

Rod A	Rod B	Voltage measured/V
copper	copper	0
P	copper	0.02
Q	copper	1
R	copper	−0.05
S	copper	0
T	copper	0.6

a) Which of metals P, Q, R, S and T is copper? Explain your answer.
b) Arrange the five metals in order of reactivity, with the most reactive metal first.

Q5 Write balanced symbolic equations for the combustion of i) ethane and ii) butane in **a)** plentiful and **b)** limited supplies of air.

Q6 For each of the following conversions
i) name a suitable reagent for carrying out the reaction
ii) state whether the reaction involves the oxidation of the substance in capitals, the reduction of the substance in capitals, or whether the substance in capitals is neither oxidised nor reduced
iii) write a balanced equation for the reaction.

a) SODIUM CARBONATE to carbon dioxide
b) IRON(II) CHLORIDE to iron(III) chloride
c) AMMONIA to nitrogen
d) AMMONIUM CHLORIDE to ammonia
e) POTASSIUM IODIDE to iodine.

Patterns of behaviour (Units 88–106)

Q1 A sample of an oxide of antimony (Sb) contained 40 g of antimony combined with 8 g of oxygen. Use this data to show the simplest formula of the oxide of antimony is Sb_2O_3.

Questions **2** and **3** refer to the following equation for the reaction between magnesium and dilute hydrochloric acid.

$$Mg(s) + 2HCl(aq) \longrightarrow MgCl_2(aq) + H_2(g)$$

Q2 What mass of anhydrous magnesium chloride would be produced from 2.4 g of magnesium?

Q3 What volume of hydrogen, at room temperature and atmospheric pressure, would be produced when 0.1 g of magnesium reacts with excess hydrochloric acid?

Q4 The graph shows the atomic radii for the first 36 elements.

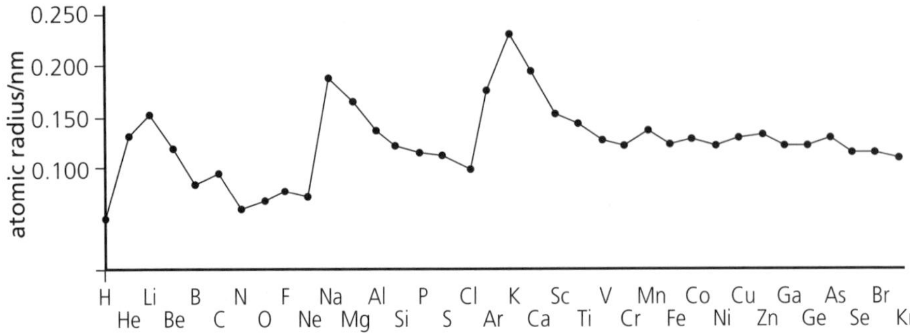

What do you notice about the atomic radii of the transition elements (Sc to Zn, atomic numbers 21–30)? How do you explain this?
What significance does this have for the reactivity of these elements?

Physical processes

107–8 Current and energy transfer

- Current is not used up by electrical devices.
- Components connected in series must always have the same current.
- In a parallel circuit the current splits at a junction; the current passing into a junction must be the same as the current passing out.
- Currents consist of moving charges that transfer energy from the electricity supply into heat, light and movement when they pass through circuit components or domestic appliances.
- In metals the charge carriers are negatively charged electrons. Both positive and negative ions can move in ionised gases and electrolytes.

Q1 Study these two circuits. Complete the following sentences, choosing words from the list to fill in the blank spaces.

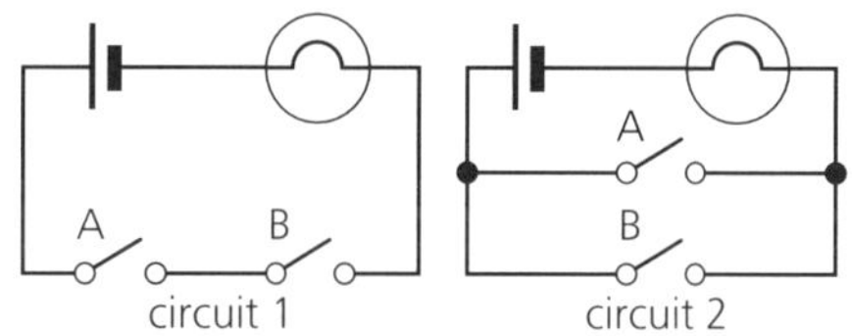

and but either neither nor or

In circuit 1, for the lamp to be on A ____________ B must be on.

In circuit 2, for the lamp to be on A ____________ B must be on.

Q2 A burglar alarm has to satisfy the following requirements:
It is switched on when either the front door or the back door is opened.
There is a master switch to switch it off.
Copy the diagram and add three switches so that it satisfies these conditions.

Q3 Write down the ammeter readings A1 to A4 in these two circuits.

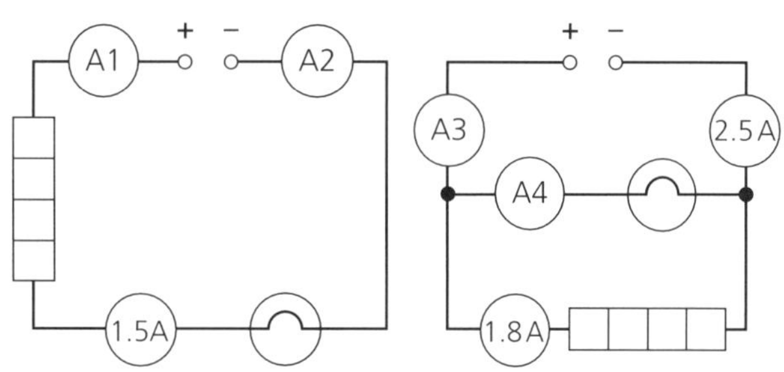

Q4 Here is a list of things which all conduct electricity. Write each item from the list in one of the columns of the table.

filament lamp vacuum cleaner sodium street light copper sulphate solution convector heater immersion heater fluorescent light neon light

Current carried by both positive and negative ions	Current carried by electrons only

Q5 Complete the paragraph below about electric current, choosing words from the list to fill in the blank spaces.

attracted collide charged divide negative positive

An electric current is a movement of ______________ particles. In a metal the particles are electrons which carry a ______________ charge. Electrons are ______________ to the positive terminal of a power supply and repelled from the negative. Energy transfer to particles of the metal happens when the electrons ______________ with these particles.

Q6 Draw diagrams to show the energy flow through:

a) a filament lamp

b) a fan heater.

Q7 When sodium chloride is molten it conducts electricity. Molten sodium chloride contains positive ions, Na^+, and negative ions, Cl^-. Use a diagram to describe what happens to these ions when two carbon rods, connected to a battery, are placed in molten sodium chloride.

109 Current and its control

- **Components in parallel must all have the same voltage across them.**
- **The sum of the voltages across the components in a series circuit is equal to the supply voltage.**
- **The size of the current in a circuit or component depends on the resistance as well as the voltage.**
- **Increasing the resistance in a circuit decreases the current. Increasing the voltage increases the current.**

Q1 Describe what the variable resistor does in each of these circuits.

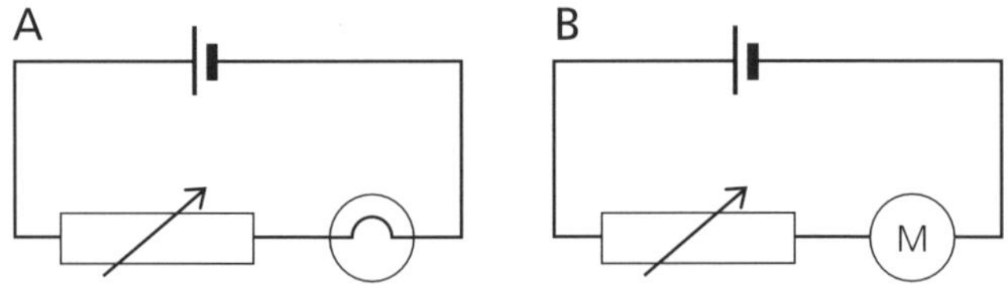

Q2 Resistance measures the amount of opposition that something has to an electric current passing through it. A lamp, a kettle and a food mixer are all operating from the mains 240 V supply. The table shows the current in each appliance.

List the appliances in order of resistance, starting with the one with the least resistance. Explain how you can tell which one has the least resistance.

Appliance	Current/A
lamp	0.25
kettle	10
food mixer	1.75

Q3 **a)** On the circuit diagram, add an ammeter and a voltmeter to measure the current in the heater and the potential difference across it.

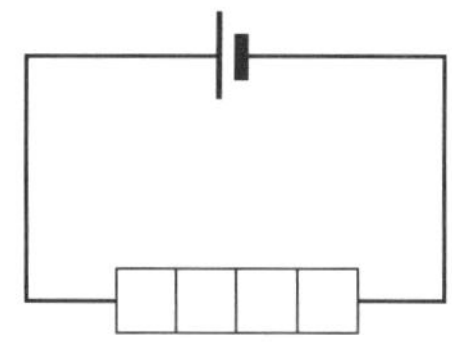

b) Explain how the current in the circuit changes when a second heater is added in series with the first one.

c) Explain how you could double the size of the current in the circuit.

Q4 Study the circuits and write down the meter readings on the ammeters A1, A2, A3, A4 and the voltmeters V1, V2 and V3.

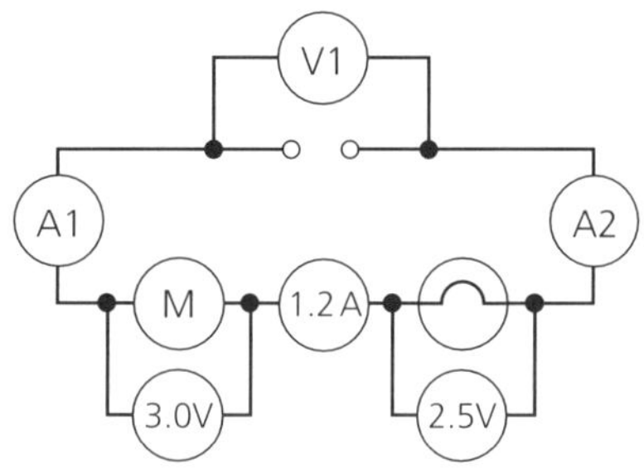

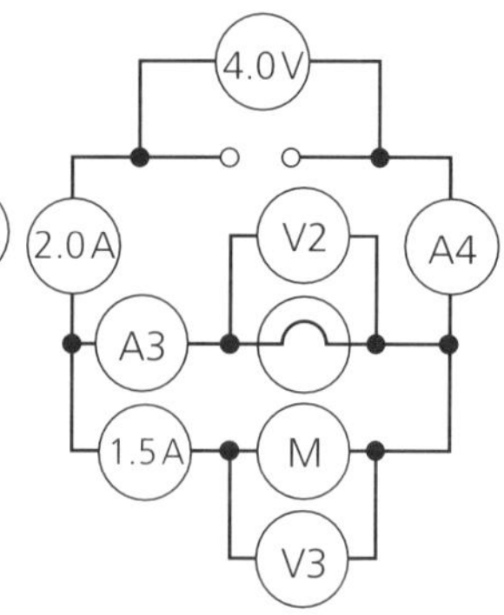

110–11 Electrical resistance

- Resistance is the opposition to electric current. It is measured in ohms (**Ω**) and calculated using the formula:

$$R = V/I$$

- The resistance of a metallic conductor has a constant value provided that the temperature stays the same. As the temperature increases, so does the resistance.
- A diode is a component that allows current to pass in one direction only. Its symbol includes an arrow which shows the direction in which current can pass.
- The resistance of thermistors and light-dependent resistors (LDRs) depends on environmental conditions. The resistance of a thermistor decreases with increasing temperature and that of an LDR decreases when the illumination increases.

Q1 Use the resistance equation to complete the table.

	Voltage/V	Current/A	Resistance/Ω
a)	12	2	
b)		4	0.5
c)	240		960
d)	20	0.25	
e)		10	12
f)	12		1.2

Q2 Here are four graphs of voltage against current:

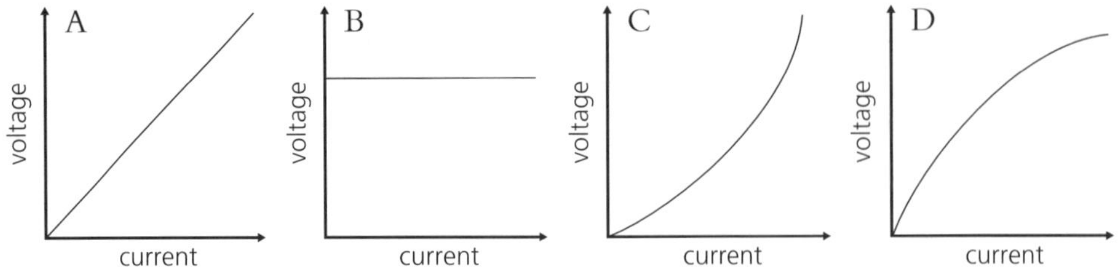

a) Which graph shows the correct relationship for a wire at a constant temperature?

b) Which graph shows the correct relationship for a filament lamp?

Q3 In which of these circuits does the lamp light?

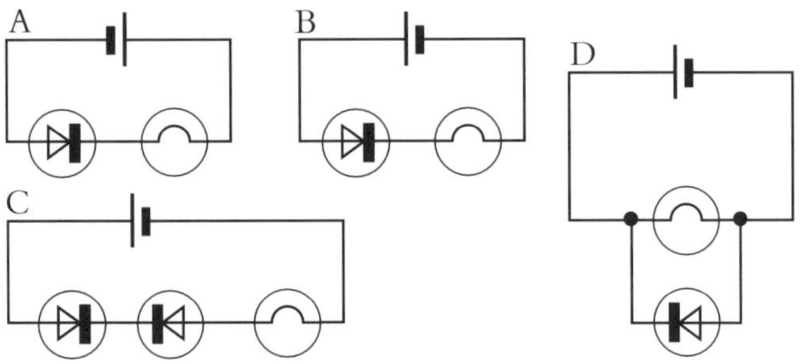

Q4 The table gives some data about a silicon diode.

Current/A	0.5	1	1.5	2	2.5	3
Voltage/V	0.68	0.72	0.74	0.76	0.78	0.79
Resistance/Ω						

a) Calculate the resistance of the diode for each pair of values of voltage and current.

b) Plot a graph of resistance (y-axis) against current (x-axis).

c) Describe how the resistance changes as the current in the diode increases.

Q5 Which line in the table gives a correct description of the resistance of a thermistor and LDR for the given environmental conditions?

	Environmental conditions	Resistance of thermistor	Resistance of LDR
A	cold and dark	high	low
B	cold and light	low	high
C	warm and dark	high	high
D	warm and light	low	low

Q6 This circuit uses a light-dependent resistor as a light sensor. In bright sunlight the resistance of the LDR is 100 Ω and in darkness it is 1000 Ω.

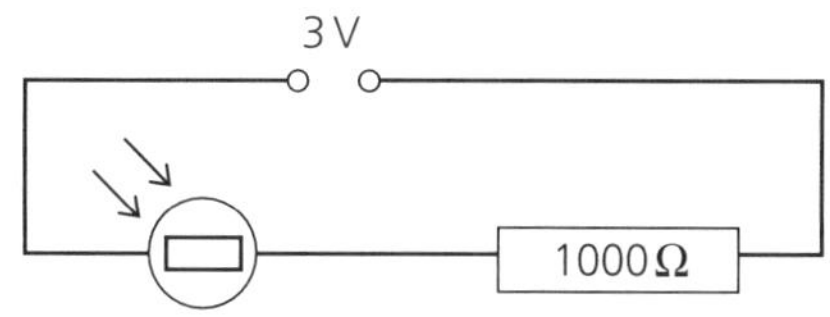

a) The total resistance of the circuit is 1100 Ω in bright sunlight and 2000 Ω in darkness.
Calculate the current in the circuit in each case.

b) Calculate the voltage across the LDR in bright sunlight and in darkness.

c) Describe what happens to the voltage across the LDR as the light level fades.

d) Transistors are the basis of many switching circuits. Together with components such as relays they can be used to switch mains devices on and off. Transistors have a threshold voltage of 0.6 V, above which they are 'on' and below which they are 'off'.
Describe how you could use the LDR circuit, together with a transistor switch, to do a useful job.

e) In switching circuits, the fixed resistor of the LDR circuit is usually replaced with a variable resistor. Explain the advantage of this.

112 Current and voltage

- **Electric current in a circuit is a flow of charge.**
- **The current in amps is equal to the rate of flow of charge in coulombs per second. Current is calculated using the formula:**

  current = charge flow ÷ time **or** $I = Q/t$
- **The energy transferred by the moving charge is measured by the voltage. One volt is an energy transfer of one joule for each coulomb of charge. Voltage is calculated using the formula:**

  voltage = energy transfer ÷ charge **or** $V = E/Q$

Q1 Which statement is correct?

A A 12 V battery supplies 12 J of energy to each amp of current.
B A 12 V battery supplies 12 J of energy to each coulomb of charge.
C A 12 V battery takes 12 J of energy from each amp of current.
D A 12 V battery takes 12 J of energy from each coulomb of charge.

Q2 Calculate the current passing in the following examples:

a) A charge of 3000 C flows through a kettle element in the 5 minutes it takes to boil.

b) 15 C flow through a 60 W lamp each minute.

c) In a lightning strike, 20 C of charge passes to earth in 1 ms (0.001 s).

d) 480 C flow through an oven element each minute.

Q3 Calculate the amount of charge which flows in the following examples:

a) 100 A pass through a car starter motor for 5 s.
b) 10 A pass in an immersion heater for 20 minutes.
c) 6 A pass in a hair dryer for 8 minutes.
d) 0.05 A passes in a low-energy lamp for 1 hour.

Q4 Use your answers to **Q3** to calculate the energy transferred by the charge in each case. The voltage is 12 V for part **a)** and 240 V for **b)**, **c)** and **d)**.

Q5 The circuit diagram shows a heater in series with a lamp and the mains supply. Write down a sentence about each meter reading.
Your sentences should explain what the meter reading means in terms of charge flow or energy transfer.

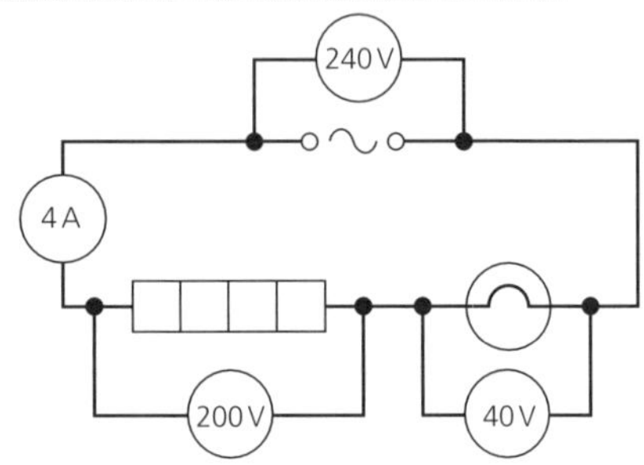

113 Power in circuits

- **Power is the rate of energy transfer in joules per second or watts (W). Power is calculated using the formula:**

  power = energy transfer ÷ time **or** $P = E/t$

- **The power of a circuit component or electrical appliance depends on both the current and the voltage.**
- **The formula for electrical power is:**

  power = voltage × current **or** $P = V \times I$

Q1 Complete the sentences.
Power is the rate of _______________ transfer.
1 watt is an energy transfer of 1 _______________ per _______________.
A 60 W lamp transfers _______________ J of energy in one minute.

Q2 Calculate the total energy transfer in the following examples:

a) A 100 W mains lamp is switched on for 30 s.
b) A 0.4 W torch is switched on for 5 minutes.
c) A 800 W vacuum cleaner is used for 3 minutes.

Q3 The oil in a frier requires 1 MJ (1 000 000 J) of energy to heat it from room temperature to the correct temperature for cooking. It is fitted with a 2 kW (2000 W) heater.

a) Calculate the time it takes to heat up to the required temperature.
b) Give two reasons why it is likely to take longer than the time you have calculated in **a)**.

Q4 Complete the table.

Device	Current/A	p.d./V	Power/W
microwave oven	4	240	
indicator lamp	2		24
clock		240	4
television	0.35	240	
model car	5.8	6	

114–15 Electricity at home

- There are three conductors in the mains supply to a house. The live wire carries the energy supplied to the house through electricity, the neutral wire completes the circuit and the earth wire is a safety wire that is connected to the ground.
- Fuses and circuit breakers protect fixed installation cables and flexible cables from overheating and possible fire risk.
- The plug fuse together with the earth wire protect the user from electrocution.
- Energy transfer in kilowatt-hours is calculated using the equation:

energy in kWh = power in kW × time in h

Q1 The diagram shows a fused, three-pin plug.

a) Which part of the appliance should the earth wire be connected to?

b) Explain how the earth wire can protect against electric shock.

c) The fuse is to protect against fire hazard. Explain how it does this.

d) The current in a lamp operating normally is 0.25 A and that in a kettle is 10 A. Which of the following fuses should be fitted to the plugs?

1 A   3 A   5 A   13 A

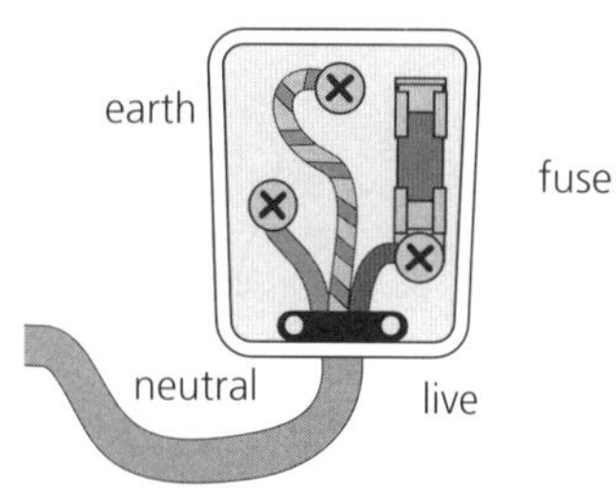

Q2 The diagram shows a switching circuit which can be used in a house.

a) Complete the table to show when the lamp is off or on.

Position of switch A	Position of switch B	Lamp off or on
1	1	
1	2	
2	2	
2	1	

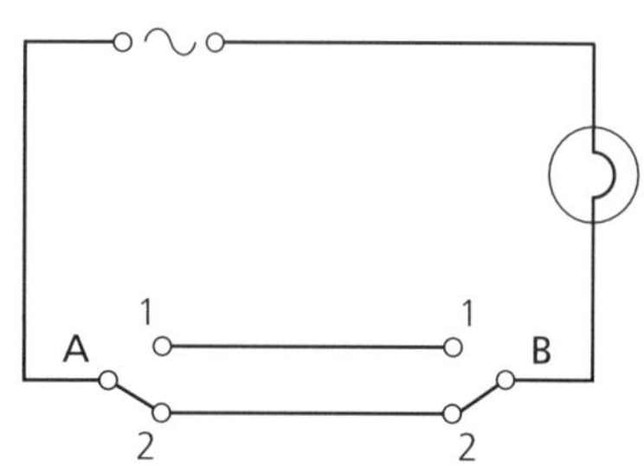

b) Describe a use for this switching circuit in a house.

c) The lights in a house are connected in parallel. Complete the circuit diagram to show how two lights in a room can be turned on and off by one switch.

d) Draw another circuit diagram using the same components to show how each light can be controlled by its own switch.

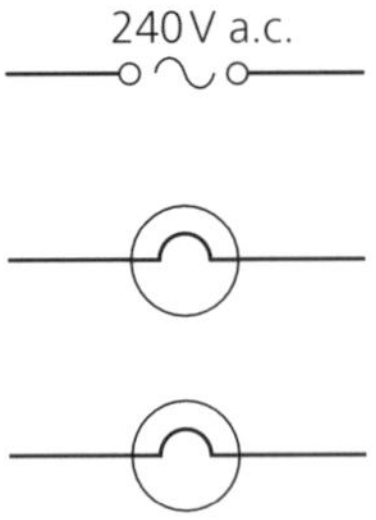

Q3 Complete the table, assuming that each kWh of energy costs 8p.

	Appliance	Power/kW	Time used/h	Energy transfer/kWh	Cost/p
a)	microwave oven	1.3	2		
b)	food frier	2	0.5		
c)	hi-fi	0.05	4		
d)	immersion heater	2.5	2		

Q4 For each heating appliance shown in the table, decide whether the main energy transfer from the heating element is by conduction, convection or radiation. Tick the appropriate columns in the table.

	Appliance	Energy transfer by		
		conduction	convection	radiation
a)	iron			
b)	convector heater			
c)	kettle			
d)	radiant heater			
e)	immersion heater			
f)	sandwich toaster			

Q5 Energy from electricity costs 8p for each kilowatt-hour. Energy from gas costs 2p for each kilowatt-hour. Suggest **three** reasons why electricity is such a popular energy source despite this price difference.

Q6 Electric storage heaters can be used to heat houses. They use cheap 'off-peak' electricity to heat blocks of concrete during the night and the energy can be released during the day.

a) Suggest why electricity companies are willing to sell energy at a cheap rate at night.

b) If you were installing central heating in a house, what advantages would electric storage heaters have over a gas-fired hot water system?

c) As a user of central heating, what disadvantages would electric storage heaters have over a gas-fired hot water system?

Q7 Use the information in **Q3** to work out how long each appliance could be switched on for it to transfer 1 kWh of energy.

116–17 Static charge

- When two materials are rubbed together, some charge in the form of electrons is transferred from one to the other.
- Insulators do not allow charge to move through them, so charge on an insulator is 'static'.
- Materials with the same type of charge repel each other. Materials with opposite types of charge attract each other.
- When charge is allowed to build up, lightning and sparks can occur due to the air becoming ionised.
- Static charge is used to do useful jobs in photocopiers, removing ash from power station waste gases, and in painting metal panels.

Q1 Charged nylon and charged polythene repel each other. What does this tell you about the types of charge on nylon and polythene?

Q2 When cellulose acetate is rubbed with a duster it becomes positively charged.

a) Explain what happens to make the acetate charged.

b) Draw a diagram to show the charge on the cellulose acetate and the charge on the duster.

Q3 When in use, the dome of a van de Graaff generator has a positive charge. A small sphere nearby is earthed.
The positive charge of the dome attracts negative charges from the Earth onto the small sphere.
The electric force from the positive dome pulls electrons from air particles, creating positive and negative ions.

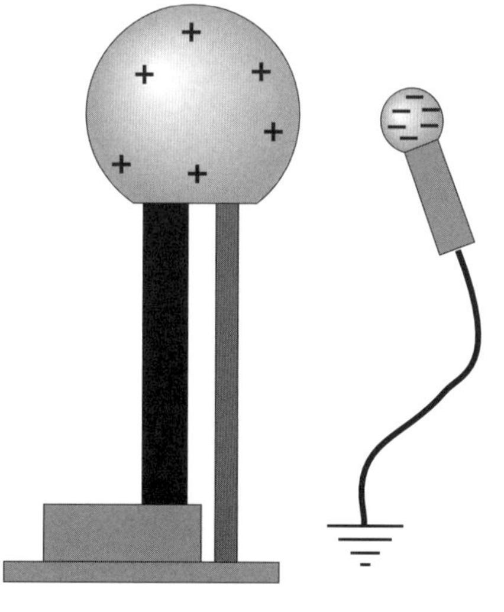

a) What do the ions consist of?

b) Explain how an electric current is conducted between the dome and the small earthed sphere.

Q4 The diagrams show what can happen when a person walks across a nylon carpet and then puts his hand near a door handle. Describe what is happening in each diagram.

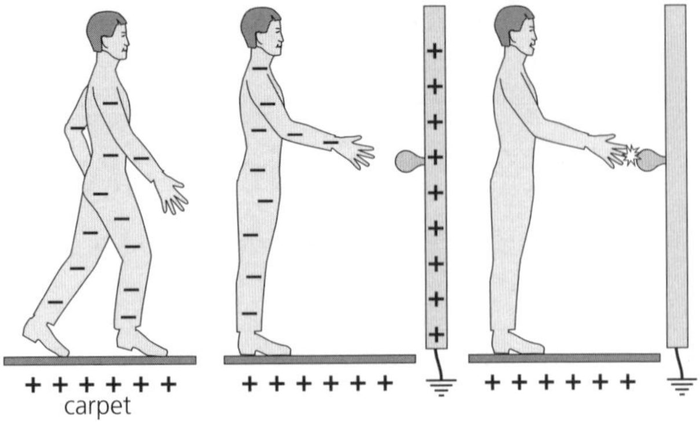

Q5 If charge is allowed to build up on a ship it could be dangerous.

a) What dangers could there be from a build-up of charge on a ship?

b) If sailors were insulated from the ship they could become charged when walking on the decks. Explain why sailors wear special shoes that conduct electricity.

Q6 **a)** Explain why a build-up of charge could be dangerous while an aircraft or car is being refuelled.

b) Aircraft become charged while flying. Explain why aircraft tyres are made using a special rubber that conducts electricity.

Q7 Crops are often sprayed with insecticide. Most of the insecticide lands on the soil and very little reaches the underside of the plant leaves. To overcome this, the spray droplets are given a positive charge as they leave the nozzle of the spray.

a) What happens to the spray drops when they are given a positive charge?

b) Why does the charging of the drops cause them to spread out after leaving the nozzle?

When the positively charged drops approach the plants, the plants gain a negative charge.

c) Explain how movement of ions gives the plants a negative charge.

d) Explain how this method of spraying crops gives better coverage of the plants and causes less insecticide to be wasted.

118 Electromagnetism

- All electric currents have their own magnetic field – this is called electromagnetism.
- A weak magnetic field exists inside and around a coil of wire that is carrying a current.
- Stronger fields can be created by wrapping the coil around an iron core.
- Electromagnets consisting of a coil of wire wrapped on an iron core are used in relays for switching.
- Electric bells use an electromagnet linked to a 'make-and-break' circuit to repeatedly switch the electromagnet on and off.

Q1 A current passing in a coil of wire is a weak electromagnet. One way of making it into a stronger electromagnet is to use an iron core.
Suggest **two** other ways of making the coil of wire into a stronger electromagnet.

Q2 An electromagnet that uses alternating current loses its magnetism very quickly when the current is switched off. Direct current electromagnets are stronger, for the same current, but do not lose their magnetism as quickly.
Explain which type of electromagnet, alternating current or direct current, you would recommend for:

a) an electromagnet that pulls splinters of iron out of a person's skin
b) an electromagnet used for moving iron scrap in a scrapyard.

Q3 The diagram shows an investigation of the magnetic field due to a coil of wire. Some small compasses have been placed inside and around the coil but the current has not yet been switched on.

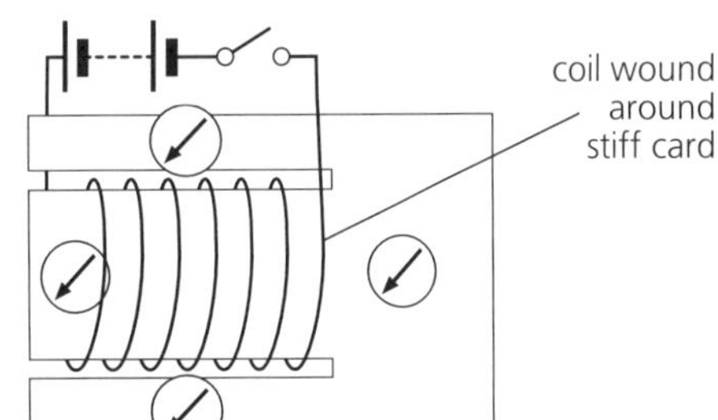

a) Explain why all the compass needles point in the same direction.

In the second diagram the current has been switched on.

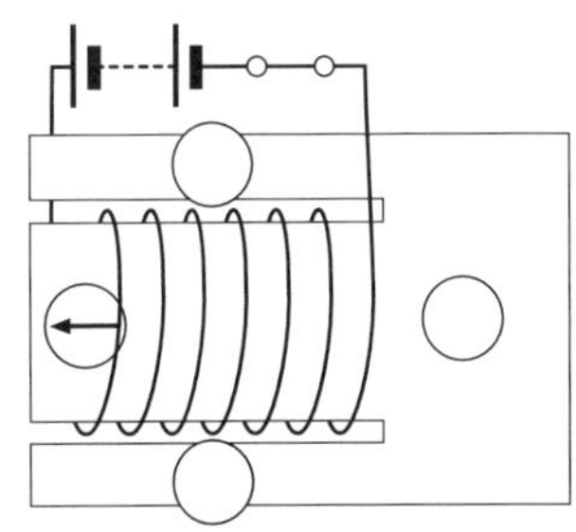

b) Add arrows to show which way you would expect the compass needles to point.

c) Describe and explain what would happen if an alternating current was used instead of a direct current.

Q4 A relay is a switch which is operated when a current passes in a coil of wire. The diagram shows a relay.

a) Describe and explain what happens when a current passes in the coil.

b) Copy and complete the circuit diagram to show how to connect a mains lamp to be switched on and off by the relay.

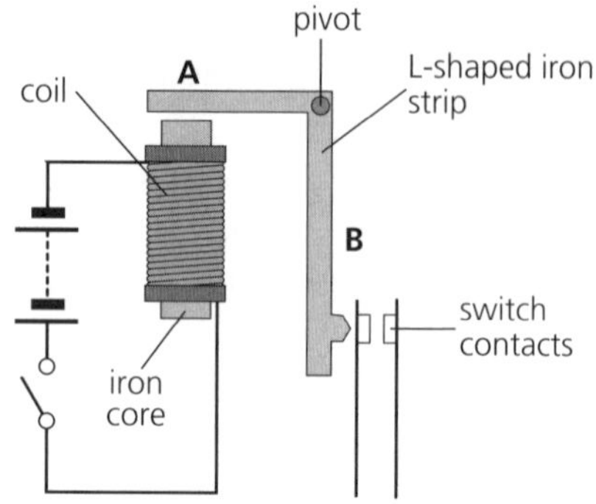

119 The d.c. motor

- **There is a force exerted on a current-carrying wire in a magnetic field.**
- **The force is at right angles to both the wire and the magnetic field.**
- **An electric motor consists of a coil of wire placed within a magnetic field. Rotation is caused by the turning effect of the forces on the sides of the coil.**
- **In a d.c. motor, connections to the coil are made by a split ring commutator. This reverses the current in the coil once each half revolution so that the coil keeps turning the same way.**

Q1 a) Draw a diagram to show how you could demonstrate the force on a current-carrying wire in a magnetic field.

b) Give two factors that the size of the force depends on.

c) Give two factors that the direction of the force depends on.

Q2 Write down two examples of devices that use electric motors to:

a) turn something round

b) move something in a straight line

c) cause something to oscillate, i.e. move up and down or from side to side.

Q3 The diagram shows part of a simple motor. The force on the left-hand side of the coil is in an upwards direction.

a) Label:

i) the direction of the magnetic field

ii) the direction of the force on the right-hand side of the coil.

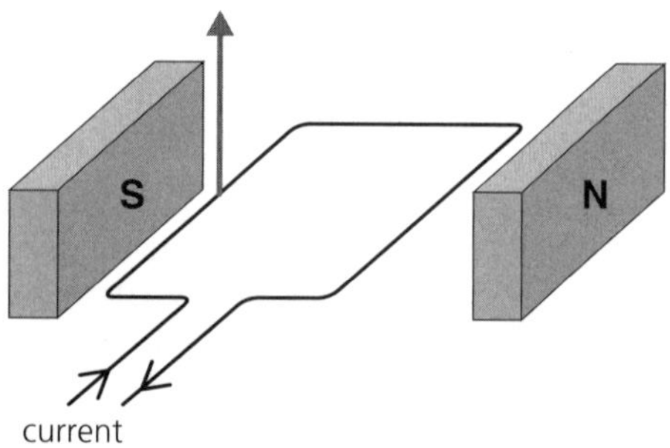

b) Sketch the coil after it has completed half a revolution. Label:
  i) the direction of the current in the coil
  ii) the direction of the magnetic field
  iii) the direction of the force on each side of the coil.

c) Use your answers to **a)** and **b)** to explain why this motor is not practical.

Q4 The diagram shows a washing machine motor. The armature has several coils wound using thick copper wire.

a) Explain why thick wire is used.

b) Suggest why several coils are wound on the armature rather than just one coil.

c) If you compared the washing machine motor with a simple motor, what other difference would you expect to find?

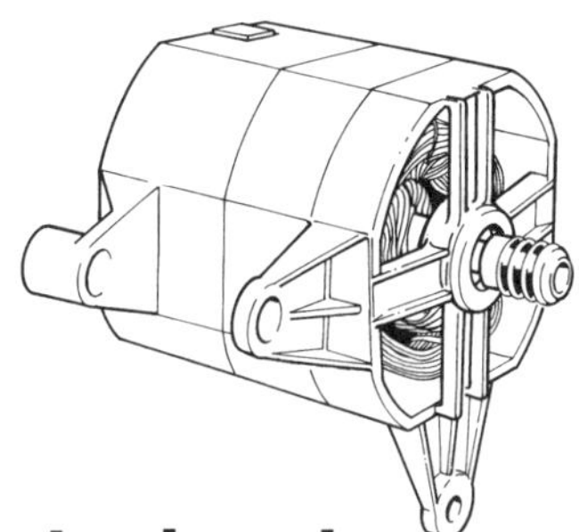

120–1 Electromagnetic induction

- **A voltage is induced in a conductor whenever the magnetic field around it changes. If there is a complete circuit, the induced voltage causes a current to pass in the conductor.**
- **The size of the induced voltage depends on the rate at which the magnetic field changes.**
- **Reversing the change causes the direction of the induced voltage to be reversed.**
- **Transformers can change the size of an alternating voltage by having different numbers of turns of wire on the primary and secondary coils.**
- **The relationships between the voltages, power and currents in the coils are given by the formulae:**

$$\frac{V_P}{V_S} = \frac{N_P}{N_S} \qquad V_P I_P = V_S I_S \qquad \frac{I_P}{I_S} = \frac{N_S}{N_P}$$

Q1 The diagrams show the results of a demonstration of electromagnetic induction. The ammeter reading is zero when the pointer is in the centre.

a) Describe in detail what each diagram shows.

b) Explain how the size and direction of the induced voltage can be changed.

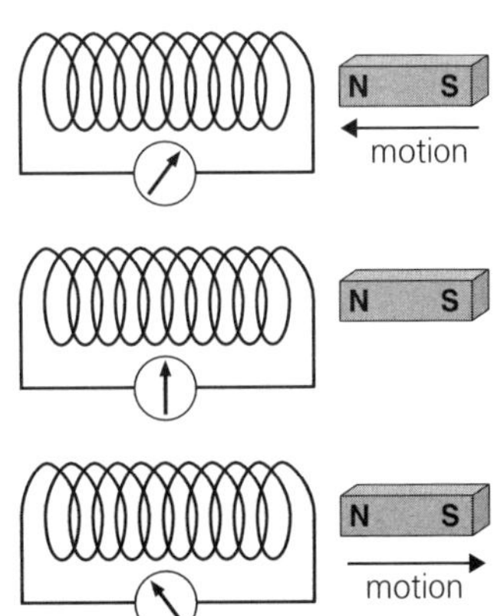

Q2 The diagram shows a loop of wire connected to a sensitive ammeter. The wire loop is placed in a magnetic field.

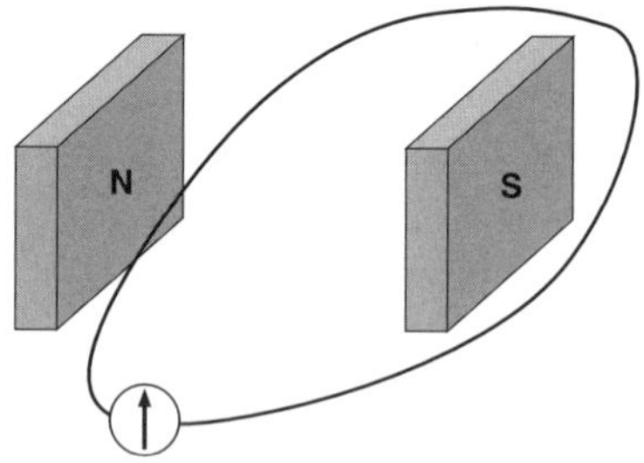

a) Describe and explain what you would expect to happen when:
  i) the wire is moved upwards slowly
  ii) the wire is moved upwards quickly
  iii) the wire is moved down
  iv) the wire is held stationary between the poles of the magnet.

b) State two ways in which the size of the induced voltage and current could be increased.

Q3 Transformers can be used to step up a voltage and step down a voltage.

a) Describe the difference in construction between a step-up transformer and a step-down transformer.

b) Give two examples of where each type of transformer is used.

Q4 Use the transformer equations to complete the table.

	Number of turns on primary coil	Number of turns on secondary coil	Primary voltage/V	Secondary voltage/V
a)	100	300	6	
b)	1000	1000		240
c)		2000	12	240
d)	400		240	4800
e)	3600		240	9
f)	1000	1	240	
g)	20 000	200 000	2500	
h)		400	450	25

Q5 A radio is powered by four cells, giving a 6 V d.c. supply. Explain why a step-down transformer on its own would not allow the radio to operate from the mains supply.

122 Power transmission

- Electricity is generated at power stations by electromagnets rotating in coils of wire.
- Alternating current at 25 000 V goes into a step-up transformer before being fed into the national grid.
- The national grid transmits power at a high voltage in order to minimise the current and keep power losses as small as possible.
- Transformers are used to reduce the voltage before the electricity is supplied to consumers.

Q1 The diagram represents part of the national grid. Electricity is generated at 25 000 V and is transmitted by the national grid at much higher voltages.

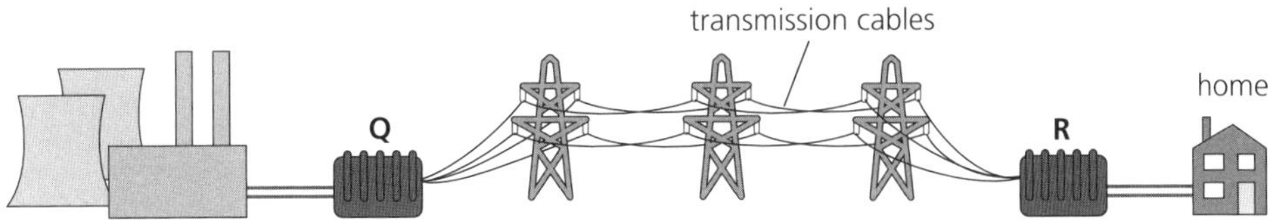

a) What is the purpose of transformer Q?
b) Describe the advantages of using transformers in the distribution of electrical energy.
c) Why is transformer R necessary?
d) The overhead transmission cables are made from aluminium. State two reasons for aluminium being a suitable material.
e) What provides the insulation between the aluminium cables and the Earth?
f) When in use the cables become hot. Describe how the excess heat energy is lost from the cables.
g) It is possible to use underground cables instead of overhead ones. Suggest two reasons why the cost of using underground cables is greater than that of overhead ones.
h) Explain why power is generated and distributed using alternating current rather than direct current.

Q2 A power station generates 100 MW (1×10^8 W) of electrical energy at 25 000 V.
a) Calculate the current which is generated.
The voltage is stepped up to 250 000 V.
b) Describe how this is done.
c) Calculate the current that is transmitted.
d) Describe the advantages and disadvantages of transmitting the power at a higher voltage and lower current.

Q3 One mile of power transmission cable has a resistance of 1.5 Ω.
a) Calculate the rate at which energy from electricity is transferred to heat (i.e. the power lost) when the current in the cable is 1000 A.
b) If the power being transmitted is 10 MW, how much of it reaches its destination?
The same power is now transmitted at 100 A.
c) Describe how this is done.
d) How much is now lost, and how much reaches its destination?
e) What are the advantages of transmitting the power at 100 A? Are there any disadvantages?

123 Changing shape

- All materials stretch when subjected to a pulling force, but some stretch more than others.
- A material is elastic if it returns to its original size and shape when the force is removed. A material is plastic if it undergoes permanent deformation.
- Some materials, such as metals, behave in a regular and predictable way when they are subjected to small forces – their extension is proportional to the force applied.
- These materials are said to obey Hooke's law, which states that the extension is proportional to the force provided that the limit of proportionality is not exceeded.

Q1 Sort the following materials into two lists – those that are elastic for small extensions and those that are plastic.

chewing gum foam rubber margarine nylon Plasticine putty rubber steel wood

Q2 The table shows the results of increasing the force on a stretched metal wire.

Force/N	10	20	30	40	50	60	70	80	90	100
Extension/mm	1.5	3.0	4.5	6.0	7.5	9.0	11.0	14.0	19.0	25.0
Does it return to its original size when the force is removed?	yes	yes	yes	yes	yes	yes	yes	yes	no	no

a) Use squared paper to plot a graph of force against extension.
b) For what range of forces does the material obey Hooke's law? Explain how you can tell.
c) For what range of forces is the material elastic? Explain how you can tell.

Q3 A forcemeter uses a spring to measure forces. The diagram shows a forcemeter.
a) Does the spring obey Hooke's law? Explain how you can tell.
b) Explain why it is important that the manufacturer of the forcemeter knows the elastic limit of the spring.

124 Gases under pressure

- Gases exert pressure due to collisions between the particles of the gas and the walls of the container.
- Compressing a gas increases the frequency of the collisions so the pressure is increased.
- For a fixed mass of gas whose temperature does not change, the pressure is inversely proportional to the volume. This is known as Boyle's law and can be written as:

$$pV = \text{constant} \quad \text{or} \quad p \propto 1/V$$

Q1 Which statement is correct?

A The particles of a gas lose energy when they hit the walls of their container.

B The particles of a gas gain energy when they hit the walls of their container.

C The particles of a gas exert a force on the container wall when they hit it.

D The particles of a gas move very slowly and do not collide with the container walls very much.

Q2 The diagram represents the particles in a sample of air.

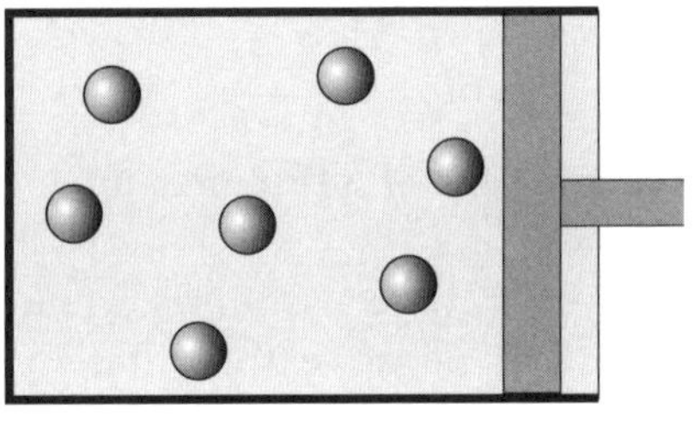

a) Add arrows to show how the particles could be moving.

The piston is pushed in so that the gas is trapped in half of the original volume.

b) Draw a diagram to show the effect this has on the air particles.

c) What effect does this have on the pressure of the air?

Q3 The table shows the results of an experiment to find out how the pressure of a trapped gas changes when its volume is reduced.

Volume/cm^3	25	18	13.5	9	7.5	5
Pressure/kPa	100	140	190	270	330	500

a) Use these results to plot a graph of pressure against volume. Draw the best curve.

b) Read off from your graph the value of the pressure when the volume is:
  i) 10 cm^3
  ii) 20 cm^3.

c) Explain whether the data you obtained from your graph in **b)** supports the statement 'if the volume of a gas is doubled, the pressure halves'.

Q4 Some aerosol cans used for food such as cream use compressed nitrous oxide to force the cream out. A full can contains 200 cm^3 of nitrous oxide at five times atmospheric pressure.

a) What volume does the nitrous oxide occupy at normal atmospheric pressure?

b) Explain why, if all the gas is allowed to escape from the can and is collected, only 800 cm^3 is obtained.

c) There is a warning printed on such cans: 'Do not expose to direct sunlight or temperatures above 50°C'. Explain why the cans should not be allowed to become hot.

125 How fast?

- **The speed of a moving object is calculated using the formula:**

$$\text{average speed} = \frac{\text{distance travelled}}{\text{time taken}} \quad \textbf{or} \quad v = \frac{d}{t}$$

- **Speed can also be calculated as the gradient of a distance–time graph.**
- **Displacement describes the distance of an object from a certain position. Displacement can be positive or negative, the different signs showing opposite directions.**
- **The gradient of a displacement–time graph represents the velocity of the moving object. Like displacement, velocity can be positive or negative depending on the direction of travel.**

Q1 Use the speed equation to complete the following table. Take care to give the correct unit with each of your answers.

	Distance travelled	Time taken	Speed
a)	10 km	2 hours	
b)	180 km	3 hours	
c)	15 km	0.25 hour	
d)		5 hours	35 mph
e)	20 miles		10 mph
f)	16 cm	12 s	
g)		3.5 hours	550 mph
h)		15 s	75 cm/s
i)	24 km		1.5 km/hour
j)	8 miles		16 mph

Q2 Here is a distance–time graph for a cycle ride.

a) Calculate the speed of the cyclist at each of the sections labelled A, B, C and D on the graph.

b) Calculate the average speed for the cycle ride.

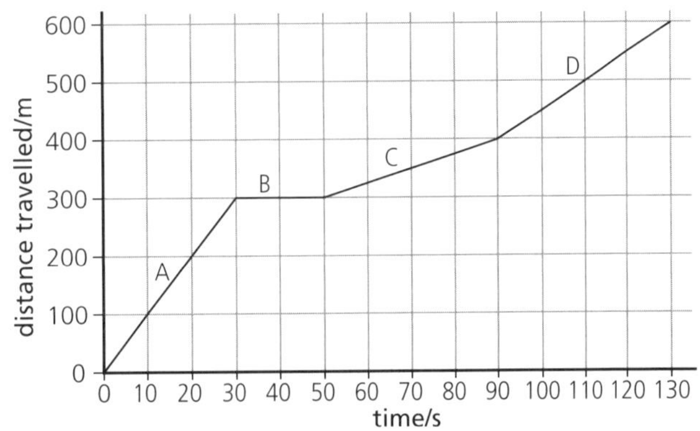

Q3 Here is a displacement–time graph for a moving object.

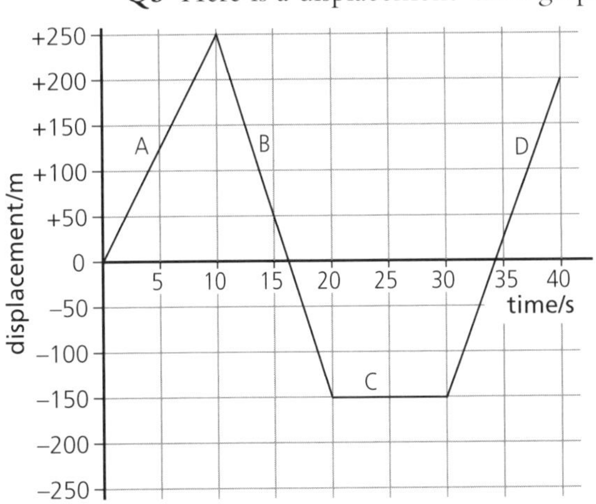

a) What was the furthest distance the object moved from its starting point?

b) At which times shown on the graph did the object return to its starting point?

c) At which labelled point on the graph was the object not moving? Explain how you can tell.

d) Calculate the velocity of the object at the parts of the graph labelled A and B. Explain how you can tell that these represent travel in opposite directions.

126–7 Stopping and starting

- The distance a vehicle travels while braking depends on several factors – the state of the driver is important, as are the road conditions and those of the tyres and brakes.
- All drivers take time to react to a changing situation. While they are reacting, their vehicle carries on moving.
- The 'stopping distance' of a vehicle is made up of both the 'thinking distance' and the 'braking distance'.
- Whether a moving object changes its speed depends on the balance of the forces that are acting.

Q1 The table shows braking distances for a typical car.

a) Use the data in the table to plot a graph of braking distance against speed.

b) Describe the shape of the graph line that you drew.

c) Use the data in the table to describe what happens to the braking distance when the speed of a car is doubled.

Speed/kph	Braking distance/m
20	2.5
40	10
60	22.5
80	40
100	62.5

Q2 The table shows how a driver's thinking distance depends on the speed at which the car is travelling.

a) Draw a graph to show how the thinking distance depends on the speed.

b) Describe the shape of your graph line. Does it show that thinking distance is proportional to speed? Explain how you can tell.

Speed/kph	Thinking distance/m
20	4
40	8
60	12
80	16
100	20

c) Explain how the thinking distance would be affected if the driver had consumed alcohol.

d) Some medicines warn: 'do not drive after taking this medicine'. Suggest why the manufacturers give this warning.

Q3 a) Use the data given in questions **1** and **2** to draw up a table showing how the stopping distance of a car depends on the speed of travel.

b) Present this information as a graph or chart. Add a slogan that you consider could make drivers take notice if your chart was presented as a roadside poster.

Q4 The diagrams show the horizontal forces acting on a cyclist moving along a level road.

a) Which diagram shows the forces acting on a cyclist who is speeding up?

b) Which diagrams show the forces acting on a cyclist who is slowing down?

c) Which diagram shows the forces acting on a cyclist who is moving at a steady speed?

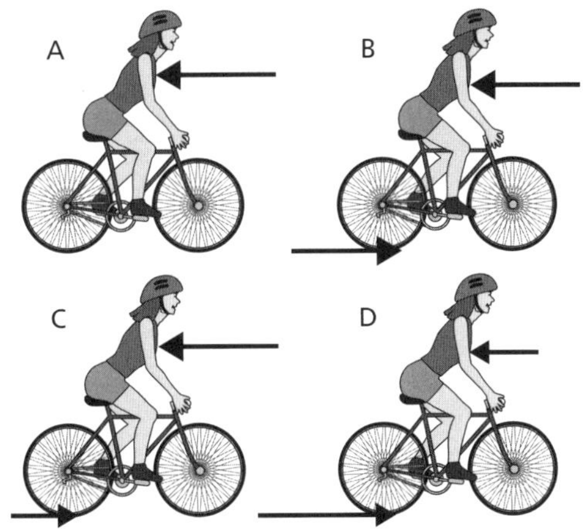

Q5 When you walk, your shoe pushes backwards on the ground.

a) What force stops your shoe from sliding over the ground?

b) Write a description of the force that pushes you forwards.

Q6 Racing cars are fitted with low-resistance tyres. These do not have the same amount of tread as a normal car tyre.
Explain why racing cars can go out of control if there is an unexpected shower during a race.

Q7 A parachutist jumps out of an aircraft. After twenty seconds she opens her parachute. Forty seconds later she lands on the Earth.

a) Describe how the forces on the parachutist change as she falls.

b) Sketch a graph to show how the speed of the parachutist changes during her fall.

128–9 Acceleration

- **Acceleration is defined as being the increase in velocity ÷ time taken and is measured in m/s^2 or m s^{-2}.**
- **Acceleration can also be calculated as the gradient of a speed–time or a velocity–time graph. If a speed–time graph has a negative gradient this represents a deceleration.**
- **A negative gradient on a velocity–time graph represents either a deceleration or an acceleration in the direction of negative velocity.**
- **If the forces on an object are unbalanced, its acceleration depends on the size of the unbalanced force and its mass:**

$$\text{force} = \text{mass} \times \text{acceleration}$$

Q1 Calculate the acceleration of:

a) a car which speeds up from 0 m/s to 15 m/s in 6 s
b) a moped which accelerates from 10 m/s to 15 m/s in 10 s
c) a train which starts from rest and reaches a speed of 60 m/s after 120 s
d) an aircraft which accelerates from 60 m/s to 120 m/s in 15 s.

Q2 Here is a speed–time graph.

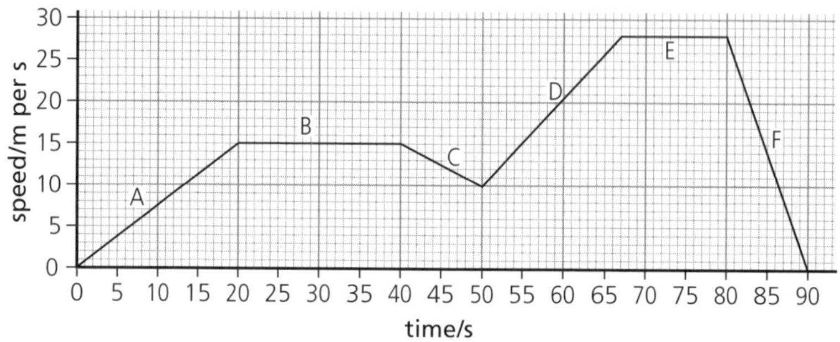

a) Describe the motion that the graph represents.
b) Which sections of the graph show no acceleration? Explain how you can tell.
c) Calculate the acceleration represented by the other sections of the graph.
d) Calculate the distance travelled during each section of the graph.
e) Use your answers to **d)** to calculate the average speed over the 90 s that the graph represents.

Q3 A driver normally drives on her own to work and back each day. When the family goes on holiday there are three extra passengers and their luggage.

a) How does this affect the performance of the car?
b) What advice would you give her about the distance she should leave between her car and the car in front?

Q4 Children sometimes carry a passenger when riding a cycle. Apart from the effect on the stability of the cycle, give one other reason why this can be dangerous.

Q5 A small, 70 000 kg rocket weighs 700 000 N. It is fitted with restrainers so that it leaves the launchpad when the upward force acting on it is 750 000 N.

a) Calculate the initial acceleration of the rocket.
b) Explain why this acceleration increases as fuel is burned.
c) When the fuel in them has been used up, the rocket jettisons some fuel tanks. Explain why this is an advantage.

Q6 Here is a speed–time graph for a cyclist from when he sets off to reaching a steady speed.

a) Describe how the acceleration changes during this time.

b) The cyclist exerts a steady force on the pedals. Explain why the acceleration changes.

c) When the cyclist is travelling at a steady speed, what is the size of the resultant (unbalanced) force acting on him?

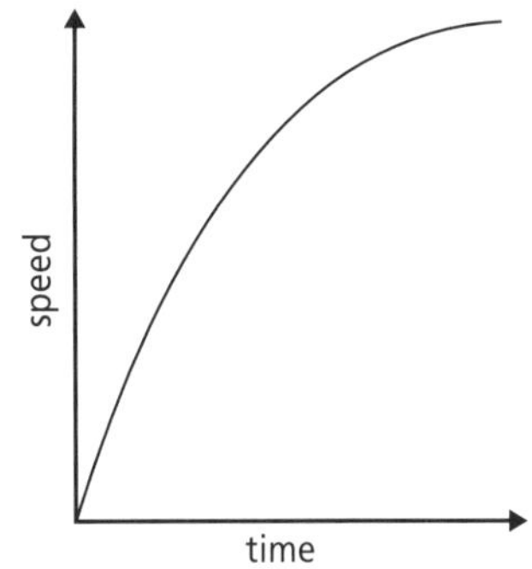

Q7 Modern railway carriages are not rigid. The undercarriage is made in a concertina shape rather than being solid. Explain how this helps to prevent injury to passengers in the event of a collision.

130 Falling down

- **Gravitational forces act between any two objects that have mass. The Earth pulls you and you pull the Earth with an equal-sized force in the opposite direction.**
- **Close to the Earth's surface, the strength of the Earth's gravitational field is 10 N/kg, meaning that each kg of mass is pulled down with a force of 10 N.**
- **The downward pull of the Earth is called an object's weight. It is calculated using the formula:**

  weight = mass × gravitational field strength
- **When an object falls freely with no resistive forces acting, the Earth's pull causes a downwards acceleration of 10 m/s^2.**

Q1 The surface gravitational field strength on Jupiter is 26 N/kg. Explain why this would make walking difficult (if you could walk on Jupiter!).

Q2 Mercury is a small planet about the size of the Earth's Moon. The gravitational field strength at its surface is 3.7 N/kg.

a) How much would a 60 kg person weigh on Mercury?

b) Scientists are hoping to send a space probe to Mercury. Mercury has very little atmosphere. Explain why the lack of atmosphere makes it difficult to land a space probe on Mercury.

Q3 It is possible to estimate the depth of a well by releasing a stone at the top and timing how long it takes it to reach the bottom.
Suppose it takes the stone 3 s. Accelerating at $10\,m/s^2$, its speed after 3 s is 30 m/s. Don't forget that its speed at the start of the 3 s interval was 0, so its average speed over the 3 s time interval was 15 m/s.

a) Calculate the distance travelled by the stone in 3 s.
b) Calculate the distance travelled if the time taken to reach the bottom is:
i) 1 s ii) 2 s iii) 4 s.
c) Is it true to say that the time it takes the stone to reach the bottom is proportional to the depth of the well?
d) Can you see a relationship between the time and the distance travelled?
e) Explain why the time it takes to reach the bottom of a well does not depend on the mass of the stone.

Q4 The Earth's gravitational pull on the Moon keeps the Moon in orbit around the Earth.

a) Draw a diagram to show the forces between the Earth and the Moon.
b) Explain why the Moon has less effect on the motion of the Earth than the Earth has on the motion of the Moon.

131 Turning forces

- **The turning effect, or moment, of a force depends on the perpendicular distance to the pivot as well as the size of the force.**
- **How effective a force is at causing rotation is measured by its moment. The moment is calculated using the formula:**

  moment = force × perpendicular distance to pivot
- **The forces acting on a static object must not only be balanced in each direction – their turning effects, or moments, must also balance.**
- **This is known as the principle of moments, which states that when an object is in equilibrium the sum of the clockwise moments about any pivot is equal to the sum of the anticlockwise moments.**

Q1 Write down **three** examples of forces being used to cause turning or rotation.

Q2 A crowbar being used to lift a heavy stone is an example of a lever that magnifies force.

a) Give **two** other examples of levers being used to magnify force.
b) Give **one** example of a lever being used to magnify movement.
c) Calculate the moment of the force acting on the lever in the diagram.

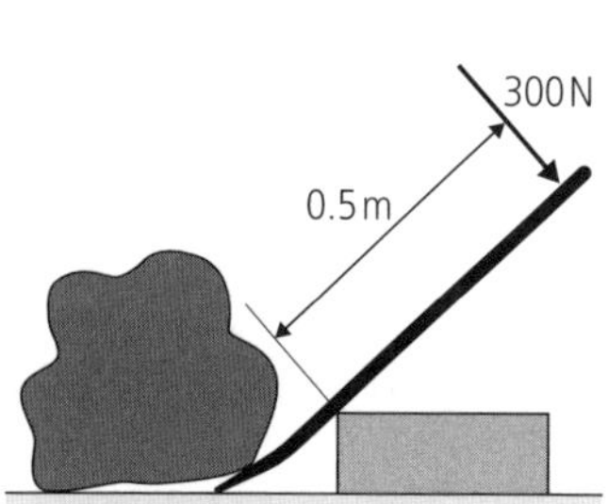

Q3 Explain why it is easiest to close a door when pushing as far away from the hinge as possible. Diagrams could help to make your answer clear.

Q4 The diagram shows the pedal and crank of a cycle. The crank of the cycle is 0.2 m long.

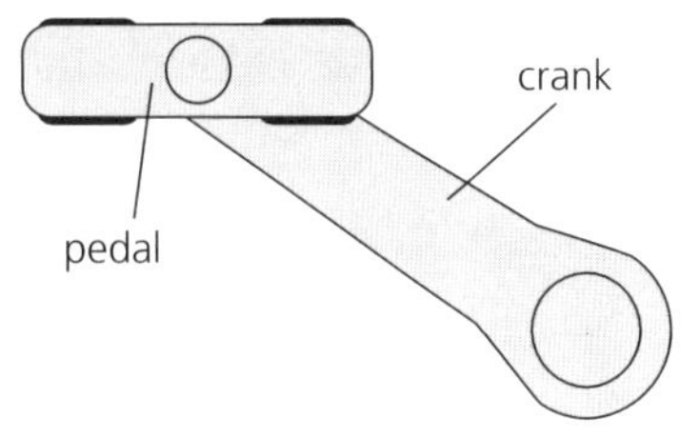

a) Calculate the maximum moment if the cyclist pushes down on the pedal with a force of 350 N.

b) Use diagrams to explain why it is difficult to produce a turning effect when the cranks are vertical.

c) Where should the cranks be to produce the maximum turning effect?

Q5 The diagram shows a fishing rod.

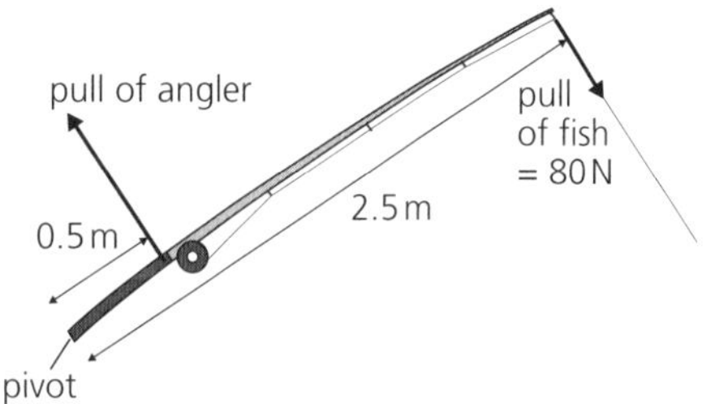

a) Explain why the angler must exert a bigger force than the fish to maintain the rod in a state of balance.

b) What advantage does the angler gain by using a rod instead of just a line?

c) Explain what happens to the rod if the angler pulls with a force of 450 N.

132–3 Wave reflections

- **The total distance travelled between a sound being emitted and its echo being received can be calculated using the formula:**

  distance = speed × time
- **Most surfaces reflect light in all directions.**
- **When light is reflected at a mirror surface the angles of incidence and reflection are equal.**
- **The image formed by a mirror is virtual, upright and the same distance behind the mirror as the object is in front.**

Q1 Which surface would give the best echo of a sound?

A a conifer hedge B a large brick wall
C a football ground 'stand' D a tennis court net

Q2 Complete the paragraph below, choosing words from the list to fill in the blank spaces.

diffused echo reflected refracted scattered 450 900 1800

A girl, standing some distance from a vertical cliff face, shouted her name. Three seconds later she heard the _________. The sound had been _________ by the cliff face. She worked out that the sound had travelled 900 m in that time, so her distance from the cliff was _________ m.

Q3 The speed of sound in sea water is 1500 m/s. A pulse of ultrasound is sent towards the sea bed from a ship. The echo returns after 0.800 s.

a) Calculate the total distance travelled by the sound.

b) How deep is the sea?

c) What would be noticed if the ship passed over a wreck on the sea bed?

Q4 Astronomers can measure the distance between the Earth and the Moon by sending a pulse of waves and timing the interval between sending the pulse and receiving the echo.
Explain why sound waves cannot be used to make the measurement.

Q5 The diagram shows light being reflected by a mirror.
Which statement about the sizes of the angles is correct?

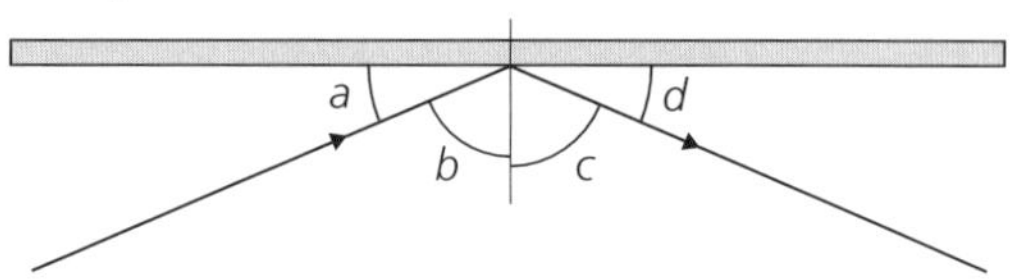

A $a = b$ B $a = c$
C $d = c$ D $d = a$

Q6 The diagram shows an eye looking into a mirror.

a) Draw the image of the eye.

b) Explain why a person standing behind the mirror would not be able to see the image.

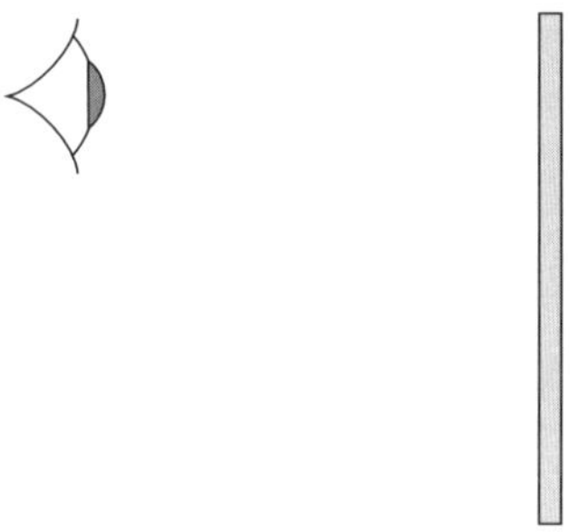

Q7 A girl stands 12 m from a mirror and looks at her image.

a) What is the distance between the girl and her image?

b) She walks towards the mirror at a speed of 2 m/s. What happens to her image?

c) At what speed are the girl and her image approaching each other?

d) How long does it take for the girl and her image to meet?

Q8 Astronauts who visited the Moon placed mirrors on the surface so that astronomers could measure the distance between the Earth and the Moon. A pulse of laser light, travelling at 3.0×10^8 m/s is sent to the Moon, and the time interval between sending the pulse and receiving the reflection is measured.

a) The distance from the Earth to the Moon is 3.84×10^8 m. Calculate the time interval between sending the pulse and receiving the reflection.

b) The radius of the Moon's orbit is thought to be increasing by four centimetres each year. Explain why this increase is very difficult to detect.

134–5 Wave measurements

- The loudness of a sound changes when the amplitude of the vibrations changes. The amplitude is the greatest displacement from the normal position.
- The wavelength, λ, of a wave motion is the length of one complete cycle of a wave – that is, a compression and rarefaction for a longitudinal wave; a crest and a trough for a transverse wave.
- The frequency, f, is the number of vibrations each second.
- Increasing the frequency of a sound wave increases the pitch.
- The wave equation:

$$\text{speed} = \text{frequency} \times \text{wavelength} \quad \text{or} \quad v = f\lambda$$

applies to all waves.

Q1 Each object in the left-hand column is a sound source. The right-hand column is a list of things that vibrate to cause the sound. Match each object on the left to the correct source of vibration on the right.

	Sound source		**Vibration source**
A	clarinet	1	air column
B	loudspeaker	2	skin
C	piano	3	reed
D	organ	4	paper cone
E	drum	5	wire

Q2 Choose the correct description of how sound travels from a loudspeaker to an ear.

A The sound is carried by air particles moving from side to side.
B Vibrating air particles travel from the loudspeaker to the ear.
C The sound is carried by longitudinal vibrations of air particles.
D The sound is carried by waves that travel around the air particles.

Q3 The graph represents the movement of an air particle transmitting a sound.

a) Mark a distance that represents the amplitude of the wave.
b) How many complete vibrations are shown on the graph?
c) Write down the time taken for one vibration to take place.
d) To the same scale, sketch a graph to show the movement of the air particle when the loudness is reduced.

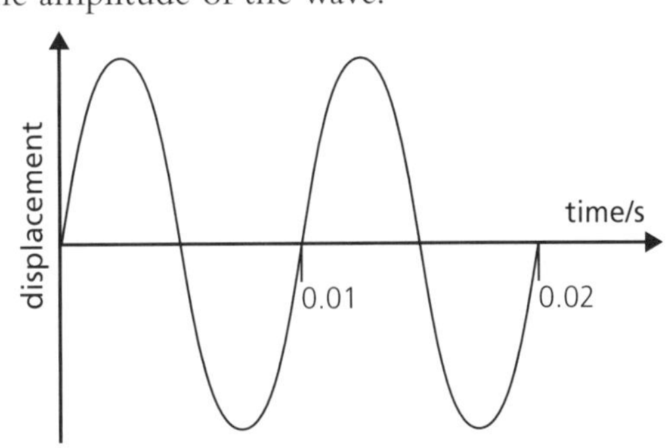

Q4 Slinky coils can be used to transmit both longitudinal and transverse waves. Sketch the appearance of a slinky coil when it is transmitting:

a) a longitudinal wave

b) a transverse wave.

Use arrows to show the direction of movement of the slinky coil and the direction of wave travel.

Q5 Sound waves transfer energy. Write down three examples of sound waves causing objects to move.

Q6 Which frequency of sound waves would give the lowest pitch?

A 30 Hz B 300 Hz C 3000 Hz D 30 000 Hz

Q7 Complete the following sentences by writing in the correct unit.

a) Amplitude is measured in ______________.

b) Wave speed is measured in ______________.

c) Wavelength is measured in ______________.

d) Frequency is measured in ______________.

Q8 Use the wave equation to work out the quantities **a)** to **f)**.

Wave speed/m per s	Frequency/Hz	Wavelength/m
a)	250	1.5
b)	3	5
200	c)	2.5
1500	d)	6
300	12	e)
2000	0.5	f)

Q9 A loudspeaker reproduces a note of frequency 320 Hz. It travels through the air with a speed of 340 m/s.

a) Calculate the wavelength of the wave in air.

b) The sound passes through water where its wavelength is 4.5 m. Calculate the speed of the sound in water (the frequency does not change).

Q10 Water waves enter a harbour at a rate of 30 crests per minute.

a) Calculate the frequency of the wave motion.

A person times a wave crest passing between two posts which are 6 m apart. It takes 2.0 s.

b) Calculate the speed and wavelength of the waves.

136 Refraction of light

- Refraction is the name given to the change in speed that occurs when a wave passes from one substance into another.
- Waves travelling in a direction at right angles to the boundary between two substances do not change their direction, but all other waves do.
- The change in direction is towards the normal line (a line drawn at right angles to the boundary) when waves slow down and away from the normal line when waves speed up.
- Virtual images are sometimes formed when light is refracted.

Q1 Which statement about refraction is true?

A When light passes from air to glass it speeds up and the wavelength decreases.

B When light passes from air to glass it slows down and the wavelength decreases.

C When light passes from air to glass it speeds up and the frequency decreases.

D When light passes from air to glass it slows down and the frequency decreases.

Q2 Which diagram shows the correct change in direction when light passes from air into glass?

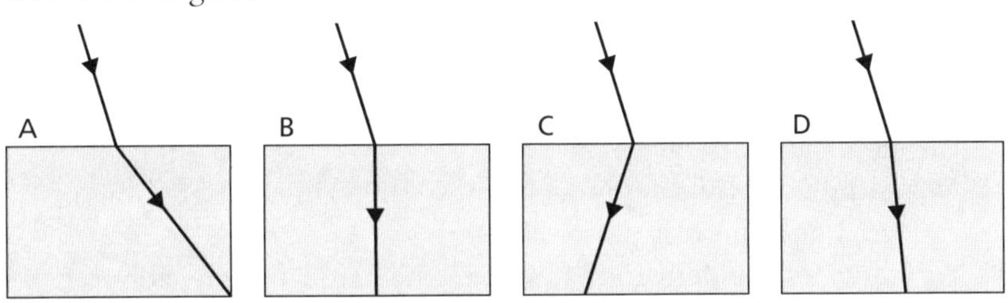

Q3 Complete the diagrams, showing what happens to the waves when light passes **through and out of** the glass.

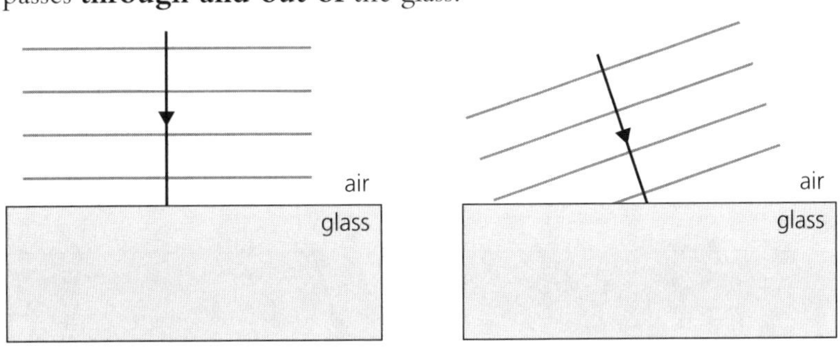

Q4 When you look at an object through glass or water, it seems to be nearer than it really is. The change in direction of light as it crosses the boundary between air and water or glass causes a virtual image to be formed.
The diagram shows light from the floor of a swimming pool changing direction as it leaves the water and enters air.
Complete the diagram, showing where the bottom of the swimming pool appears to be.

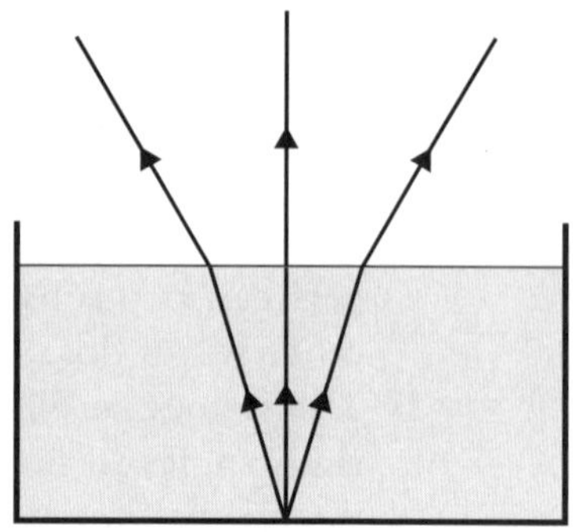

Q5 When viewed through glass, objects appear to be nearer by approximately one-third of the thickness of the glass. Standard window glass is 4 mm thick and safety glass is 6 mm thick.
A person inside a room looks at a tree which is 10 m from the window. Explain why there is no apparent difference when the object is viewed through a single pane of standard glass and a double-glazed window of safety glass.

Q6 Green light in air has a wavelength of 0.5 μm (1 μm = 1×10^{-6} m).
In water, green light has a wavelength of 0.4 μm.
Explain why colours look the same when viewed in air and under water.

137 Using TIR

- **Light travelling from glass or water towards air does not always pass through the boundary.**
- **When light hits the boundary below the critical angle, some is reflected and the rest passes through.**
- **At angles of incidence greater than the critical angle, about 42° for glass, all the light is reflected internally.**
- **Total internal reflection (TIR) is used in prisms to turn light round corners and in fibres for communication and endoscopy.**

Q1 The diagrams show light passing through a right-angled glass prism.
Which diagram is correct?

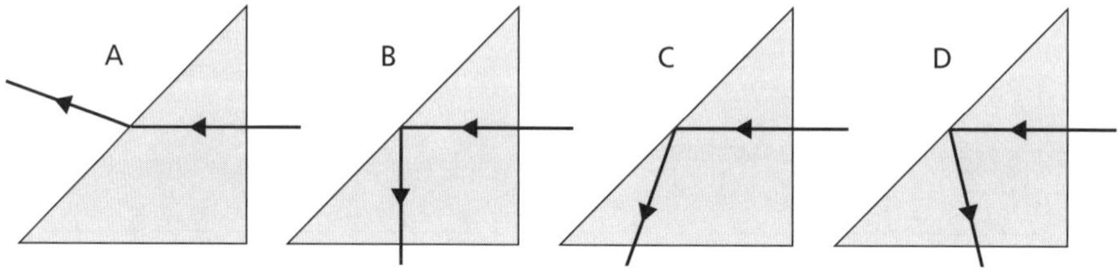

Q2 Cycle reflectors and binoculars use prisms to turn light through 180°. Complete the diagram, showing the light passing through and out of the prism.

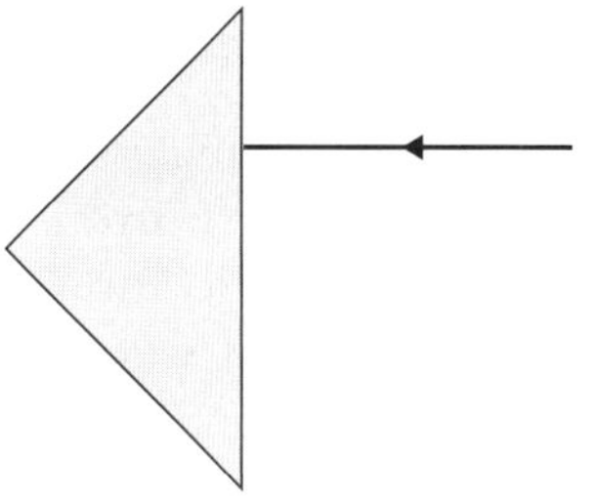

Q3 The diagrams show light hitting a glass–air surface. In A the angle of incidence is less than the critical angle, and in B it is greater than the critical angle. Complete the diagrams, showing what happens to the light after it meets the surface.

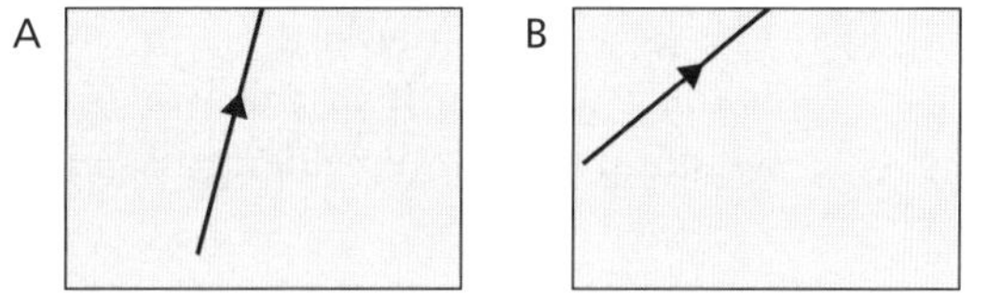

Q4 **a)** Complete the diagram, showing how light can travel round a bend in a fibre.

b) Complete the sentence to explain why the light does not leave the fibre.
Light travels in the fibre in a series of ______________ lines. When it hits the edge of the fibre the angle of incidence is always ______________ than the critical angle and so all the light is ______________ internally.

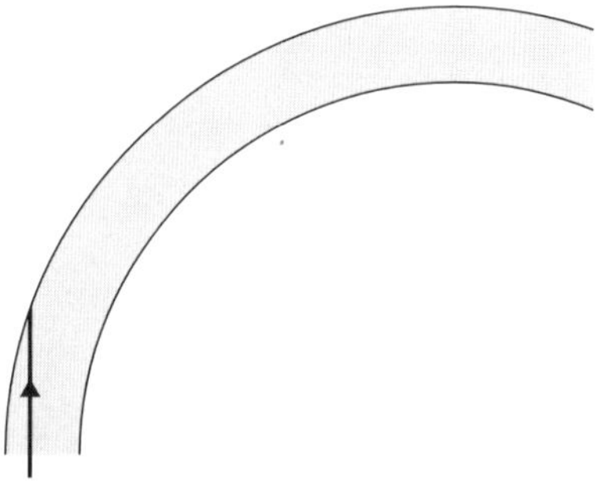

Q5 The diagram shows light in two different directions entering a long optical fibre.

a) Explain why light travelling in the direction of A takes longer to travel along the same length of fibre than the light travelling in the direction of B.

In communications, information is sent along fibres in digital form using pulses of light.

b) Explain how a pulse can become spread out as it travels down a fibre.

c) Explain why this spreading can limit the range of a fibre used in communications.

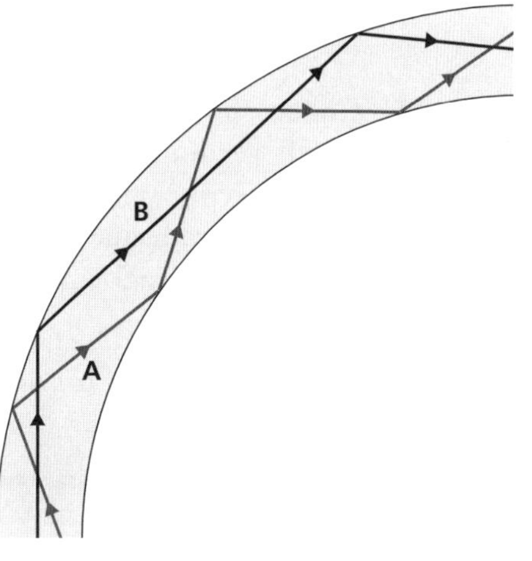

138 A family of waves

- The electromagnetic spectrum is a family of transverse waves ranging in wavelength from less than 1×10^{-12} m (a millionth of a millionth of a metre) to thousands of metres.
- The shortest waves are X-rays and gamma rays, followed by ultraviolet and then light.
- Waves longer than light are infrared, microwaves and radio waves.
- Diffraction is the spreading out of waves when they pass an obstacle or go through a gap.
- The greatest spreading occurs when the size of the gap is the same as the wavelength of the waves. Very little spreading occurs at gaps which are many wavelengths wide.

Q1 Some of the waves that make up the electromagnetic spectrum are shown in the left-hand column. Some uses of these waves are shown in the right-hand column. Match each wave type on the left with an appropriate use on the right.

	Wave		**Use**
A	X-ray	1	long-distance communication
B	ultraviolet	2	examining cracked bones
C	light	3	sunbeds
D	infrared	4	taking photographs
E	radio	5	cooking using a grill

Q2 Which type of electromagnetic wave:

a) has a wavelength between that of infrared and radio waves
b) is given off by radioactive substances
c) is used by remote controls for televisions
d) affects the retina of a human eye
e) is absorbed by the ozone layer?

Q3 Choose the correct statement.

A All electromagnetic waves travel at the same speed in a vacuum.
B All electromagnetic waves travel at the same speed in glass.
C All electromagnetic waves are dangerous to humans.
D All electromagnetic waves are longitudinal waves.

Q4 Some people keep hi-fi equipment in a glass-fronted cabinet. Special glass has to be used to allow the hi-fi to be operated by remote control. Suggest why ordinary window glass is not used in these cabinets.

Q5 The diagram represents sound waves travelling towards an open doorway. The wavelength of the waves is equal to the width of the doorway.

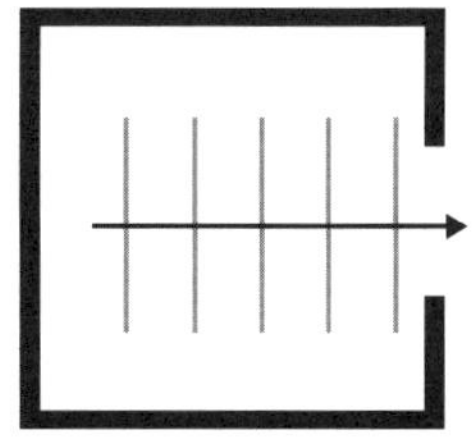

a) Draw a diagram to show the effects of diffraction as the sound passes through the doorway.

The next diagram shows how the light from a lamp passes through the same doorway.

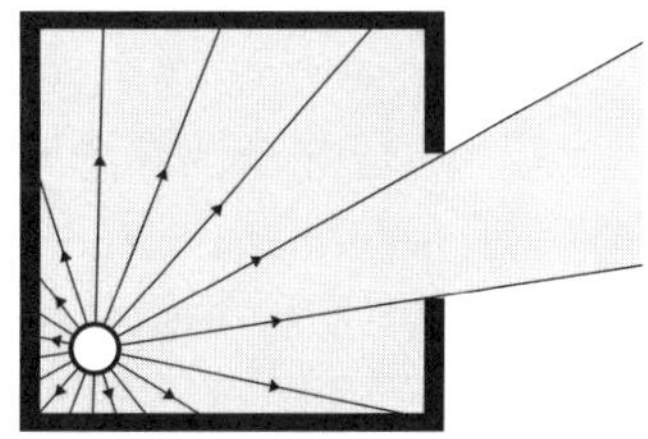

b) Explain why the light does not spread out as it passes through the doorway.

139–41 Using electromagnetic waves

- **Microwaves are short wavelength radio waves which are absorbed by water and salt molecules in food, causing heating.**
- **Infrared radiation has a wavelength shorter than that of microwaves but longer than that of light. It also causes heating when absorbed by objects.**
- **Ultraviolet radiation has a wavelength shorter than that of light. It is given out when an electric current passes through mercury vapour and is used in fluorescent tubes for lighting.**
- **Short wavelength radio waves are used to transmit information in a narrow beam. Radio and broadcasts use waves ranging from less than a metre to hundreds of metres.**
- **X-rays are used to take photographs. They pass through body tissue but are absorbed by bone.**
- **Gamma ray sources are used as medical tracers to show blood flow or to concentrate in one particular organ.**

Q1 Which list shows ultraviolet, microwave and infrared radiation in the correct order of increasing wavelength?

A	ultraviolet	infrared	microwave
B	infrared	ultraviolet	microwave
C	microwave	infrared	ultraviolet
D	infrared	microwave	ultraviolet

Q2 Explain why food should not be wrapped in aluminium foil when it is cooked under a grill.

Q3 People who run marathons often have very little energy reserve left at the end of a race. Their bodies can be very hot. Explain how an aluminium foil cape can help to keep energy in their bodies.

Q4 When food is cooked in a microwave cooker, the energy penetrates the food to a depth of 3 to 4 cm.

a) How can a microwave cooker be used to cook pieces of food larger than this?

b) What size is the largest piece of food which can be cooked effectively in a microwave cooker?

Q5 Suppose that a friend of yours spends half an hour each day getting a 'tan' by lying on a sunbed. Write a paragraph describing the possible dangers and giving advice about the use of a sunbed.

Q6 VHF (very high frequency) waves are used to broadcast some radio and television stations. VHF waves travel in straight lines. Long wavelength, lower frequency radio waves can follow the Earth's curvature and be diffracted through openings and round obstacles.
Use diagrams to explain why some householders living in hilly areas can receive long wavelength waves clearly but have a very poor reception of short wavelength waves.

Q7 Radio dials can be calibrated in terms of frequency or wavelength. Radio stations sometimes advertise the frequency of their broadcasts and sometimes the wavelength.
The wave equation $v = f\lambda$ can be used to calculate the frequency if the wavelength is known, or calculate the wavelength if the frequency is known.
Use the wave equation, taking the speed of radio waves as 3×10^8 m/s, to work out the quantities not shown in the table.

	Radio station	Frequency/Hz	Wavelength/m
a)	Radio 1	97.6×10^6	
b)	Virgin Radio		247
c)	Classic FM	1.00×10^8	
d)	Radio 4		1515
e)	Radio 5	6.93×10^8	

Q8 Which option describes the difference between X-rays and gamma rays?

A Gamma rays travel faster than X-rays.

B Gamma rays have a longer wavelength than X-rays.

C Gamma rays do not affect photographic film.

D Gamma rays and X-rays have different sources.

Q9 X-rays and light both affect photographic film. Describe the difference between the way in which an X-ray photograph is taken and the way in which a 'normal' photograph is taken.

Q10 Photographic film is blackened when light or X-rays affect it. Explain why bones show up as white on an X-ray photograph but flesh shows up as black.

Q11 Ultraviolet radiation causes some substances to fluoresce. Fluorescence occurs when waves of a higher frequency and shorter wavelength than light are absorbed and re-emitted as visible radiation.

a) Which other waves in the electromagnetic spectrum could cause fluorescence?

b) Explain why infrared radiation cannot make substances fluoresce.

Q12 Technetium-99 is used extensively as a gamma emitter for medical purposes. Used together with other chemicals, it can be directed to certain parts of the body. Explain the advantages of concentrating the technetium-99 in one organ rather than distributing it throughout the body.

142 Earth waves

- **Earth tremors cause waves to travel to parts of the Earth's surface.**
- **Longitudinal waves, or P-waves, can travel through solids and liquids and they are detected all over the Earth's surface.**
- **S-waves are transverse and cannot travel through liquids. The fact that S-waves do not travel through the centre of the Earth gives evidence that the Earth's outer core is liquid.**
- **L-waves are long wavelength waves that travel through the Earth's crust.**

Q1 Which type of wave from an earthquake:

a) would cause the greatest damage to buildings

b) travels through the Earth's core

c) does not travel to points on the Earth's surface directly opposite the earthquake?

Q2 Which line in the table shows the changes in pressure and temperature that occur on going from the Earth's crust to its core?

	Change in pressure	Change in temperature
A	increases	decreases
B	decreases	decreases
C	decreases	increases
D	increases	increases

Q3 The time taken for P-waves to travel from an Earth tremor to a point on the Earth's surface directly opposite the source of the tremor is approximately 20 minutes (1200 s). The diameter of the Earth is 12 750 km.

a) Calculate the average speed of the P-waves through the body of the Earth.

b) The speed of a wave increases with increasing density and stiffness of the material it travels through. P-waves start their journey through the crust at a speed of 8 km/s, rapidly speeding up to 14 km/s. What can you deduce about how the mantle changes, going from the crust towards the core?

c) The speed of P-waves falls to 7.5 km/s as they enter the outer core. What difference in property between a liquid and a solid could account for this?

d) Explain how you would expect the speed of the P-waves to change as they enter the inner core.

Q4 The diagram shows a seismographic record of an earthquake.

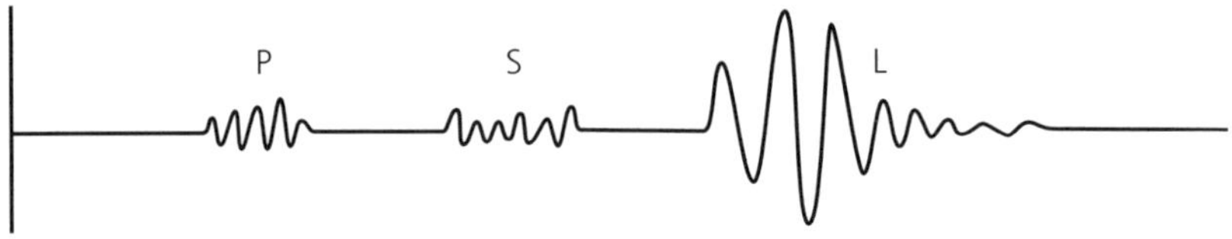

The P-waves arrived at the seismometer 300 s after the earthquake took place.

a) If the average speed of the P-waves was 12 km/s, how far from the earthquake centre was the seismometer?

b) The average speed of the S-waves is 7 km/s. How long after the earthquake occurred did they arrive at the seismometer?

c) Give two reasons why the L-waves arrived after both the S-waves and the P-waves.

d) Describe and explain how a seismographic record of the same earthquake, taken at a point on the Earth's surface directly opposite the earthquake, would be different from the one shown in the diagram.

143 Plate tectonics

- The rocks in the Earth's crust are constantly being broken down by weathering or erosion. These processes are caused by the action of wind and rain, water and ice.
- Rocks are being constantly broken down and new rocks are being formed.
- The theory of plate tectonics proposed that the Earth's crust had cracked into huge sections called plates which move slowly (about 1–2 cm each year) floating on the liquid mantle.
- When two plates are moving apart, hot molten rock from the magma comes to the surface of the Earth and forms new rocks. This is called a constructive plate margin.
- When two plates collide, the rocks are squeezed together and one of the plates is pushed back into the magma. This is called a destructive plate margin.

Q1 Identify 1–7 in the diagram using words from the following list.

erosion   high temperature and high pressure   compacting   cooling   melting

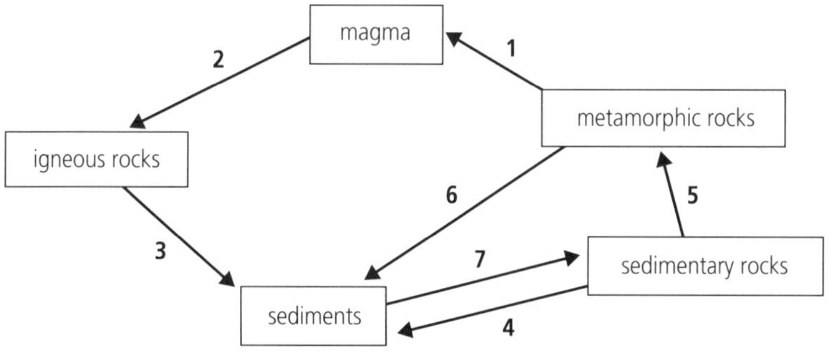

Q2 Complete the passage below, using words from the list to fill in the blank spaces.

erosion   igneous   metamorphic   magma   sedimentary

________ rocks are formed when sediments are deposited. The effect of high temperature and high pressure turns ________ rocks into ________ rocks.

Igneous rocks are formed when the ________ cools and crystallises. Weathering or ________ of rocks produces sediments which can be used to make new rocks.

Q3 Draw and label a diagram to show a destructive plate margin.

Q4 The Mid-Atlantic Ridge is an underwater ridge which runs north–south along the floor of the Atlantic Ocean. At different distances from this ridge studies were carried out to find the age of the oldest sea floor sediments. The results are shown in the table.

Distance from ridge/km	Age of oldest sediments /millions of years
250	10
500	23
750	36
1000	49
1500	75

a) Plot a graph of distance from the ridge (on the *y*-axis) and the age of the oldest sediments (on the *x*-axis).

b) i) Explain how the graph can be used to estimate the rate at which the ocean floor has spread apart in the past.

ii) From the graph, estimate the age of the oldest sediments 900 km from the ridge.

c) The spreading apart of the ocean floor on either side of the ridge can be explained by the theory of plate tectonics. Use the diagram to explain the formation of volcanoes at ocean ridges.

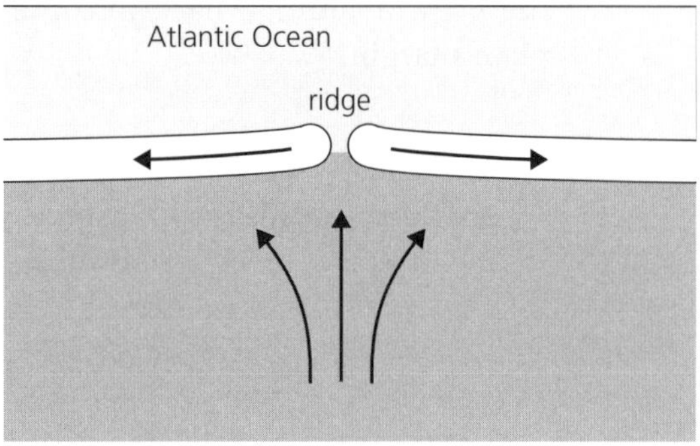

144–5 Gravitational forces

- There are nine known planets in orbit around our Sun. The four inner planets are dense and rocky.
- Asteroids are rocky fragments that orbit the Sun inbetween the inner and outer planets.
- The five outer planets are cooler than the inner ones. They are thought to be made up largely of gases and ice.
- Gravitational forces are attractive forces that exist between massive objects.
- The Sun's gravitational pull on the planets, asteroids and comets keeps them in orbit. Moons are kept in orbit by the gravitational pull of their planet.
- The strength a body's gravitational field decreases with increasing distance from the body.

Q1 The four inner planets are, in order from the Sun: Mercury, Venus, Earth and Mars. Although all the orbits are ellipses, those of Venus, Earth and Mars are almost circular.

a) Draw a diagram to show the relative positions of the four innermost planets and the Sun.

b) Give two reasons why Mercury takes the least time to orbit the Sun.

c) Two of the innermost planets have moons. How long does it take the Earth's moon to travel once around the Sun?

Q2 Collisions between asteroids in the asteroid belt can cause pieces of rock to leave their orbit and move nearer to the Sun. Some of these strike the Earth and its moon, as well as other planets.

The Earth has an atmosphere and its surface is covered in water. The Moon has neither atmosphere nor water.

a) Explain why very few of the rocks that strike the Earth reach its surface.

b) Explain why impact craters due to rocks hitting the Moon may remain for millions of years.

Q3 The table gives some information about the planets.

Planet	Diameter, Earth = 1	Mass, Earth = 1	Surface gravitational pull, Earth = 1	Density (g/cm^3)	Average distance from Sun, Sun – Earth = 1	Period of orbit (years)	Number of moons
Earth	1	1	1	5.5	1	1	1
Jupiter	11.2	318	2.6	1.3	5.2	11.9	16
Mars	0.5	0.1	0.4	4	1.5	1.9	2
Mercury	0.4	0.06	0.4	5.4	0.4	0.2	0
Neptune	3.8	17	1.2	2.3	30	165	8
Pluto	0.2	0.002	0.2	0.4	39	248	1
Saturn	9.5	95	1.1	0.7	9.5	29.5	>20
Uranus	3.9	15	0.9	1.6	19	84	5
Venus	0.95	0.8	0.9	5.2	0.7	0.6	0

a) List the planets in order of mass, starting with the most massive.

b) On which planet does 1 kg have the greatest weight?

c) Explain why, if an astronaut were to visit Mars, she would be able to jump much higher than she can on Earth.

d) Jupiter is less dense than the Earth. Explain why Jupiter is more massive than the Earth.

Q4 The diagram represents the Earth and Moon in two positions of their orbit around the Sun.

a) Draw arrows to show:

i) the Sun's gravitational pull on the Earth in each position shown

ii) the Earth's gravitational pull on the Moon in each position shown.

b) Complete the paragraph below, choosing words from the list to fill in the blank spaces.

attractive Earth Moon repulsive Sun

The Moon orbits the _____________ and the Earth orbits the _____________. Planets and moons are kept in orbit by the _____________ gravitational forces between massive objects.

Q5 The data in the table concern the orbits of the five outer planets.

Planet	Mean distance from Sun (Earth = 1)	Mean orbital speed (km / s)
Jupiter	5.2	13.1
Saturn	9.5	9.6
Uranus	19.1	6.8
Neptune	30.0	
Pluto	39.5	4.7

a) Describe the link between orbital speed and distance from the Sun.

b) Draw a graph of orbital speed (y-axis) against distance from the Sun (x-axis). Use your graph to predict the orbital speed of Neptune.

Q6 Comets go round the Sun in elliptical orbits. The diagram represents the orbit of a comet.

a) Describe and explain how the speed of the comet is changing at each of positions X and Y.

b) Explain why comets are only visible for a few weeks of the hundreds of years that it may take to complete an orbit.

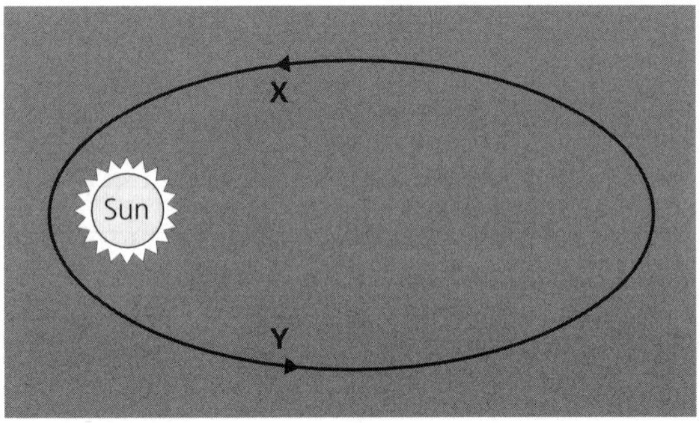

Q7 The diagram shows how the orbit of a comet can change as it passes Jupiter.

a) Describe and explain the change in the comet's orbit.

b) Explain how the orbit time of the comet is different in the new orbit.

c) Why is Jupiter more likely than any other planet to have this effect on a comet?

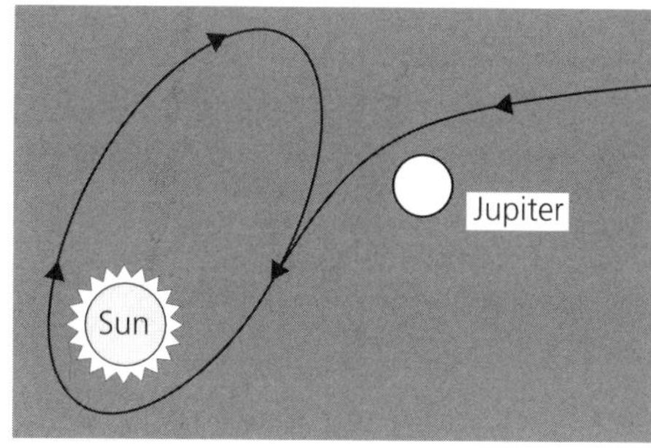

146–7 Stars and galaxies

- Stars form in clouds of dust and gas, drawn together by gravitational forces.
- After a star's main sequence, it expands and cools, becoming a red giant. A small star then contracts to become a white dwarf.
- Large stars can become blue supergiants, forming the more massive elements by the fusion of helium nuclei. Once these reactions cease, the star expands, then contracts and glows very brightly as a supernova before exploding.
- New stars can be formed from the remnants of an exploded supernova.
- The Universe is known to be expanding. The rate of expansion is estimated by measuring the 'red shift' of light from stars.
- Time may have started with an enormous explosion, called the 'big bang'.
- The future of the Universe depends on whether the gravitational forces are strong enough to stop the expansion.

Q1 a) The list contains the stages in the life cycle of a star. Put them in the order in which they occur.

collapse of dust cloud   blue supergiant   explosion
main sequence   red giant   supernova

b) In which stage is the main reaction the fusion of hydrogen nuclei into helium nuclei?

c) In which stage can carbon and oxygen be formed?

d) How does the composition of the Earth provide evidence that our Solar System is formed from the remnants of an exploded supernova?

Q2 Imagine that you are watching an exploding supernova. Write and illustrate a newspaper article that describes what you might see.

Q3 The colour a star appears to be depends on its surface temperature. Blue stars are hotter than white stars, which in turn are hotter than red stars.

a) What happens to the surface temperature of a star when it expands?

b) The fusion reaction in a white dwarf is very slow and releases less energy than the star radiates. Explain what is likely to happen to the colour of a white dwarf as it cools.

c) The majority of stars in the Milky Way are red dwarfs. Explain why red dwarfs are difficult to see.

d) Astronomers have predicted that there could be a phase in a star's life when it becomes a black dwarf. Suggest how a black dwarf is likely to evolve.

Q4 Which is the correct description of 'red shift'?

A Red stars are moving faster than white stars.

B Red stars are moving slower than white stars.

C The frequency of the light detected from a star is lower than the frequency of light that the star emits.

D The frequency of the light detected from a star is greater than the frequency of light that the star emits.

Q5 Hubble noticed that all the galaxies are moving away from each other, with the most distant ones receding at the greatest rate.

a) Use a diagram to explain how all the galaxies could have started at one point.

b) Hubble's constant measures the rate of expansion of the Universe. Why is a knowledge of Hubble's constant important to astronomers?

c) Suggest why Hubble's constant is difficult to measure.

Q6 There are several possibilities for the future of the Universe. It may continue to expand, it may reach a steady, constant size, or it may stop expanding and start to contract.

a) What could cause the expansion of the Universe to slow down?

b) The future of the Universe depends on its mass, which is unknown. Explain how the amount of mass in the Universe could affect its future.

148–9 Convection and conduction

- **Convection currents transfer energy by movement of parts of a fluid (liquid or gas).**
- **Parts of the fluid that have been warmed expand and become less dense than the surrounding fluid. Parts that have been cooled become denser than their surroundings and so sink.**

- In the process of conduction, the more energetic molecules in the warmer part of the material pass on some of their energy to neighbouring molecules.
- Conduction is a much slower process in gases than it is in solids and liquids because the molecules are spread more widely.
- Metals are much better conductors than non-metals. Metals have free electrons that can move rapidly and transfer the energy to all parts of the metal.

Q1 Which of the following materials allow energy to be transferred through them by convection currents?

air brick concrete water wood

Q2 Complete the paragraph below about convection currents, choosing words from the list to fill in the blank spaces.

contract decreases expand fall gases increases rise solids

Convection currents can only occur in liquids and ______________. When part of a fluid is heated, it expands and its density ______________, which causes it to ______________. Cooling part of a fluid causes it to ______________ and ______________.

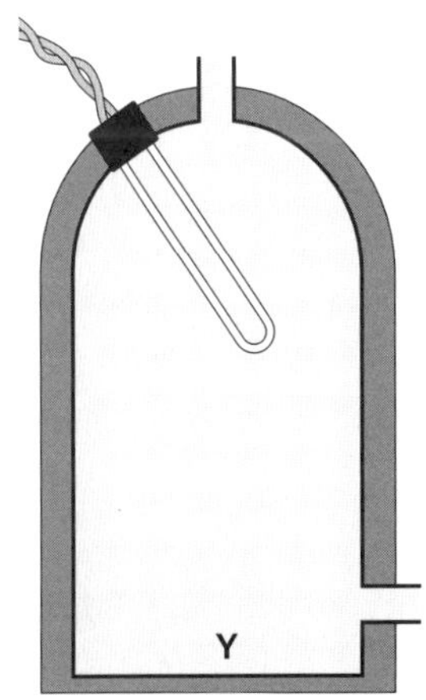

Q3 The diagram shows an immersion heater in a hot water tank.

a) Sketch the convection currents in the water when the heater is switched on.

b) Would you expect the water at Y to be hot or cold? Explain why you think this.

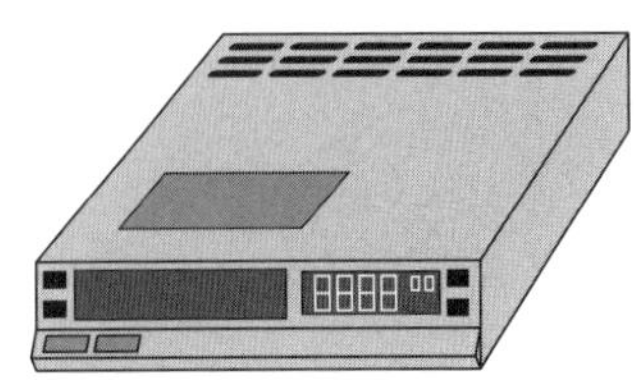

Q4 The casing of a video recorder has slots at the back. There are slots both at the bottom and at the top.

a) What is the purpose of the slots at the top?

b) What is the purpose of the slots at the bottom?

c) Explain how the slots help to keep the inside of the video recorder cool.

d) A sticker on a video recorder next to these slots reads 'Do not cover'. Why is it important that the slots are not covered? What could happen if the slots were covered?

Q5 Which of the following statements is true?

A Conduction only occurs in metals.

B Conduction only occurs in solids.

C Conduction does not apply to gases.

D Conduction cannot take place through a vacuum.

Q6 Complete the paragraph below about conduction, choosing words from the list to fill in the blank spaces.

best convection electrons molecules
protons radiation worst

Metals are the best conductors of thermal energy because they have free ____________ which can move. Non-metallic solids rely on the energy being transferred through the vibrations of ____________ which are in fixed positions. Gases are the ____________ conductors but they are good at transferring energy by ____________.

Q7 For each of the following, state whether it is better to use a good or a poor conductor. Give a reason for your answer in each case.

a) the tiles that cover the outside of the space shuttle
b) a kettle used on a gas ring
c) a bath
d) the liquid in a thermometer.

Q8 The conductivity of a building material is described by its *U*-value. The higher the *U*-value, the better the conductor. The *U*-value is the energy flow each second through 1 m^2 of material for each °C difference in temperature. The table shows some *U*-values of insulated and uninsulated parts of a house.

Material	*U*-value/W m^{-2} $°C^{-1}$
uninsulated cavity wall	1.4
foam-insulated cavity wall	0.7
single-glazed window	5.5
double-glazed window	2.8
uninsulated roofspace	2.2
fibreglass-insulated roofspace	0.5

a) List the materials in order, with the best insulator at the top of your list and the worst at the bottom.
b) A room has an outside wall with an area of 9 m^2. It is a foam-insulated cavity wall. How much energy flows through the wall each second when the temperature inside is 20°C and the temperature outside is 5°C?
c) A second outside wall in the same room has the same total area, but 2 m^2 is taken up by a single-glazed window. Calculate the total energy flow per second through the wall and window.
d) The inside walls of the room have a *U*-value of 3.3. Suggest why this is much higher than that of an uninsulated cavity wall.
e) Suggest why very little energy flows through the inside walls of the room.

150 Radiant energy

- Everything emits and absorbs infrared radiation.
- The hotter the object, the more energy it emits each second.
- Dark, dull surfaces are better than light, shiny surfaces at giving out and absorbing infrared radiation.
- Foil can be effective at keeping things hot or cold because it reflects infrared radiation in the same way that it reflects light.

Q1 Here is a list of things:

black skirt **mirror** **tarmac road** **white tee-shirt**

a) Which two things are the best **emitters** of infrared radiation?
b) Which two things are the best **absorbers** of infrared radiation?

Q2 Which is the best description of infrared radiation?

A a longitudinal wave with a wavelength longer than that of light
B a longitudinal wave with a wavelength shorter than that of light
C a transverse wave with a wavelength longer than that of light
D a transverse wave with a wavelength shorter than that of light

Q3 Infrared radiation can be detected by its heating effect when it is absorbed.

a) An ordinary mercury-in-glass thermometer is not a good detector of infrared radiation. Explain why.
b) How can a mercury-in-glass thermometer be adapted to make it a better detector of infrared radiation? Explain how your method improves the thermometer as a detector of infrared radiation.

Q4 Explain the reasons for the following.

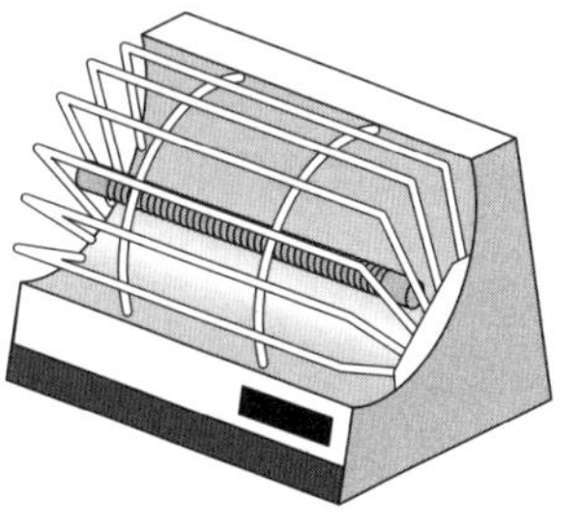

a) Manufacturers of lightweight sleeping bags put a layer of fabric which has been sprayed with aluminium paint just inside the sleeping bag lining.
b) Electric radiant heaters have concave reflectors fitted behind the heating element.
c) In southern Europe, houses are often painted white or other light colours.

Q5 In summer, gliders can stay airborne for hours by using thermals. These are upward-moving air currents that can often be found rising from large areas of tarmac.

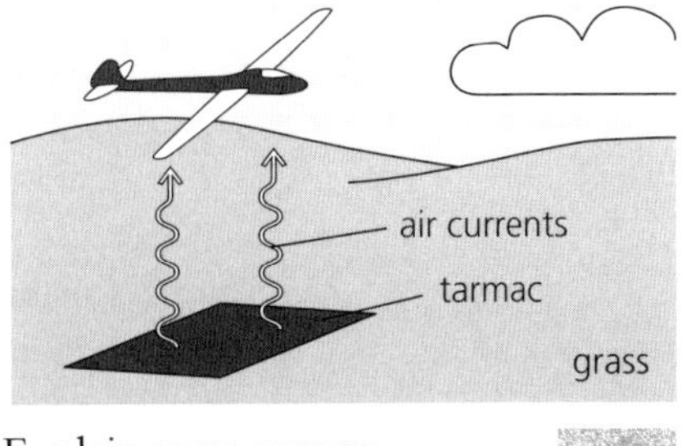

a) Use your knowledge of radiation and convection to explain how these thermals are formed.
b) What air movements would you expect to find at ground level around the tarmac? Explain your answer.

151 Evaporation

- Evaporation happens when energetic molecules leave a liquid and form a vapour.
- As a liquid evaporates it cools and takes in energy from its surroundings. This is an important process in the control of body temperature.
- Thermal insulation is designed to reduce energy losses by convection, conduction, radiation and evaporation.
- Effective insulation involves using a combination of lids and covers, foil and trapped air.

Q1 Which of the following are examples of **evaporation**?

A warm air rising from a radiator B steam rising from a hot drink
C water forming on the inside of a bathroom window
D smoke rising from a chimney E a puddle drying up

Q2 A molecule can only escape from a liquid surface if it has enough energy to overcome the forces from the other molecules.

a) Do the molecules in a liquid attract or repel each other? Explain how you can tell.

b) Explain why water at 50°C evaporates more rapidly than water at 10°C.

Q3 When swimmers get out of a swimming bath, they often feel cold even though the air is warm. Explain how this is caused by evaporation.

Q4 The cost of heating a swimming pool can be reduced if the pool is covered at night. A simple polythene roll-up cover is normally used. Explain how this reduces the energy lost from the water.

Q5 Cool boxes can keep food cool in hot weather for several hours. The diagrams show the construction of two cool boxes.

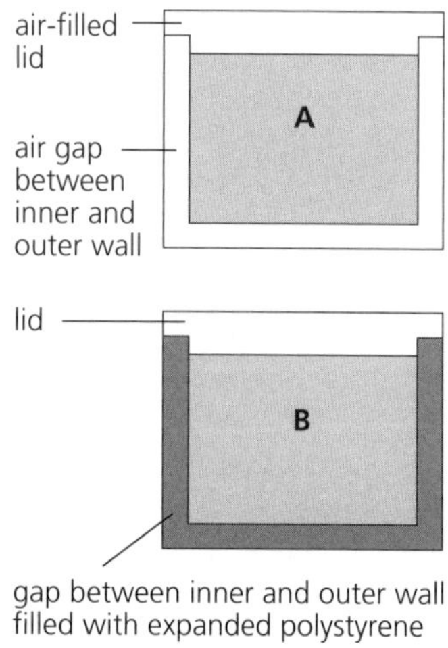

a) Explain how convection currents could transfer energy between the inner and outer walls in container A.

b) Explain why the expanded polystyrene in container B is a better insulator than the air gap in A.

c) Why is it not necessary to fill container B's lid with expanded polystyrene?

d) Cool boxes are available in a variety of colours. What additional insulation would you recommend a manufacturer to use with dark-coloured containers? Explain why you would recommend this.

152 Insulating a house

- Energy is lost from warm houses in a variety of ways.
- Draughts can remove warm air through badly-fitting doors and windows.
- Energy is transferred by conduction and convection through walls, the roof, windows and floors.
- All parts of a house radiate energy.
- Common methods of insulating a house include double glazing and loft and cavity wall insulation.

Q1 By which method – conduction, convection or radiation – does energy flow through:

a) the bricks of a wall

b) the air gap between the inner and outer walls in an uninsulated cavity wall

c) the glass of a window

d) the air gap between the panes of a double-glazed window

e) a plasterboard ceiling?

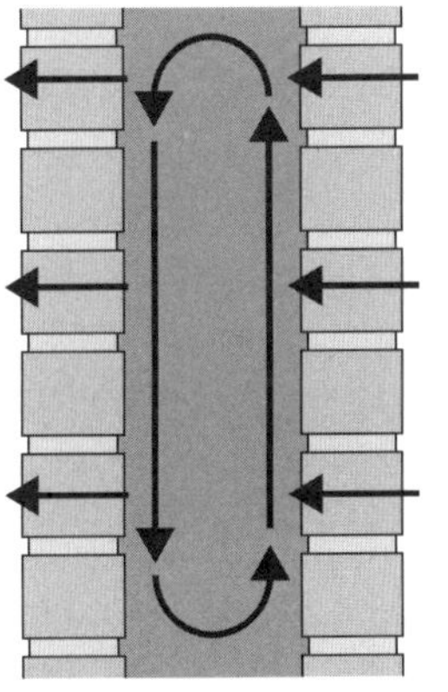

Q2 The diagram represents the energy transfer through an uninsulated cavity wall.

a) Name the method of transfer:

i) in the bricks ii) in the cavity.

b) Explain how cavity wall insulation reduces the energy lost from a house through its walls.

Q3 Many modern houses are built on solid concrete floors. These are very difficult to insulate.

a) How is energy transferred through concrete?

b) Explain how using carpet and underlay together can reduce the energy lost through a floor.

Q4 Central heating radiators are available in standard lengths and heights. The table shows the power output of radiators of the same height but different lengths.

a) Use squared paper to plot a line graph of power output (y-axis) against length (x-axis).

b) Describe the pattern that the graph shows.

c) Use the information from the graph to estimate the power output of a 2.5 m radiator.

d) Apart from height and length, what other factors determine the power output of a radiator?

Length/m	Power output/W
0.48	530
0.64	700
0.80	880
0.96	1060
1.12	1230
1.28	1410

153 Using energy resources

- Our limited fuel reserves will last longer if they are used more efficiently.
- The **efficiency** of an energy transfer is the percentage of the available energy that is transferred to a useful output.
- Most power stations operate at an efficiency of less than 50%, with more than half of the available energy being wasted as heat in the surroundings.
- Many of our current methods of using renewable energy sources are expensive to manufacture and have a low efficiency, so limiting their use.

Q1 a) Complete the following paragraph.
An ordinary filament lamp has an efficiency of 5%. This means that, out of every 100 J of energy supplied to it, 5 J are transferred to ______________. The remaining ______________ J are transferred to ______________.

b) Fluorescent lights are more efficient than filament lamps. Explain why fluorescent lights do not get as hot as filament lamps.

Q2 A householder replaces an old gas central heating boiler with a new, more efficient one.

a) What does 'more efficient' mean, when used to describe a central heating boiler?

b) State two benefits of burning gas more efficiently.

c) What happens to the energy from the gas that is not transferred to the hot water in the boiler?

Q3 In the 1950s we used more coal than any other fuel. In the 1990s we use more petroleum than any other fuel.

a) Give two reasons why we use less coal now than we did in the 1950s.

b) Give one reason why we use more petroleum now than we did in the 1950s.

Q4 A combined heat and power plant (CHP) burns fuel to produce electricity and supply hot water for heating houses, schools, hospitals and workplaces. The diagram compares the energy flow through a CHP and a coal-fired power station.

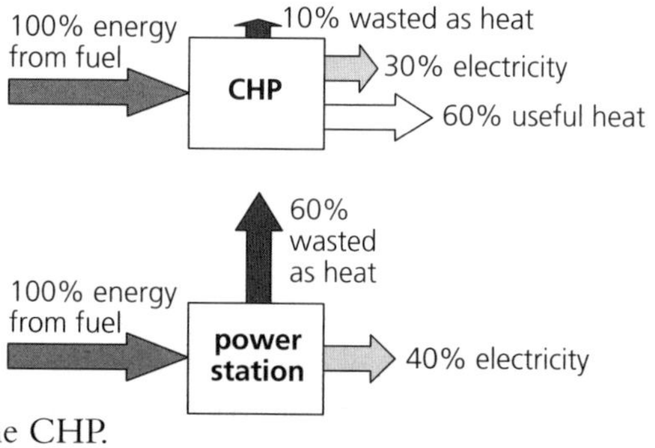

a) Describe the advantages of the CHP.

b) Think about where a CHP needs to be built, the demand for electricity and heat at different times of the year and different times of the day, and the need to repair and maintain the CHP boiler. Describe the disadvantages of using a CHP to provide both electricity and heat to the local community.

Q5 We all depend on energy from electricity and energy from fuels. The table shows the percentages of the total energy supplied in one year that go to different sectors of the community.

a) Present this information as a bar chart or a pie chart.

b) Name two types of energy consumers that are classified as 'other'.

c) In recent years the percentage of total energy supplied to 'domestic' and 'other' consumers has hardly changed. Industry has made big improvements in its efficiency of energy transfer and the number of cars on the road has increased dramatically.
What differences would there be in your chart if you had used data from the 1970s instead of the 1990s?

Sector	Percentage of total energy
industry	28
transport	32
domestic	27
other	13

Q6 The bar chart shows the maximum efficiency with which electricity can be generated from renewable sources. Describe the advantages and disadvantages of each of the renewable sources of energy shown in the bar chart.

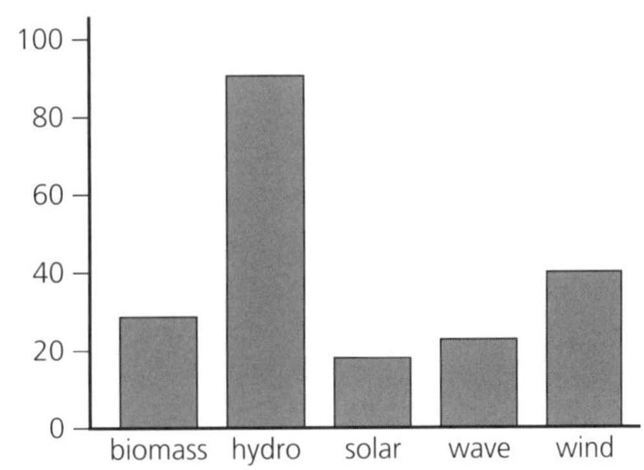

154–5 Work, energy and power

- **When a force causes movement, it does work and transfers energy.**
- **Work and energy transfer are measured in joules (J) and are calculated using the formula:**

work done or energy transfer = force × distance moved in its own direction

or $W = f \times d$

- **The power of a device describes the amount of work done or energy transferred each second. Power is measured in watts (W) and is calculated using the formula:**

power = work done or energy transferred ÷ time taken or $P = E/t$

Q1 Which of the following forces are working?
A the upward push of the floor on a person in a stationary lift
B the upward push of the floor in a lift moving upwards
C the upward push from a wall on a shelf
D the horizontal push of air pressure on a window
E the downward pull of the Earth on a falling leaf

Q2 Calculate the amount of work done (energy transferred) when:
a) a boy who weighs 650 N climbs through a vertical distance of 3 m
b) a father pushes a pram with a force of 80 N for 350 m
c) a braking force of 1200 N acts on a car as it travels for 25 m.

Q3 A boy pushes a supermarket trolley 120 m, using an average force of 90 N. How much work has he done ?

Q4 Electricity generating boards store energy by pumping water from a low reservoir to a higher one. How much energy is stored by each tonne of water (1 tonne weighs 10 000 N) which is pumped to a height of 120 m?

Q5 Use the power equation in one of the three forms $P = E/t$, $E = Pt$, $t = E/P$ to complete the table.

	Power/W	Energy transfer/J	Time/s
a)		200	5
b)		240	60
c)	250		300
d)	60		12
e)	5	550	
f)	2500		120

Q6 Calculate the power of:
a) a lamp which transfers 3600 J of energy from electricity into heat and light in one minute
b) a motor which does 900 J of work in 1 second
c) a bricklayer who weighs 800 N carries a 450 N load of bricks through a height of 3 m in 15 seconds.

Q7 A fork lift truck lifts a 12 000 N crate of food onto a shelf 2.8 m above the ground. The speed of the lift is $0.2\,m\,s^{-1}$.
a) How much work is done to the lift?
b) How long does it take to lift the food?
c) Calculate the output power of the truck.

Q8 A diesel engine used for lifting rocks has a power output of 50 kW.
a) How much work does the engine do when it lifts a 25 000 N rock through a height of 18 m?
b) How long does it take to lift the rock?

156 K.e. and p.e.

- When an object is moved away from the Earth's surface it gains **gravitational potential energy**, or potential energy (p.e.) for short.
- Falling objects lose potential energy as they lose height.
- The energy transfer due to such a change in position is calculated using the formula:

  change in potential energy E_p = weight × change in height = $mg\Delta h$
- Moving objects have kinetic energy (k.e.). Kinetic energy depends on the mass of the object and its (speed)^2.
- Kinetic energy is calculated using the formula:

  kinetic energy $E_k = \frac{1}{2} \times \text{mass} \times (\text{speed})^2 = \frac{1}{2}mv^2$
- If an object is falling or rising freely with no other forces acting, energy is transferred between kinetic and potential. The gain in kinetic energy is exactly balanced by the loss in potential energy for a falling object and vice versa for a rising object.

In the following questions, take g = 10 N/kg.

Q1 Calculate the change in potential energy for each of the following.

a) A car of mass 850 kg goes through a vertical height of 120 m in climbing a hill.

b) A high-jumper of mass 65 kg lifts her body weight through a vertical distance of 0.8 m.

c) A parachutist of total mass 120 kg falls a distance of 1200 m.

Q2 Calculate the kinetic energy of the following:

a) a tenpin bowling ball of mass 8 kg travelling at 2.5 m/s

b) a 7000 kg bus travelling at 15 m/s

c) a 7000 kg bus travelling at 15 m/s and carrying 60 passengers of average mass 60 kg.

Q3 Explain why the braking distance of a car travelling at a speed of 20 m/s is four times the braking distance of the same car travelling at 10 m/s.

Q4 Use your answers to question **2 b)** and **c)** to explain how the acceleration and braking of a bus full of passengers is different to that of a bus without passengers.

Q5 A 5 kg mass falls vertically through a distance of 8 m. Calculate:

a) the loss in potential energy

b) the gain in kinetic energy

c) the speed of the mass when it reaches the ground.

Q6 Repeat question **5** for a 10 kg mass. Do your answers support Galileo's idea that, in the absence of air resistance, all objects fall freely at the same rate?

Q7 **a)** Calculate the kinetic energy of a 0.8 kg ball which is thrown upwards at 15 m s^{-1}.

b) How much potential energy does it have at its maximum height?

c) How high does it go?

157–8 Radioactive emissions

- **Alpha particles consist of two neutrons and two protons. They are intensely ionising but not very penetrative.**
- **Beta particles are fast-moving electrons. They also cause ionisation and are more penetrative than alpha particles.**
- **Gamma rays are short-wavelength, electromagnetic radiation. They are weakly ionising and very penetrative.**
- **Radioactive decay is a random process. The decay of a particular unstable nucleus cannot be predicted but, statistically, the rate of decay of a sample of radioactive material depends on the number of unstable nuclei present.**
- **The half-life of a radioactive material is the average time for the number of undecayed nuclei in a sample of the material to halve.**

Q1 Which type of radioactive emission:

a) is negatively charged **b)** has no charge

c) can pass through lead **d)** is totally absorbed by paper

e) is sometimes called a helium nucleus?

Q2 Some people think that alpha radiation is relatively harmless because it is not very penetrative. Explain why this is not true.

Q3 Which line in the table describes the effect on the mass and atomic number when a nucleus emits an alpha particle?

	Change in mass number	Change in atomic number
A	+2	−2
B	−4	−2
C	−2	−4
D	−2	+2

Q4 Match each description to one type of nuclear radiation.

a) passes easily through paper and aluminium

b) absorbed by 5 cm of air

c) absorbed by 3 mm aluminium.

Q5 Which of the following can detect nuclear radiation?
A Geiger-Müller tube
B voltmeter
C manometer
D photographic film
E oscilloscope.

Q6 Radon gas decays by emitting alpha particles. It seeps into buildings from underground, where it is produced by radioactive decay in rocks.
Explain why the presence of radon gas in buildings is a health hazard.

Q7 The table shows the origins of background radiation in the United Kingdom.
a) Present the data as a bar or pie chart.
b) What percentage of the background radiation can be described as being from natural sources?
c) The table omits some sources which contribute very little to the overall background radiation in the UK but may have a significant effect in certain areas. Suggest one such source of background radiation.

Source	% of background radiation
air	38
ground	19
food	17
cosmic rays	14
medical	12

Q8 The table shows the results of a laboratory experiment to measure the half-life of radon-220.

Time/s	0	10	20	30	40	50	60	70	80	90	100	110	120
Activity /counts per s	1000	870	769	670	577	516	451	388	340	300	268	233	202

a) Use the data to plot a graph of activity (y-axis) against time (x-axis) and draw the best smooth curve.
b) Explain why all the points do not lie exactly on the curve.
c) Use your graph to find the average time for the activity of the radon sample to halve.
d) Estimate the time from the beginning of the experiment when the activity of the sample will have fallen to 50 counts/s.

Q9 **a)** Radium-224 decays by emitting an alpha particle. Complete the equation that describes the decay of radium-224 into radon and an alpha particle.

$$^{224}_{88}\text{Ra} \longrightarrow \quad \text{Rn} +$$

b) Protactinium-234 decays by beta emission, forming uranium-234. Complete the equation that describes the decay of protactinium.

$$^{234}_{91}\text{Pa} \longrightarrow \quad \text{U} +$$

159–60 Using radioactivity

- All living things are radioactive due to the presence of carbon-14 in the atmosphere.
- The age of a dead object can be estimated from the proportion of carbon-14 in the object or by measuring the radioactivity of the object.
- Rocks can be dated by measuring the proportions of radioactive materials and materials that form when radioactive decay occurs.
- Radioactive materials are commonly used as tracers, thickness gauges and to generate electricity.
- When choosing a radioactive isotope for a particular purpose, the half-life and type of emission need to be considered.

Q1 To compare their age, the radioactivity of two different rocks is measured.

a) What factors other than the age of the rocks could affect their radioactivity?

b) What must be done to make a reliable comparison?

Q2 Wood contains carbon. When the radioactivity of carbon from new wood is measured, it is found to decay at the rate of 15.3 counts per minute for each gram of carbon.

a) Describe the precautions that need to be taken when measuring the radioactivity of carbon.

b) The half-life of carbon-14, the isotope responsible for the radioactivity, is 5730 years. Draw an activity–time graph for carbon-14, using a time scale up to 20 000 years.

c) The carbon in a sample of wood has an activity of 10.5 counts per gram of carbon. Estimate the age of the wood.

Q3 The table shows some radioactive materials found in rocks, with their half-lives and the substances formed when they decay.
The age of the Earth is thought to be 4600 million years.

a) Explain why very little strontium-87 is found in rocks.

b) Why is it not possible to date a rock by comparing the relative amounts of potassium-40 and argon-40?

c) Explain why uranium-238 is useful in dating rocks thought to have an age similar to that of the Earth.

Isotope	Substance formed	Half-life in millions of years
rubidium-87	strontium-87	49 000
thorium-232	lead-208	14 000
uranium-238	lead-206	4500
potassium-40	argon-40	1250
uranium-235	lead-207	704
iodine-129	xenon-129	17

Q4 The diagram shows how a weld joining two steel pipes together can be checked for faults.

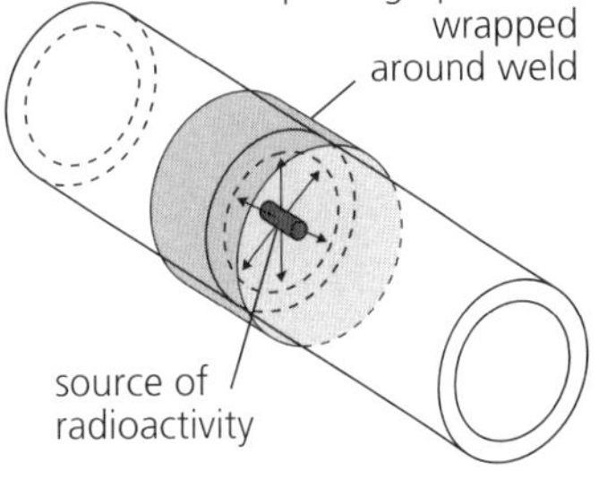

a) What is the purpose of the photographic film?
b) What type of radiation should the source emit?
c) Explain how a weak spot in the weld could be detected by this method.
d) X-rays can also be used to check welds. Explain the advantage of using radioactivity rather than X-rays in this example.
e) What advantage do X-rays have when metal structures are being tested?

Q5 Beta emitters are used in thickness gauges to control the thickness of paper in a paper mill.
a) Explain why alpha and gamma radiation could not be used to control the thickness of paper.
b) Draw a diagram to show how the source and detector are arranged.
c) What could be the consequences of using a source with a half-life of one year?

Q6 The thyroid gland can be examined using iodine-123. Iodine-123 is a gamma emitter which concentrates in the thyroid gland when injected into the body. The diagram shows how the radiation from the thyroid gland can be detected.

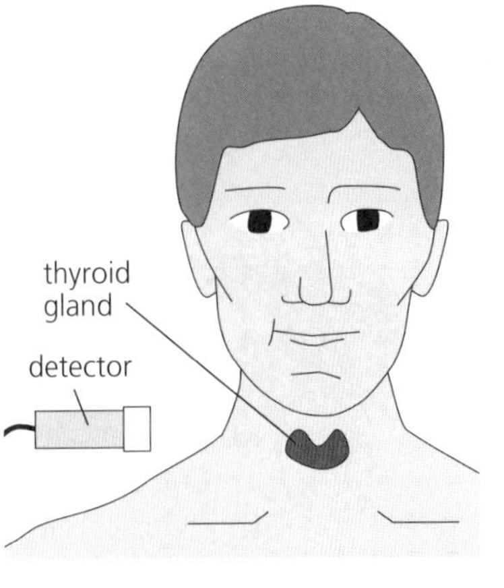

a) Explain why a gamma emitter is suitable for this purpose.
b) The half-life of iodine-123 is 13 hours. Explain why this is a suitable half-life for use in a human body.

Iodine-131 can also be used to examine the thyroid gland. It emits beta and gamma radiation and has a half-life of 8 days.
c) Explain why alpha and beta emitters should not be used inside a human body.
d) Explain why the half-life of iodine-131 is too long for it to be used for this purpose.

Review questions

Electricity and magnetism (Units 107–22)

Q1 Draw a diagram of a circuit that has two lamps and two switches so that each lamp can be switched on and off without affecting the other.

Q2 The table shows the results of an experiment to measure the current in a pencil lead (a mixture of graphite and clay) for different values of the voltage across it.

Voltage/V	1.5	3.0	4.5	6.0
Current/A	0.20	0.45	0.82	1.50

a) Calculate the resistance of the pencil lead for each pair of values of current and voltage.
b) Describe how the resistance changes when the voltage is increased.
c) Plot a graph of voltage (y-axis) against current (x-axis). What do you notice about the slope of the graph?
d) It is possible that the change in resistance of the pencil lead was due to it getting hotter. Describe how you could test this idea.

Q3 a) Calculate the power of:
i) a 240V lamp when the current in the filament is 0.25 A.
ii) a 12V lamp when the current in the filament is 5 A.
b) Many domestic lamps and car headlamps have a power of 60 W. Explain why a 60 W car headlamp needs thicker cable and a larger value protective fuse than a 60 W domestic lamp.

Forces and motion (Units 123–31)

Q1 A pressurised container contains carbon dioxide gas at a pressure of 1 000 000 Pa.
a) The surface area of the inner walls of the container is 0.02 m^2. Calculate the force on the walls of the container due to the gas pressure.
b) Explain how the gas particles are able to exert such a large pressure.
c) Describe and explain the effect on the gas pressure if the temperature of the gas increases.

Q2 A car of mass 800 kg is travelling at 15 m/s on a level road. The car brakes and comes to a halt after 4.5 s.

a) Calculate the deceleration (negative acceleration) of the car.

b) Calculate the size of the braking force needed to cause this deceleration.

c) How far does the car travel during braking?

d) Explain how the braking distance of a car is affected by rain falling on the road.

Waves (Units 132–42)

Q1 The graph shows how the displacement of an air molecule changes during one cycle of a sound wave that has a frequency of 200 Hz.

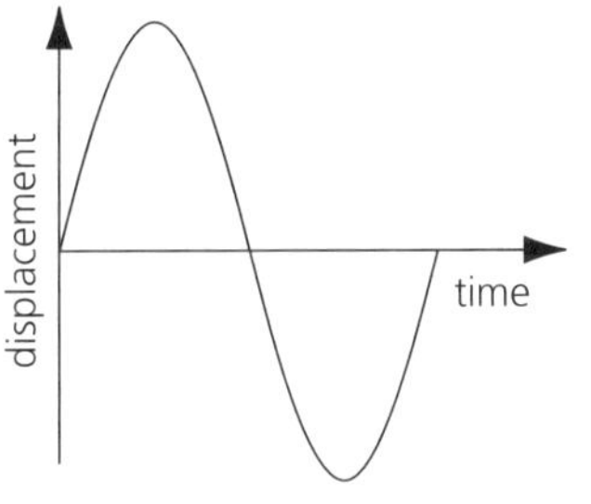

a) Sketch a graph which shows the displacement of the air molecule when the volume of the sound is increased with the frequency unaltered.

b) Sketch a graph which shows the displacement of the air molecule with the volume at its original level when the frequency is increased to 400 Hz.

c) Sound waves travel in air with a speed of 330 m/s. Calculate the wavelength of a sound wave which has a frequency of 200 Hz.

Q2 a) Sound travels in air at 330 m/s. Calculate the wavelength of a sound which has a frequency of 18 000 Hz.

b) Loudspeakers are designed so that high frequency, short wavelength sounds are emitted by a speaker with a small opening. Explain why loudspeakers are designed in this way.

The Earth and beyond (Units 143–7)

Q1 The diagram represents the motion of the two innermost planets, Mercury (M) and Venus (V).

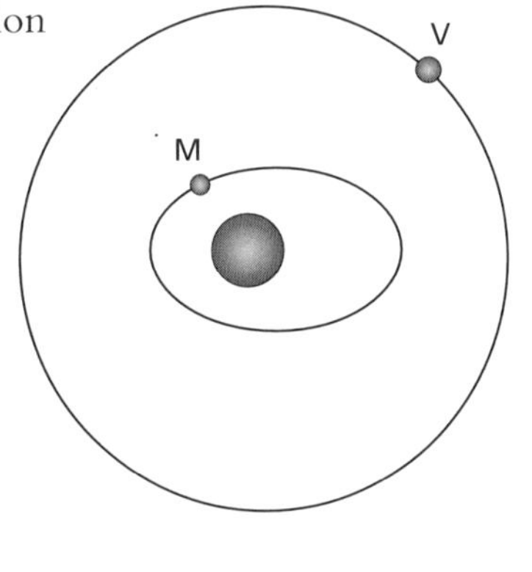

The table gives some data about these planets.

	Mercury	Venus
mass/kg	3.3×10^{23}	4.9×10^{24}
radius/m	2.4×10^{6}	6.1×10^{6}
density/g per cm^3	5.4	5.3
orbital period/Earth days	88	224
distance from Sun compared to Earth	0.39	0.72
mean orbital speed/km per s	48	35
atmosphere	none	carbon dioxide with sulphuric acid clouds

Use the diagram and the information in the table to answer the questions that follow.

a) The speed of Venus in its orbit around the Sun hardly changes but that of Mercury varies considerably. Suggest why this is.

b) Describe and explain how you would expect the speed of Mercury to change as it orbits the Sun.

c) Suggest **two** reasons why the time taken to complete one orbit of the Sun is longer for Venus than for Mercury.

d) Venus is similar in size and mass to the Earth. What does this information tell you about the densities of the three innermost planets?

e) Mercury and the Earth's Moon both show evidence of many collisions with meteors. These are thought to have occurred in the early part of the Solar System's lifetime. Suggest **three** reasons why there is little evidence of collisions on Earth and Venus.

Energy resources and energy transfer (Units 148–56)

Q1 The diagram represents an uninsulated cavity wall of a house.

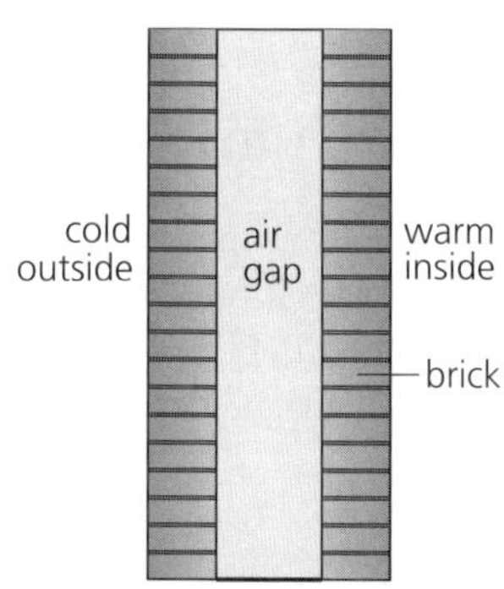

a) Explain how conduction and convection are involved in transferring energy from the warm inside to the cold outside.

b) Explain the effect of filling the air gap with mineral wool.

c) In rainy weather the outside bricks can get wet. Explain why this can cause cooling of the inside of the house.

Q2 In a pumped storage system, water is pumped from a low reservoir to a high one during the night. At times of peak demand during the day the water can be released so that it falls back into the lower reservoir, generating electricity as it passes through turbines.

a) Explain why the water is pumped up at night rather than during the day.

b) Calculate how much potential energy is transferred to kinetic energy when 1 tonne (10 000 N) of water falls through a height of 80 m.

c) Explain why it is not possible to transfer all the kinetic energy of the water into electricity.

d) 1 000 000 J (1 MJ) of energy is needed to pump 1 tonne of water up through a height of 80 m. Explain why the energy needed to pump the water up is greater than the energy released when the water falls down.

e) Pumped storage systems absorb more energy than they provide. Describe **two** advantages of using these systems to generate electricity.

Radioactivity (Units 157–60)

Q1 The activity of a sample of polonium-214 is recorded at intervals of 1 minute. The results are shown in the table.

Time/min	0	1	2	3	4	5	6	7	8
Activity/counts per s	600	491	408	333	270	228	185	148	121

a) Plot a graph of activity (y-axis) against time (x-axis) and draw the best curve.

b) Use your graph to obtain a value for the half-life of polonium-214.

c) Estimate the activity of the sample 30 minutes after the start of the measurements.

Reference section

Glossary

A

Absolute temperature There is a minimum temperature below which it will never be possible to cool anything. This is called **absolute zero** and is –273°C. This is the starting point for the Kelvin temperature scale. 0°C is the same as 273 K on the Kelvin scale.

Acceleration Increase in velocity (or speed) per second.

Accommodation Process during which the shape of the lens and the size of the pupil change to focus the eye on near or distant objects.

Acid A substance that dissolves in water to form a solution with a pH below 7. An acid contains hydrogen which can be replaced by a metal to form a salt.

Acid rain Rain which contains above normal amounts of sulphur dioxide and nitrogen oxide gases.

Active transport The process which enables movement of particles across a membrane, often against a concentration gradient. Requires respiratory energy (ATP).

Adenosine triphosphate (ATP) An energy-rich compound which transfers energy at the cell level.

Aerobic respiration The release of energy from food in the presence of oxygen.

Air resistance The force from the air that acts in the opposite direction to motion.

Alcohol An alcohol is an organic compound containing an OH group. A common alcohol is C_2H_5OH, ethanol.

Alkali An alkali is a base that dissolves in water to form a solution with a pH above 7. Alkalis are neutralised by acids to form salts. Common alkalis include sodium hydroxide, NaOH, potassium hydroxide, KOH and calcium hydroxide, $Ca(OH)_2$.

Alkali metal A metal in group I of the Periodic Table, e.g. sodium, potassium.

Alkaline-earth metal A metal in group II of the Periodic Table, e.g. magnesium, calcium.

Alkane A family of hydrocarbons with a general formula of C_nH_{2n+2}. The simplest alkane is methane, CH_4, the main constituent of natural gas.

Alkene A family of hydrocarbons with a general formula of C_nH_{2n}. The simplest alkene is ethene, C_2H_4. Alkenes contain carbon–carbon double bonds.

Allele A gene may exist in more than one form. Each form is known as an allele.

Allotropy When an element can exist in two or more forms in the same physical state, it is said to show allotropy. The different forms are called allotropes. Diamond and graphite are two solid allotropes of carbon. Different allotropes exist because of different arrangements of atoms.

Alloy A metal made by mixing two or more metals together, e.g. brass is an alloy of copper and zinc.

Alpha particle A particle consisting of two neutrons and two protons emitted from a decaying nucleus.

Amalgam Many metals form alloys when mixed with mercury. These alloys are called amalgams. They are used for fillings in teeth.

Ammeter Instrument that measures electric current.

Amorphous Without definite or regular shape.

Ampere The unit of electric current.

Amplitude Maximum displacement of a wave from the undisturbed position.

Anaerobic respiration The release of energy from food in the absence of oxygen.

Analysis Finding out the elements present in a substance is called **qualitative analysis**. **Quantitative analysis** is finding out how much of each element is present.

Angle of incidence The angle between light hitting a surface and the normal line.

Angle of reflection The angle between light reflected by a surface and the normal line.

Angle of refraction The angle between light that has passed through a surface and the normal line.

Anhydrous A substance without water. Often it is used to describe salts which have lost water of crystallisation.

Anion A negatively charged ion, e.g. Cl^-, which moves towards the anode during electrolysis.

Anode The positively charged electrode in electrolysis.

Anorexia nervosa An eating disorder where a person has minimal intake of food over prolonged periods of time.

Antagonistic pair Two muscles which work as a pair, with each reversing the action of the other.

Antibodies Proteins produced by lymphocytes which help to neutralise the effect of antigens.

Antigens Foreign cells or substances present in the body.

Antitoxins Substances produced by lymphocytes to neutralise toxins produced by pathogens.

Aqueous solution A solution made by dissolving a substance in water.

Armature Rotating part of an electric motor.

Asexual reproduction The process where new individuals are formed from parts of parental tissue.

Asteroid Piece of rock found in the asteroid belt, between Mars and Jupiter.

Atom The smallest particle of an element which can exist.

Atomic number The atomic number is the number of protons in the nucleus of an atom.

Auxin A substance which controls the growth of a plant.

B

Background radiation Radiation from the ground, the atmosphere and space that is present all the time.

Balanced diet All the necessary daily food requirements in the correct proportions for an individual.

Base A metal oxide which reacts with an acid to form a salt and water only.

Battery farming Farming technique where animals are provided with a controlled environment.

Beta particle An electron emitted from a decaying nucleus.

Big bang Theory that the Universe started with a tremendous explosion.

Boiling point A liquid turns rapidly to its vapour at a fixed temperature called the boiling point, which varies with pressure. The lower the pressure the lower the boiling point.

Boyle's law Describes the relationship between the pressure and the volume of a gas at constant temperature.

Braking distance The distance travelled while the brakes bring a vehicle to rest.

Bulimia An eating disorder where one of the symptoms is the intake of huge amounts of food followed by induced vomiting.

Burning See **combustion**.

C

Carbohydrates Compounds of carbon, hydrogen and oxygen with a general formula $C_xH_{2y}O_y$.

Carbon cycle The processes involved in the fixing and release of carbon.

Carcinogen Something which causes cancer.

Carnivore An animal which kills and feeds on other animals.

Carrier An individual who is heterozygous for a genetic disease or disorder, but appears to be normal.

Catalyst A substance that alters the rate of a reaction without being used up.

Cathode The negatively charged electrode in electrolysis.

Cation A positively charged ion, e.g. H^+, which moves towards the cathode during electrolysis.

Cell The basic unit of life.

CFCs Chlorofluorocarbons, atmospheric pollutants.

Chromatography A way of separating mixtures, especially coloured substances, by letting them spread across a filter paper or through a powder.

Chromosome number Number of chromosomes present in haploid nucleus, e.g. 23 in humans.

Cilia Microscopic hair-like structures, can be found in the respiratory system.

Circuit breaker Device that cuts off the electricity supply if a fault develops.

Clone A group of organisms with identical genetics.

Combination The joining together of atoms of different elements to form a compound (see **synthesis**).

Combustion (burning) The combination of a substance with oxygen to produce energy.

Community A group of populations of plants and animals living in a habitat.

Compass Small pivoted magnet that points towards magnetic North.

Compensation point Point where photosynthetic production of glucose exactly balances the glucose used by respiration.

Competition The interaction between organisms for the resources found in the environment.

Complementary base pair Organic bases which always form pairs in a nucleic acid, e.g. adenine / thymine and cytosine / guanine.

Compound A substance formed by joining atoms of different elements together.

Concentration gradient A measure of the difference in concentration between two places.

Condensation reaction A reaction between two smaller molecules to form a larger molecule accompanied by the formation of water.

Conduction (of energy) A mechanism of transfer of heat or electricity.

Conduction (of water in plants) The transport of water in the xylem tissue of plants.

Conductor A conductor will allow electricity to pass through it (electrical conductor) or heat to pass through it (heat conductor).

Consumer An organism which feeds on ready-made food, i.e. other organisms, typical of animals.

Convection Movement of currents in a fluid due to differences in density.

Corrosion The wearing away of the surface of a metal by chemical reaction with oxygen and water. Rusting is an example of corrosion.

Coulomb The unit of electric charge.

Cracking The breaking down of long-chain hydrocarbon molecules with heat and/or a catalyst to produce short molecules useful for making polymers.

Crumple zone The part of a vehicle designed to protect passengers by absorbing the energy of an impact as it crumples.

Crust The outer layer of the Earth.

Crystal A piece of a solid substance that has a regular shape. Slow crystallisation will produce larger crystals.

Current A flow of electric charge.

D

Decay The process of decomposition brought about by microscopic organisms, e.g. bacteria and fungi.

Decomposer A microscopic organism which reduces organic matter to inorganic matter.

Decomposition A chemical reaction that results in the breaking down of substances into simpler ones.

Dehydration A reaction where water (or the elements of water – hydrogen and oxygen) are removed.

Denitrifying bacteria Soil bacteria which break down nitrates releasing nitrogen gas into the air.

Density The mass of a given volume of a substance. It has units of kg/m^3 or g/cm^3. When the density is high the particles are closely packed together.

Detergent A detergent is a cleaning agent There are two main types – soaps and soapless detergents.

Diatomic An element whose molecules are composed of two atoms is said to be diatomic. Common gases, e.g. H_2,O_2, Cl_2 and N_2 are all diatomic.

Diffraction The spreading out of a wave as it passes through an opening or by the edge of an obstacle.

Diffusion The spreading out of a substance due to the kinetic energy of its particles to fill all of the available space.

Diffusion gradient A measure of the rate at which particles will diffuse in a particular direction.

Diode A device that allows electric current to pass in one direction only.

Diploid A diploid nucleus contains two of each kind of chromosome, $2n$, e.g. 23 pairs in humans (see also **haploid**).

Discharging The conversion of an ion to a neutral atom at an electrode during electrolysis.

Displacement Is the change of position of an object.

Dissolving The process that occurs when a solute is added to a solvent and the solute disappears. The particles of the solute fit between the particles of the solvent. The solute can be recovered by evaporation.

Distillation A process of purification involving boiling followed by condensation.

Division of labour The way in which a living system, cell or organism, shares out the work load needed to stay alive.

DNA Deoxyribonucelic acid, found in chromosomes. Provides the genetic code.

Dominant A dominant allele always expresses itself (works) whether it is partnered with another like itself or with a recessive allele.

Doppler effect The change in apparent wavelength and frequency of light or sound due to movement of an object or an observer.

Double circulation Blood passes through the heart twice on each complete circuit of the mammalian body.

Double helix The arrangement of the two nucleotide strands in DNA.

Double insulation The situation when the wires and the casing of an electrical device are insulated.

Ductile Metals are said to be ductile because they can be drawn into thin wires.

Dynamo A device for generating electricity, consisting of a magnet that rotates inside a coil of wire.

E

Earth wire A safety wire, connecting the metal case of an appliance to the earth.

Echo A reflection of a sound.

Ecosystem The sum total of all the living organisms and non-living factors in an environment.

Effector A muscle or gland which brings about a change.

Effervescence If a gas is produced during a chemical reaction, bubbles of gas can be seen to escape from the solution. This 'fizzing' is called effervescence. (The word is frequently confused with efflorescence, which is the loss of water of crystallisation from a hydrated compound.)

Efficiency The proportion of energy input that is transferred to a useful output.

Elastic The property of regaining shape after deformation.

Elastic limit The maximum force that can be applied to an object while it remains elastic.

Electrode The conducting rod or plate which carries electricity in and out of an electrolyte during electrolysis.

Electrolysis The splitting up of an electrolyte, either molten or in aqueous solution, by electricity.

Electrolyte A chemical compound which, in aqueous solution or when molten, conducts electricity and is split up by it. Acids, bases, alkalis and salts are electrolytes.

Electromagnet A magnet whose magnetic field is caused by a current passing in a coil of wire.

Electromagnetic induction Producing a voltage or current in a conductor due to the change of a magnetic field.

Electromagnetic spectrum The family of electromagnetic waves arranged in order of frequency.

Electromagnetic wave A wave consisting of oscillating electric and magnetic fields at right angles to each other.

Electron Negatively charged particle that is responsible for electrical conduction in metals.

Electron micrograph Photograph of an image produced by an electron microscope.

Element A pure substance that cannot be split up into anything simpler.

Endoscope A medical device that uses optical fibres for seeing inside the body.

Endothermic reaction A reaction which takes in energy from the surroundings.

Energy The ability to do work, e.g. cause motion.

Environment The surroundings of a cell or organism.

Enzyme A protein molecule which acts as a biological catalyst.

Essential amino acids Amino acids which mammals cannot make and therefore must have as part of their diet.

Eutrophication The result of the introduction of excessive amounts of nutrients, often nitrates and phosphates, into an aquatic ecosystem.

Evaporation The process by which a liquid changes to a vapour, due to particles leaving the surface of the liquid. This happens at temperatures below the boiling point but is fastest when the liquid is boiling.

Evolution A theory which offers an explanation of the way organisms present on Earth today came to be there.

Exothermic reaction A reaction which gives out energy to the surroundings.

Extracellular Outside the cell, e.g. gut enzymes are extracellular.

F

F_1 generation The first generation of offspring produced by two parents.

F_2 generation The second generation of offspring, the offspring being the 'grandchildren' of the original parents studied.

Fermentation The process in which enzymes in yeast convert glucose into ethanol and carbon dioxide.

Fertilisation The fusion of the nuclei of two different gametes (sex cells).

Filament lamp A lamp that gives out light from a heated filament.

Filtration (or filtering) A method of separating a solid from a liquid.

Fission The splitting of an atomic nucleus into two smaller atoms, with the release of neutrons and energy.

Flammable Describes a substance, e.g. petrol, which catches alight easily.

Fluid A liquid or a gas.

Fluorescent lamp A lamp that gives out light from an ionised gas.

Food chain A sequence of organisms in a feeding relationship.

Food web Arises when one producer or consumer can be eaten by more than one consumer, i.e. interconnected food chains.

Fossil The remains of plant and animal bodies which have not decayed and disappeared but have been preserved. Fossil fuels include coal, oil and natural gas.

Fractional distillation A method of separating miscible liquids with different boiling points .

Free-fall Vertical motion with no resistive forces acting.

Freezing When a liquid changes to a solid at the freezing point.

Friction A force that opposes the movement of objects sliding over or past each other.

Fuel A substance which burns to produce energy.

Fuse A thin wire that melts to cut off the supply to a circuit when the current exceeds a stated value. Thus the fuse acts as a safety device.

Fusion Process by which large nuclei are formed when smaller nuclei merge.

G

Galaxy A collection of stars held together by gravitational forces.

Gamma ray Short wavelength electromagnetic radiation emitted from a nucleus.

Gaseous exchange The exchange of gases needed for biological processes such as respiration and photosynthesis.

Geiger-Müller tube A detector of radioactive emissions.

Gene A section of the nucleic acid of a chromosome, which on its own, or with associated genes, is responsible for a particular characteristic.

Generator Generates electricity by an electromagnet spinning inside a coil of wire.

Genetic engineering Technology which allows a gene (DNA) from one organism to be introduced into another organism.

Genotype Symbols representing the alleles present for a particular gene.

Geotropism Plant growth in response to gravity. Roots are positively geotropic and shoots are negatively geotropic.

Giant structure This is a crystal structure in which all of the particles are linked together by a network of bonds extending through the crystal, e.g. diamond.

Gravitational force An attractive force between any two objects that have mass.

Greenhouse effect Caused by the increase in concentration of atmospheric carbon dioxide, resulting in global warming.

Group Vertical column in the Periodic Table.

H

Haemoglobin Pigment which combines reversibly with oxygen. Found in red blood cells.

Half-life Half-life is the average time for the number of undecayed atoms to fall to half the original number.

Halogen An element in group VII of the Periodic Table. The word halogen means salt-producer. Common halogens are chlorine, bromine and iodine.

Haploid A haploid nucleus contains only one of each kind of chromosome, *n*, e.g. 23 singles in humans (see also **diploid**).

Herbivore An animal which feeds exclusively on plant material.

Hertz The unit of frequency.

Heterozygous A condition where the alleles for a particular gene are different.

Hibernate The body chemistry of a hibernating organism slows down, enabling the organism to survive periods of low temperature.

Homeostasis The maintenance of a stable environment or steady state.

Homiothermic Warm-blooded, having a constant body temperature.

Homologous series A family of organic compounds, e.g. alkanes.

Homozygous A condition where both alleles for a particular gene are the same.

Hooke's law Describes the behaviour of some materials when they are deformed.

Hydrated A hydrated substance contains water.

Hydraulic Uses liquids to transmit pressure.

Hydrocarbon Compounds made up from the elements carbon and hydrogen only.

Hydrolysis A reaction in which a large molecule is split into two smaller molecules by reaction with a water molecule, e.g. digestion.

I

Igneous Rocks that have cooled and solidified as crystals from molten rock produced deep in the earth, e.g. granite.

Immiscible Two liquids which do not mix, e.g. oil and water.

Indicator A chemical that can show if a substance is acid or alkaline by changing colour. For example, litmus is red in acids and blue in alkalis.

Infrared Electromagnetic radiation given out by all objects.

Inhibitor Something, e.g. a poison, which slows down or stops a process.

Insulation Reduces the flow of heat or prevents the flow of charge.

In vitro fertilisation (IVF) Eggs taken from a female are fertilised outside the body before being returned to a receptive uterus.

Ion A positively or negatively charged particle formed when an atom or a group of atoms loses or gains electrons.

Ion exchange A process where ions which cause hard water (Ca^{2+} and Mg^{2+}) are taken out of water and replaced with sodium ions which do not cause hardness.

Isotope These are atoms with the same atomic number, but different mass numbers.

J

Joule The unit of work and energy.

Joulemeter Measures energy transfer from electricity.

K

Kilowatt-hour The domestic unit of energy from electricity.

Kinetic energy Energy due to the movement of an object.

L

Leaching The removal of soluble material by a solvent, e.g. removal of nutrients from soils by rainwater.

Left-hand rule Used to predict the direction of motion of the coil of an electric motor.

Lever A device for changing the size of a force or the movement caused by a force.

Light-dependent resistor An electronic component whose resistance depends on its illumination.

Limiting factor Something which holds back a process, e.g. low light intensity can limit the rate of photosynthesis.

Limit of proportionality The force at which an object stops following Hooke's law.

Live wire The wire that supplies energy to an electrical device.

Locus The specific position on a chromosome occupied by a gene (gene locus).

Longitudinal A wave in which the vibrations are parallel to the direction of motion.

M

Magnetic field A region around a magnet where its magnetic force acts.

Malleable Metals are malleable because they can be beaten into a different shape.

Malnutrition Condition caused by an inappropriate diet.

Mantle The part of the Earth between the core and the crust.

Meiosis (reduction division) Cell division which produces cells which have half the number of chromosomes of the parent cell, achieved by the separation of the members of pairs, important in the formation of gametes (sex cells).

Melt A solid changes to a liquid at the melting point.

Meristem Region of cell division in plants, e.g. found at the tips of roots and shoots.

Metabolism The total chemistry of a living organism.

Metamorphic Rocks that were originally either igneous or sedimentary and which have been altered by the effects of high temperatures and pressures, e.g. marble.

Micropropagation Technique to produce a large clone from a small piece of parent tissue.

Microwave Short wavelength radio wave used in cooking, relaying telephone conversations, and radio and television.

Milky Way The galaxy containing our Sun.

Mineral A naturally occurring substance of which rocks are made.

Mitosis Cell division which produces two identical copies of the parent cell (replication).

Molecule The smallest part of an element or compound which can exist on its own.

Moment The turning effect of a force.

Monoculture Farming practice where large areas of land are given over to one type of crop, often in successive years, e.g. large areas of cereal.

Monohybrid Feature controlled by a single gene.

Multicellular An organism composed of many cells.

Mutation Usually random process of genetic change, sometimes caused by a factor known as a mutagen. The product is known as a mutant.

N

National grid The network of cables and transformers that distributes electricity around the country.

Natural selection The hypothesis which Darwin used to explain evolution.

Nebula A cloud of gas and dust.

Negative feedback By producing more of something, the source eventually causes its own shut-down.

Neutralisation A reaction in which an acid reacts with a base or alkali.

Neutral wire The wire that completes a mains circuit.

Nitrifying bacteria Group of soil bacteria which convert ammonia to nitrates.

Nitrogen-fixing bacteria Group of bacteria which fix gaseous nitrogen into nitrogen-containing substances, making the nitrogen available to plants.

Nitrogen cycle The processes involved in the fixing and release of nitrogen.

Normal line A line drawn at right angles to a surface.

Nucleus Site of the chromosomes, the control centre of the cell.

O

Obesity Eating disorder where the individual becomes extremely overweight.

Optical fibre A glass or plastic fibre that transmits light.

Orbit The path of an object that goes around another object.

Organ Group of tissues with a specific function.

Organelle A very small structure (e.g. a mitochondrion) found within a cell and having a specific function. Many are not visible with the light microscope.

Organism Collection of organ systems.

Organ system Group of organs with a specific function.

Oscillation A vibration or to-and-fro motion.

Osmoreceptor Structure sensitive to changing proportion of water and dissolved material in an organism.

Osmosis Net movement of water through a selectively permeable membrane from a region of higher water concentration to one of lower water concentration.

Oxidation A reaction where a substance gains oxygen, loses hydrogen or loses electrons. The opposite of **reduction**.

Oxide Compound of an element with oxygen. A basic oxide is an oxide of a metal. A neutral oxide, e.g. carbon monoxide, has no reaction with acids or alkalis and has a pH of 7. Acidic oxides are non-metal oxides which react with alkalis to form a salt and water. An amphoteric oxide, e.g. aluminium oxide, can act as an acidic or a basic oxide depending upon conditions.

Oxidising agent An oxidising agent, e.g. chlorine, oxidises another substance.

Oxygen debt The situation which arises when a muscle cell has to continue to respire anaerobically. It is paid back by continued, raised breathing rate after the exercise has finished.

P **Parallel circuit** A circuit containing more than one current path.

Pathogen Disease-causing organism.

Perennating organ An organ which allows a plant to overwinter, e.g. a bulb.

Period A horizontal row in the Periodic Table.

Peristalsis Movement caused by alternate, antagonistic contractions of circular and longitudinal muscles in the walls of tubes, e.g. gut movements.

Pesticide Chemical used to kill pests.

pH A scale measuring acidity and alkalinity.

Phagocytosis Feeding process typical of phagocytes, which engulf bacteria so forming food vacuoles.

Phenotype The outcome of a particular gene – the feature shown.

Photomicrograph Photograph of an image formed by a light microscope.

Phototropism Plant growth in response to light. Shoots are positively phototropic and roots are negatively phototropic.

Pivot A point that objects turn around.

Planet A large body that orbits a star.

Plastic An object that is permanently deformed when a force is applied.

Polymer A long chain molecule built up of a large number of small units, called monomers, joined together by a process called polymerisation.

Polymerisation Repetitive chemical combination of small molecules to form a large chain known as a polymer.

Potential energy Energy due to position relative to the surface of the Earth.

Power The rate of energy transfer or doing work.

Precipitate An insoluble substance formed in a chemical reaction involving solutions.

Predator Carnivore which kills and eats, other animals.

Pressure The force per unit area. Pressure is measured in N/m^2.

Prey Animal which forms the food of a predator.

Producer An organism which produces organic compounds (food) from inorganic raw materials, typical of green plants.

Prokaryotes Classification group (Kingdom) which includes bacteria.

Properties A description of a substance and how it behaves. Physical properties include density and melting point. Chemical properties describe chemical changes.

Protoctists Classification group (Kingdom) which includes algae and protozoa (single-celled animals).

Protoplasm Chemical components of living material, includes cytoplasm and the nucleus.

Pulmonary circuit Blood vessels which take blood from the heart to the lungs and back again.

Pure substance A single substance that contains nothing apart from the substance itself. Pure substances have definite melting and boiling points.

Pyramid of number and biomass The numbers of individuals or the total biomass at each trophic level of a food chain can be graphed. The results produce a pyramid-shaped graph.

Q **Qualitative** A qualitative study is one which depends upon changes in appearance only.

Quantitative A quantitative study involves studies of quantities, e.g. mass, volume.

R **Radioactivity** The spontaneous break-up (decay) of atoms with the emission of alpha, beta or gamma rays.

Radio wave Long-wavelength electromagnetic wave.
Random With no set order or pattern.
Reaction time The time lapse between an event and a person reacting to it.
Real image An image that can be projected on a screen.
Recessive A recessive allele works only when it is partnered by another like itself (except for X-linked recessives which are not partnered by a functional allele on the Y chromosome).
Redox reaction A reaction where both oxidation and reduction take place.
Red shift The change in frequency of light caused by an object moving away from an observer.
Reduction A reaction where a substance gains hydrogen, loses oxygen or gains electrons. The opposite of **oxidation**.
Refraction The change in speed of a wave due to a change in the medium that the wave is travelling through.
Relay An electromagnetic switch.
Replication The process which provides an exact copy of DNA and a duplicate set of chromosomes prior to cell division.
Resistance The opposition to charge flow provided by a resistor.
Resultant force The overall force when two or more forces act on an object.
Reverberation A sound continuing to be heard due to reflections from the walls and surfaces of a room.
Reversible reaction A reaction which can go forwards or backwards depending upon the conditions.

S

Salt A substance which is formed as a product of neutralisation.
Saturated compound A saturated compound is a compound which contains only single bonds, e.g. ethane, C_2H_6.
Saturated solution A solution in which no more solute will dissolve providing the temperature remains unchanged.
Sedimentary Rocks that are composed of compacting fragments of older rocks and other minerals which have accumulated in layers on the floor of an ancient sea or lake, e.g. sandstone.
Seismic wave A wave that travels through the Earth.
Seismometer A device for recording seismic waves.
Selective breeding Artificial selection process used by Man to develop improved breeds of wheat, cattle, roses, etc.
Selectively permeable membrane Allows some particles and not others to pass through it.
Selective reabsorption The process which allows some substances, filtered from the blood in the kidney, to be removed from the urine and returned to the blood before the urine leaves the kidney tubules.
Selective weedkiller Chemical used to kill some plants and not others.
Series circuit A circuit in which there is only one current path.
Sexual reproduction The process which involves the fusion of the nuclei (fertilisation) of two different gametes, in contrast to asexual reproduction.
Solubility The number of grams of a solute that will dissolve in 100 g of solvent at a particular temperature.
Speed The distance travelled per second.
Star A large mass that gives out light due to heating caused by nuclear fusion.
Stiffness How difficult it is to deform an object.

Stimulus A change in the environment which is registered and initiates a response.

Stopping distance The total distance travelled by a vehicle between an event happening and the vehicle coming to rest.

Sublimation When a solid changes straight from a gas to a solid or solid to a gas, missing out the liquid state. The solid collected is called the sublimate.

Supernova A star shining very brightly at the end of its main sequence.

Survival of the fittest Variation exists in sexually produced offspring. Some of these offspring have advantages over others (are fitter), so they survive.

Symbiosis A feeding relationship where an organism of one species lives in or on another organism of a different species, with both partners benefiting.

Synthesis The formation of a compound from the elements that make it up. This is usually accompanied by a loss of energy.

Systemic circuit The blood vessels which take blood from the heart to the various organs of the body and return it to the heart.

T

Target cell Cell which is sensitive to a particular hormone.

Thermistor A component whose resistance depends on its temperature.

Thinking distance The distance travelled by a vehicle during the driver's reaction time.

Tissue Group of cells of the same type having a specific function.

Tissue fluid Plasma which leaks from capillaries.

Titration A method of investigating the volumes of solutions that react together.

Total internal reflection (TIR) All the light meeting the boundary between two transparent substances is reflected.

Toxin Poisonous protein produced by a pathogen.

Tracer A radioactive substance used to track the path of a fluid.

Transformer A device for changing the size of an alternating voltage.

Transistor An electronic device used for switching and amplification.

Transition metal The block of metals between the two parts of the main block in the Periodic Table. Transition metals are usually dense metals that are much less reactive than alkali metals.

Transpiration Evaporation of water from leaves of plants.

Transverse A wave motion where the vibrations are at right angles to the direction of wave travel.

Trophic level Level of feeding in a food chain, e.g. producers will be at level 1.

Tropism Plant growth response where the direction of the response is related to the direction of the stimulus.

Turgor Water pressure which 'inflates' a cell, important in the support of plants.

Turning effect The effect a force has in causing rotation.

U

Ultrafiltration The separation of molecules and ions from the blood in the kidney leading to the formation of urine.

Ultrasound Sound waves that have a frequency above the range of human hearing.

Ultraviolet Electromagnetic waves with a wavelength shorter than that of light.

Unicellular Composed of one cell only.

Universe Everything that exists.

V

Vapour A vapour is a gas that will condense to a liquid on cooling to room temperature.

Variable resistor A component whose resistance can be changed, usually using a slider or a knob.

Variation Differences which arise in the offspring of a sexually reproducing organism.

Vasoconstriction and vasodilation Changes shown by blood capillaries in the skin, involved in temperature regulation; either a decrease in diameter (vasoconstriction) or an increase (vasodilation).

Vegetative reproduction Asexual reproduction in plants.

Velocity The speed and direction of a moving object.

Vertebrates Animals which have a vertebral column (backbone).

Vibration An oscillation or to-and-fro motion.

Virtual image An image that cannot be projected onto a screen.

Volatile This describes a liquid which easily turns to a vapour, e.g. petrol.

Volt The unit of voltage or potential difference.

Voltmeter An instrument for measuring voltage or potential difference.

W

Water of crystallisation Water which forms part of the structure in a crystal e.g. $CuSO_4.5H_2O$.

Water potential The tendency for water to move away from a particular place. Pure water has the maximum water potential, while adding solutes lowers the water potential.

Watt The unit of power.

Wavelength The length of one cycle of a wave motion.

Weight The force of the Earth's gravitational pull on an object.

Work Work is done when a force causes motion; it is always accompanied by an energy transfer.

X

X-ray Short wavelength electromagnetic radiation that penetrates flesh and is partially absorbed by bone.

Z

Zygote A cell formed by the fusion of two gametes which divides to form an embryo.

Formulae you should know

Here is a list of formulae that you may need to know in answering physics questions. Note that these formulae will not be given to you either on the examination paper or on a separate formula sheet.

average speed = distance ÷ time	$v = \frac{d}{t}$
acceleration = increase in velocity ÷ time	$a = \frac{v_2 - v_1}{t}$
force = mass × acceleration	$F = ma$
density = mass ÷ volume	$d = \frac{m}{V}$
work done = energy transfer = force × distance moved in its own direction	$W = fd$
kinetic energy = $\frac{1}{2}$ × mass × speed^2	$E_k = \frac{1}{2}mv^2$
change in potential energy = mass × gravitational field strength × change in height	$E_p = mgh$
weight = mass × gravitational field strength	$W = mg$
pressure = force ÷ area	$P = \frac{F}{A}$
moment = force × perpendicular distance from pivot	
charge = current × time	$Q = It$
voltage = current × resistance	$V = IR$
power = voltage × current	$P = VI$
wave speed = frequency × wavelength	$v = f\lambda$
for a transformer: $\frac{\text{primary voltage}}{\text{secondary voltage}} = \frac{\text{number of primary turns}}{\text{number of secondary turns}}$	$\frac{V_p}{V_s} = \frac{N_p}{N_s}$

In addition, candidates for AQA examinations need to know the following:

energy transfer = power × time	$E = Pt$
cost of energy = number of units × cost per unit	
efficiency = useful energy transferred by device ÷ total energy supplied to device	
power = work done ÷ time	$P = \frac{W}{t}$
energy transfer = voltage × charge	$E = VQ$

Physical quantities and their units

Physical quantity		Unit	
name	**symbol**	**name**	**symbol**
acceleration	a	metres per second in one second	m/s^2
charge	Q	coulomb	C
current	I	ampere	A
distance	d	metre	m
energy	E	joule	J
force	F	newton	N
frequency	f	hertz	Hz
mass	m	kilogram	kg
power	P	watt	W
pressure	p	pascal	Pa or N/m^2
resistance	R	ohm	$\vert$
speed, velocity	v	metres per second	m/s
temperature	t	degree Celsius	°C
time	t	second	s
voltage	V	volt	V
wavelength	λ	metre	m
work	W	joule	J

Periodic table

1	2											3	4	5	6	7	0
					1 **H** Hydrogen 1												4 **He** Helium 2
7 **Li** Lithium 3	9 **Be** Beryllium 4											11 **B** Boron 5	12 **C** Carbon 6	14 **N** Nitrogen 7	16 **O** Oxygen 8	19 **F** Fluorine 9	20 **Ne** Neon 10
23 **Na** Sodium 11	24 **Mg** Magnesium 12											27 **Al** Aluminium 13	28 **Si** Silicon 14	31 **P** Phosphorus 15	32 **S** Sulphur 16	35.5 **Cl** Chlorine 17	40 **Ar** Argon 18
39 **K** Potassium 19	40 **Ca** Calcium 20	45 **Sc** Scandium 21	48 **Ti** Titanium 22	51 **V** Vanadium 23	52 **Cr** Chromium 24	55 **Mn** Manganese 25	56 **Fe** Iron 26	59 **Co** Cobalt 27	59 **Ni** Nickel 28	64 **Cu** Copper 29	65 **Zn** Zinc 30	70 **Ga** Gallium 31	73 **Ge** Germanium 32	75 **As** Arsenic 33	79 **Se** Selenium 34	80 **Br** Bromine 35	84 **Kr** Krypton 36
85.5 **Rb** Rubidium 37	88 **Sr** Strontium 38	89 **Y** Yttrium 39	91 **Zr** Zirconium 40	93 **Nb** Niobium 41	96 **Mo** Molybdenum 42	99 **Tc** Technetium 43	101 **Ru** Ruthenium 44	103 **Rh** Rhodium 45	106 **Pd** Palladium 46	108 **Ag** Silver 47	112 **Cd** Cadmium 48	115 **In** Indium 49	119 **Sn** Tin 50	122 **Sb** Antimony 51	128 **Te** Tellurium 52	127 **I** Iodine 53	131 **Xe** Xenon 54
133 **Cs** Caesium 55	137 **Ba** Barium 56	139 **La** Lanthanum 57	178.5 **Hf** Hafnium 72	181 **Ta** Tantalum 73	184 **W** Tungsten 74	186 **Re** Rhenium 75	190 **Os** Osmium 76	192 **Ir** Iridium 77	195 **Pt** Platinum 78	197 **Au** Gold 79	201 **Hg** Mercury 80	204 **Tl** Thallium 81	207 **Pb** Lead 82	209 **Bi** Bismuth 83	210 **Po** Polonium 84	210 **At** Astatine 85	222 **Rn** Radon 86
223 **Fr** Francium 87	226 **Ra** Radium 88	227 **Ac** Actinium 89	– **Db** Dubnium 104	– **Jl** Joliotium 105	– **Rf** Rutherfordium 106	– **Bh** Bohrium 107	– **Hn** Hahnium 108	– **Mt** Meitnerium 109									

d-block transition elements

f-block

139 **La** Lanthanum 57	140 **Ce** Cerium 58	141 **Pr** Praseodymium 59	144 **Nd** Neodymium 60	147 **Pm** Promethium 61	150 **Sm** Samarium 62	152 **Eu** Europium 63	157 **Gd** Gadolinium 64	159 **Tb** Terbium 65	162.5 **Dy** Dysprosium 66	165 **Ho** Holmium 67	167 **Er** Erbium 68	169 **Tm** Thulium 69	173 **Yb** Ytterbium 70	175 **Lu** Lutetium 71
227 **Ac** Actinium 89	232 **Th** Thorium 90	231 **Pa** Protactinium 91	238 **U** Uranium 92	237 **Np** Neptunium 93	242 **Pu** Plutonium 94	243 **Am** Americium 95	247 **Cm** Curium 96	247 **Bk** Berkelium 97	251 **Cf** Californium 98	254 **Es** Einsteinium 99	253 **Fm** Fermium 100	256 **Md** Mendelevium 101	254 **No** Nobelium 102	257 **Lr** Lawrencium 103

key

atomic mass
symbol
name
atomic number